CAVES OF ICE

THE AUTHOR

CAVES OF ICE

JAMES LEES-MILNE

CHATTO & WINDUS

THE HOGARTH PRESS

LONDON

Published by
Chatto and Windus
The Hogarth Press
40 William IV Street
London WC2N 4DF

★

Clarke, Irwin and Co. Ltd.
Toronto

British Library Cataloguing in Publication Data

Lees-Milne, James
Caves of ice.
1. Lees-Milne, James   2. National Trust
I. Title
924.0854′092′4   DA655

ISBN 0-7011-2657-4

Printed in Great Britain by
Redwood Burn Ltd
Trowbridge, Wiltshire.

The shadow of the dome of pleasure
Floated midway on the waves;
Where was heard the mingled measure
From the fountain and the caves.
It was a miracle of rare device,
A sunny pleasure-dome with caves of ice!

SAMUEL TAYLOR COLERIDGE
Kubla Khan

CONTENTS

Endpapers

Nostell Priory, Yorkshire (front)
The property of the National Trust

Cotehele House, Cornwall (back)
The property of the National Trust

Those readers who may wonder why, after bringing my diary to an abrupt close at the end of the war in 1945, I resumed it in 1946 will find the answer under the date January 6th of that year – if they get so far.

I would like to point out that today I do not necessarily endorse every view and opinion which I held in 1946 and 1947, especially the foolish ones.

I was living at No 17 Alexander Place, S.W.7, until September 1946 when I moved to No 20 Thurloe Square, S.W.7.

J. L–M.

1946

No one asked me to a party last night, so I dined at home and went to bed early. At midnight heard the sirens and distant cheering. The idiocy of it. Buried my head in the pillow and turned over.

Went to the dentist who said it *is* trench mouth that I am suffering from. It sounds too disgusting, and I haven't been near a trench. I am destined to suffer from sins uncommitted. Dentist painted the affected area and told me to gargle daily with peroxide. Had tea with dear Lady Throckmorton whose nephew Nicholas Throckmorton, Robert's heir, called. Consequently I couldn't talk with her as intimately about Coughton as I would have liked.

Wednesday, 2nd January

One of the coldest of days. Midi [Gascoigne] lunched, or rather didn't lunch with me. We could not get a table anywhere so finally went to her club where she gave me a scratch meal at 1.45. She says poor Timmie [Buxton, her sister] is fearfully ill and must have another operation to enable her stomach to evacuate through an artificial hole. Ghastly for her; and what is trench mouth compared to this affliction? Drank sherry with old Logan [Pearsall Smith], aged eighty, lying on his bed in his cosy room. He calls it a deathbed cocktail party. He told me a long story of an American cousin of Henry James who stayed with James in Paris. The cousin was known to all as the Sir Galahad of the New World. He invited the novelist to sleep with him. I longed to hear the sequel but Logan was overtaken by a fit of coughing.

Friday, 4th January

Dined with the Moores. Emerald [Cunard] there in bad form. Also present Denis Rickett who after dinner told us that atomic power would not be harnessed to anything useful for years to come and that motors would still be petrol-driven. In other words atomic power is all my eye.

An explanation is now called for. Why do I resume this diary which three months ago I brought to an end? There is no explanation. I merely missed it like an old friend. It has never intentionally been a confessor, to whom I suppose a good Catholic tells all. And being a bad Catholic I used, when I went to confession, to skate lightly over sins I had a mind to while emphasising those I was less inclined to, and fancied I might with an effort abandon altogether. So too, being cowardly, I treated, and shall continue treating, my diary like an intimate friend who mustn't know everything. If a man has no constant lover who shares his soul as well as his body he must have a diary – a poor substitute, but better than nothing. That is all there is to it in my case.

Began the day in a filthy mood. Was very abrupt with Miss Hall's sister because the spout of the coffee pot was as filthy as my mood. Then I refused to get off a bus when the conductress said, 'No standing'. There were two people standing already. I slipped upstairs where luckily I found an empty seat. When I came down and proffered my 2*d*., demanding a halfpenny change, I thought she would explode with suppressed rage. Went to the National Gallery which was so full the rooms stank and I thought I should faint. Looked at the Paul Klees. They are pretty designs that would do well for bathroom curtains. Met Kathleen Kennet who invited me to the Priestleys' party on Wed. evening.

Had a talk with the Berwicks over a drink. They were sparring with each other. No wonder she gets irritated by his slowness and prevarications, sweet man though he is. Found myself humming a desperate tune of my own invention out of embarrassment. When the sparring stopped Lady B. said, 'Where is that noise coming from?' Then went to Clarissa Churchill's, she prettier than ever. James [Pope-Hennessy] came in fresh from Ireland in a beautiful thick tweed suit made for him over there. He was very proud of it although nearly dying of heat.

To Charlecote Park for the day by train. Motored from Banbury station by Stilgoe the temporary agent. I interviewed the new caretaker, Wicker, and his wife. Delightful couple. He has been a gentleman's servant and has good references. So I engaged them straight away at £4 a week, to rise to £4.10.0, which added to two women working three mornings a week at 10s. each is enough for us to pay. Alianore Fairfax-Lucy gave Stilgoe and me luncheon and was most kind. She is a splendid woman, invaluable as a kind of foreman working with the men.

On my return went to a large cocktail party given by Mrs. Hawker and Roger Cary. She, his grandmother, most welcoming. Lady Ravensdale told me how her flat was burgled. While she was out the burglar telephoned asking the maid to meet Lady R at Paddington and leave the key under the mat. The police know the man to be a certain Kavanagh 'who moves in social circles', but they cannot prove it. A sister of Lord Scarsdale, good-natured but plain, pushed me onto a sofa with her fist, like a pugilist's, so that I sat down heavily. She said, 'I have had three husbands. Now tell me what you have done.' 'Very little,' I answered haltingly.

A meeting of the Historic Buildings Committee this morning. The Committee turned down Hever Castle as a gross fake, and it will be interesting to see whether the Executive Committee endorses this. I lunched with Lord Esher and he agreed to support me in appointing Robin Fedden curator of Polesden Lacey; also agreed that I should write the guide book to the place.

Esher spoke most eloquently about the Civil Service mind as we crossed St. James's Park – the foot-bridge is closed for they are digging a bomb from beneath it. Began by saying he never believed in hari-kiri. Many people after 1911 thought the House of Lords was doomed and gave up the struggle, whereas it still survives. He believes it fulfils today another but no less necessary function than it did in 1910. The same could be said of the Monarchy, now that it is constitutional. This is why he believes the National Trust will survive, and profoundly disagrees with [George] Mallaby's, the new Secretary's, memo on the National Parks question. It advocates defeatism in assuming that the Government are bound eventually to take over the Trust's activities. He, Esher, said this attitude was typical of the Civil Service mind, which is perfectionist. He said the aristocratic mind was quite different. It was pragmatical. It made the best out of indifferent materials. He referred to a *parvenu* millionaire's ball he once went to, where banks of flowers were flood-lit in the garden. He touched a lily. It was made of paper; the other flowers were natural. That betrayed the perfectionist mind at work. The aristocracy would never do a thing like that. I was much impressed.

Thursday, 10th January

Professor Richardson entertained me at Brooks's where I ran across him. He gave me names of some young architects suitable for National Trust work. Talked of his visit to Ireland and showed me his sketch-book of various scenes and incidents (sea-sickness on the boat) and elevations of buildings. Said the Irish are the only civilized people left. They evidently enjoyed his jokes. One man said to him over the telephone, 'I cannot dine with you tonight. My horse has a cold.' 'Ah!' said the Professor, 'he has become a little hoarse.' When he left the country the customs asked if he had anything to declare. 'Yes, lots,' said the Professor, 'but you can't get at it. It'll all in my head.'

Friday, 11th January

I had a curious luncheon today at Gow's Restaurant with a Mr. Eland, an antiquarian, and three other men who looked like commercial travellers. Eland was my host, to whom I had written asking questions about Shardeloes. He had a shaven black head, no legs, only feet encased in vast boots; aged about seventy; very cultivated, intelligent and modest. He gave me several papers about Shardeloes and Leadbetter's activities there. Has proved to his satisfaction that Leadbetter was the architect. The three commercials never once uttered throughout the meal. Were they a sort of bodyguard?

James dined at Brooks's. He was his enchanting old self,

indiscreet and communicative. He is madly in love with a Communist Pole who won't allow J. to go in a taxi because it is patrician. J. being a masochist enjoys this sort of treatment. In his book on Lord Houghton he intends to have a show-down of the upper classes for their cruelty. The Pole's influence of course. J. says he has no manners at all. When bored in other people's houses he takes up a paper and reads. Sounds hell to me.

Saturday, 12th January

Motored in the office Morris to Uppark in Sussex, where [Hubert] Smith and [Ivan] Hills had arrived before me. Lady Meade-Fetherstonhaugh kindly gave me coffee – stone cold – from a pot she held over a log fire. She was welcoming and friendly and most anxious that our scheme should succeed. The country here is heavenly, rolling downs under a pellucid sea-light. Backed by a belt of trees the house commands a panoramic view of sheep-cropped sward and the sea. A romantic house, yet it disappoints me a little. Perhaps because it is so tumbledown, and the slate roof is shiny purple and the elliptical dormers are too spotty. Lady M.-F. showed me all round. She has done wonders repairing the curtains and stuffs and bringing back their old colours by dye from her herb garden. Saponaria is her great secret. She is a first-rate needle-woman and, before the war interrupted her work, spent years labouring away. During the war she had to do her own house work and so the fabric repairs were neglected. She showed me one curtain which was a heap of dull silk tatters, and another, which she has retrieved from a like state. It is a deep, live mulberry colour, minutely hemmed and stitched. The contents of the house are marvellous. She told me that Eddie Winterton was ruled out of inheritance by old Miss Fetherstonhaugh before she died in 1895. He was brought there as a child by his mother and was rather rude; asked his mother why Miss F. dropped her h's, and if he was to own the place one day. The Lady Leconfield of the day was ruled out too. Miss F. asked her what she would do with the silver, if the place were left to her. 'Take it to Petworth of course,' she said. There are no servants in the house now at all. Lady M.-F. and the Admiral gave us luncheon and tea in the basement. Their lives are completely and utterly sacrificed to the house, and they and their son love it. Mr. Cook's agent, Hill, is determined they shall part with *all* the contents for the inclusive offer of £50,000, with which sum they have to endow the house. So they, poor things, will get nothing in cash out of the transaction.

Got back in time to dine with Bridget [Parsons] and Patsy Ward. Very enjoyable evening. Heated arguments after dinner; they both attacking the Catholic Church, and then Bridget and I attacking P's socialism. One uneasy moment when frayed tempers nearly snapped.

Monday, 14th January

Martineau [the N.T. solicitor] ill with mumps and the Secretary cross for reasons unknown. Grandy Jersey lunched but when alone with me is apt to fall asleep like a large and beautiful dormouse. I got back home at 4.30 and there was Lady Esher sitting in my room over a fire so hot that the marble chimneypiece had cracked and was splitting from the wall, and she was trying to screen herself behind the tea table. She had motored all the way from Oxfordshire to meet Doreen [Colston-Baynes] who fortunately remembered to turn up. The three of us munched dainty little cakes provided by Miss Hall. The two ladies liked each other and the meeting was a success. Lady E. brought her copy of *The Regent and His Daughter* from which Doreen transcribed a note that Lady E. had written in pencil at the end. The note was given her by Princess Helena Victoria to the effect that Charlotte Princess of Wales had been poisoned by the Duke of Cumberland. It was a common belief in Queen Victoria's family. Darling Doreen wearing a too short skirt and an old frowsy black hat. She was very forthcoming and communicative.

Went to Cecil Beaton's birthday cocktail party. Talked to Daisy [Fellowes] who had been to Strawberry Hill, and Loelia [Westminster] who introduced me to her beau, Whitney Straight. Talked to a charming young Norwegian over here with his delegation to UNO. Said I would be surprised if I knew how stupid most of the delegates were, especially M. Spaak. I left with Jamesey who was in tears because his Pole has been recalled to Warsaw. J. now hates Stalinism because he says the individual is sacrificed to the Party (i.e. his Pole is recalled by the Comintern). I could have told him that before.

Made a regrettable and most extraordinary discovery this morning. *Pediculus pubis* Dr. Black's dictionary calls it, or them, in its genteel phraseology. Now this honestly is not through physical contacts for I have had *none*. I can suggest only the proverbial lavatory seat, perhaps the one in the train last Friday. Public places and conveyances these days are absolutely filthy. I know curates invariably give these reasons and excuses. But I am not a curate with a necessity to lie. Anyway it is a sad record, trench mouth and creepy-crawlies within a fortnight.

Walking down the street I saw my motor driven towards me by that odious Mr. Marcus. He drew up and said, 'You can have the old bus on Friday.' The cheek of it. Instead of saying 'Go to hell and keep it,' I mutely consented. Mustn't become a worm.

Lord Newton lunched at Brooks's to talk about Lyme [Park], for tomorrow he goes to Stockport to consult with the Town Council. I primed the simple man with data. Then went to Hampstead to tea with my lover Lady Binning whose reason for getting me there was to look at her china, now all displayed. But it is nice being loved so much. Then a drink with Pam Chichester because Hamish [St. Clair-Erskine] is in England for a week, returning to Italy on Saturday. Dined with the Subercaseaux's which was a success. Sat next to Emerald, and being rather drunk actually shouted her down. Behaved the same way with Daisy after dinner.

God, I am worn out today. Own fault. Mallaby and I had an interview in the morning with Sir Somebody Robinson and Dr. Raby. The first is permanent head of the Ministry of Works. Briefly, he postulated that the Government were just as fit persons to hold country houses as the National Trust, if it was a case of their having to provide funds. Mallaby, being a civil servant, was about to agree, but I gave him no chance to do so, interjecting, 'By heaven, you're not' rather rudely, then explained why. Quite pleased with myself. Michael Rosse, Bridget and Clarissa dined with me at a new restaurant, the Lyric, in Dean Street. No one spoke much. Michael in his table-tapping mood. Clarissa, obviously bored, kept yawning. I was longing to go to bed. A bad host. Before this lamentable meal I went to Uncle Ian Hamilton's ninety-third birthday party at 1 Hyde Park Gardens. When I went to say goodbye he did not recognize me. Watched him sitting amongst the boys of the Gordon Highlanders, as obsessed with the conjuror as they. Several dreary old friends; and poor Bligh, the parlour-maid, in her pale blue uniform, crippled now with arthritis. The ghost of darling Aunt Jean still hovers in that house of Roger Fry's pitch black and green.

Thursday, 17th January

Sir Richard Graham called this morning to discuss Norton Conyers, his house in Yorkshire, which is entailed. The situation is, legally, complicated. Then Michael R. lunched at Brooks's and we arranged a tour to visit one or two places in Yorkshire, and Little Moreton Hall. I called on Daisy at six and sat on her bed reading to her about Strawberry Hill, eating plum cake and drinking whisky.

Friday, 18th January

A Rolls-Royce is the only car that has aesthetic merits. It has solidity, dignity and beauty even when fifteen years old. It purrs and it glides.

Saturday, 19th January

Bitter cold and frozen snow in patches along the street. Got through very little of my book this weekend. Very dissatisfied with what I have so far written. That intolerably stilted, cumbersome style of mine when I try too hard. Motored to lunch with Keith Miller-Jones at his house in Chelsea Square. Just ourselves and Theodora Benson. Who she is I can't make out. Novelist I fancy. Speaks slowly, as though drugged, with eyes shut. I envy Keith this easy, homely, little modern house with its countryfied air.

Mass. Work at book. Albert Hall concert in Bridget's box. Emerald and foreigners there. Bridget came back to tea, and then Daisy arrived in her black motor with chauffeur.

Lunched with John Wilton at Wilton's. He took me in his luxurious black Rolls to my office, we sitting in the back under rugs, driven by a chauffeur. Surprisingly sybaritic young man. Dined at Sibyl's [Colefax] Ordinary and sat next to Lady Esher and Daisy. Lady E. said, 'You are sitting next the siren. I shan't be allowed to talk to you, you see.' Only too true. Promptly Daisy ordered champagne for herself and her other neighbour, Lord Hood, who had Barbara Ward on his right. I wish I could have talked to this brilliant young woman. John Russell's new wife, a plain, dark girl there, and John fatter, more prosperous than of yore, the etherial Shelleyan looks gone already.

Picked up Robin Fedden and Ben Nicolson and motored them down to Polesden. Fedden serious in his wish to be curator of Polesden. I think he will do very well. We picknicked in the little room next to the library. I left them there and went to Worplesdon to collect some books and letters and a lacquer work-box, Goethe's present to the Carlyles for their wedding. On my return the telephone rang. It was Rick [Stewart-Jones] back from Palestine. So I put off my home work, and gave him dinner and Australian burgundy at Brooks's. Came back here and talked till 12.30.

Set off on tour of the Eastern counties – not perhaps the time of year most people would choose. I don't choose. Stupidly got lost somewhere near the Alexandra Palace. Finally reached Hatfield Forest where I ate my sandwiches under the N.T. symbol, but could not find the Shell Cottage or my way about. Did my job however and continued to Cambridge. At

3.30 met Lord Fairhaven and a member of the Folk Museum Committee at the Abbey House off Newmarket road. Lord F has given the house to the Museum on condition that the Trust holds covenants over it. Not an important building, but picturesque; about 1674 of red brick; big chimney stack and curly gable; some contemporary wainscoting. It will do for covenants but not for ownership. We should protect all we can in this negative way, I maintain.

Walked in the court at King's and got to Anglesey Abbey for tea. Wonderfully appointed house, soft-treading carpets; full of semi-works of art, over-heated, over-flowered, and I do not covet it or anything in it. We had a frugal tea but sumptuous dinner prefaced by whisky and epilogued by port. Lord F is precise, complacent and dogmatic. But hospitable and kind, although aloof and pleased with his noble position. Who is he anyway? The son of an American oil magnate. We talked till midnight and groaned delightedly over the way the nation is going to the dogs.

Saturday, 26th January

Woke with slight hangover from whisky and port, and my over-heated bedroom. I don't like radiators in bedrooms, but like to sleep with the windows shut in winter. The chauffeur who has two Rolls-Royces here discovered my clutch was slipping and put it right for me. Very obliging. Why do clutches always slip?

I left this hedonistic household and drove to Willingham. Met a Mr. and Miss Ingle, elderly yeoman type. They took me into their windmill. Hitherto I have always a little despised windmills, and their whimsy, flimsy construction. This one, not much to look at outside, a tarred brick base and weather-boarded top, retains its heavy wooden machinery. You climb countless ladders to a great height. There are cogs, wheels, shafts and vents for the grain. The top crowned by a wooden ball, the roof onion-shaped, which should be painted white, revolves with the wind and turns the whole gigantic machinery in rotation. This mill no longer works, alas, and is deteriorating. But the greatness, rudeness and strength of its inside makes me feel proud of my ancestry, for we were yeomen. I suppose it dates from about 1800.

I reached Huntingdon and Hinchingbrooke at one o'c. What a

contrast to the Hollywood Anglesey Abbey. No answer from the front door bell, so I drove round to the back. Walked in and wound my way through a labyrinth of passages, finally emerging into the square oak room at the corner where Hinch was squatting over an inadequate fire. He greeted me with, 'My dear Jimmie, has no one helped you find the way in?' He and Rosemary most welcoming. Gave me sherry and a rabbit pie cooked by Rosemary, for the staff consists of army batmen and wives, not trained servants at all, and no cook. The Hinchingbrookes are picnicking in the house, still full of hospital beds and furniture. The hospital has only just vacated. Hinch took me round the outside and inside of the house. The gatehouse and nunnery, with gables, and the large 1602 bay window are the best features. Hinch has contracted for £400 to have the 1880 wing of red brick pulled down; also the ugly pepper-box tower of that date. This will make the house far more manageable and improve its appearance. It will also reveal the nunnery from the gardens, all sloping gently down to a lake with fine elm trees close to the house. The raised terrace overlooking the road is a Jacobean conceit. There is absolutely nothing to see inside the house, apart from the Charles II dado of the staircase.

At 3.30 I found Rosemary on hands and knees scrubbing the kitchen floor, and I helped her swab it over. We went to tea with the Sandwiches, now living in the dower house. Lady S. of enormous girth. Lord S. very distinguished with two prominent wall eyes. He showed me his pictures, ranging from Etty down to present times. Really a superb collection of French Impressionists and English school. We got on well. He rather disapproves of Hinch's intention to make over the place to the N.T. under the 1939 Act.

The kind Hinchingbrookes made me stay the night in the house, so I cancelled my room at the George Inn. Very cold and most primitive bathroom with no bath mat, no soap, etc. Rosemary a true bohemian, untidy and slapdash; and for this reason admirable, and tough. She is like a very jolly able-bodied seaman. Has four children and intends to have lots more. After dinner she showed me the contents of the crops of three pigeons shot that afternoon. Gave a precise anatomical lecture as she tore open their guts, squeezing out undigested acorns and berries. Then started on the gizzards and stomachs, by which time I felt rather sick and turned away. She has studied medicine and wanted to become a qualified doctor, but Hinch put a stop to that. She is robust, intelligent and affectionate.

Sunday, 27th January

At midday arrived at Woolsthorpe Manor, now empty but left very clean. The spirit of Isaac Newton still hovers shadowy against the panelled walls watching for that apple to drop. Met Mr. Smith, a retired electrician who wishes to rent the house. Then on to Grantham and lunched at The Angel where I wrote up diary. Today brilliantly sunny, crisp and cold. A lovely day for my tour. Got to Gunby [Hall] by tea-time. The dear old Field Marshal [Montgomery-Massingberd] seems older, slower and more ponderous. By midnight I was worn out by ceaseless talk about Gunby affairs. The Field Marshal much worried about his health for he has a stoppage. They have no indoor servants apart from the wonderful Waltons, and old Lady Massingberd polishes the stairs on hands and knees every morning. She is seventy-five. Still we had an excellent dinner, waited on by Walton in tail coat and white tie, I of course in dinner jacket.

Monday, 28th January

Pottered with the Field Marshal this morning round the estate until I became blue with cold. Left at twelve, always sad to leave Gunby. Lunched at Tattershall with Mr. Black, Secretary to the Local Committee, at his villa, a sort of county council cottage, in the village. Mrs. Black gave a sumptuous luncheon of boiled chicken stuffed with sage – she called it Irish stuffing. Black and I went to the Castle which the Ministry of Works have now emptied of their stuffed birds and fossils. They have not yet removed the wooden hoarding from the chimneypieces. We climbed to the roof where there is a light on each of the four turrets for the aircraft, not very sightly things on account of the stays and struts. Left at 3.30 for Womersley [Park] but did not arrive until 7, losing my way after Doncaster in the dark and rain. Still no signposts on the lesser roads. Only Michael and Anne, and Susan [Armstrong-Jones] there. Delicious food and wines as usual.

Soon after ten Michael and I set forth, motoring across the Pennines, up and down little hills through Penistone, Glossop and Macclesfield, in deluging rain. At Little Moreton Hall we were given eggs and bacon. I was cross that nothing which I had recommended during my previous visit had been done. But the house was clean and well polished.

My petrol allowance falling low, today we got Mr. Woodward to motor us to Steeton. The colliery owners offer us this most interesting late fourteenth-century gatehouse of limestone, with perfect window openings, chimney-shaft and stack. Groined vaulting over main entrance. It is a really remarkable specimen of medieval architecture.

On through Leeds and horrible, lugubrious Airedale, to East Riddlesden Hall, where we met Bruce Thompson. Very cold, snowy day. All agreed this property to be dilapidated, depressing and mismanaged – a discredit to the Trust. Ate sandwiches over a fire. Awful caretaker. On to Kildwick Hall to look at the oak furniture left us by the Briggses. The old brothers have all died and the removal vans were at the door. House on superb site overlooking Wharfedale. Late seventeenth-century gate-piers and wooden paling across the road, and the seventeenth-century garden house good. House itself Jacobean with some plaster ceilings.

Michael and I set off again in Mr. Woodward's car and drove straight to Clumber. It was a fine crisp morning which turned to raw, drenching rain in the afternoon. Stopped at the main entrance gates which must be by James Paine. Michael took photographs. We noted that the ivy ought to come off the lodges and the heraldic supporters on the piers to be repaired. The long lime avenue is intact; the plantations on either side are devastated. The ornamental trees in the garden untouched, merely neglected like the whole place. Michael had not been here since his great-uncle the Duke's death. There is not one vestige of the house left, nor of the terraces, nor the foundations, so that you can barely tell where the house stood. We walked through the neglected garden down to the lake. Found two garden temples, the one nearer to the house by Paine surviving. The bridge over the lake probably Paine's, and also the charming gate-piers at the Thoresby entrance.

We arrived at Clifton Hall for luncheon which we were given by Mrs. Clifton and her son, Peter, home from Palestine and about to command a battalion of the Grenadier Guards. He was on compassionate leave on account of a threat by the Nottingham Corporation to his property. He told us he had to sell some of the property to pay for death duties. We liked them both and the house enormously. Hardly saw the outside because of the rain. But the inside is very fine. There are rooms of four periods – the Jacobean drawing-room upstairs, 1620, with huge marble chimneypiece of touchstone and deep plaster frieze with heads and masks; and the painted wainscot room of this date, with pilasters gilded and remarkable panels of men doing halbert drill, a room comparable with the one I saw in Holland House: a bedroom ceiling of 1680 with deeply under-cut fruits in conventional compartments of the finest description: several chimneypieces of the Kent period, including a panelled room, now painted red and used as another drawing-room: fourthly, John Carr's work, consisting of the octagon hall, one of the finest apartments I have ever seen, the rococo plasterwork of the eight domed ceiling compartments very fine; and two excellent staircases of this period, the crinoline one enchanting.

They gave us chicken, and pancakes filled with treacle and cream; also port wine out of an 1800 port bottle with family crest embossed on it.

We left in the rain at 3.15 for our next destination, Pallis Hall, Norwell, near Newark, which we found in the dark after much searching. It turned out to be a house comprising three tenement hovels. Some half-timbering, but nothing of merit. We never saw the owner, who the villagers assured us was not in her right senses. Michael absolutely refused to look for her or even discuss the proposition. When we got back to Womersley I had to pay £9.10.0. for hire of the car for two days.

Left Womersley for Ripon. On the way stopped at Sharow. A child pointed out to me what was the Sanctuary Cross. All that is visible is a stone plinth and a stump about a foot in height – not a very prepossessing N.T. property. Cathedral at Ripon much restored by Blore and Scott. Splendid monument to William Weddell of Newby with bust by Nollekens; refined, delicate features. At 2.30 reached Norton Conyers, a sunny, pleasant house facing due south across a wide expanse of open park towards Ripon and framed in a broad background of expanding trees. The south front has several curved Jacobean gables and is roughcast, which gives it a somewhat naked appearance. The last Graham baronet stripped off the rough-cast to reveal red brick, but soon replaced it when he experienced the damp. Lady Graham, mother of the present baronet, received me. A capable, outspoken and blunt woman, with whom before I left I made friends, but who to start with was hostile. She manages the property of some 18,000 acres for her son who is not agriculturally-minded. At once she made it plain that she did not like her daughter-in-law. Charlotte Brontë stayed here and made it the scene of Rochester's house in *Jane Eyre*. A lunatic Lady Graham was once incarcerated in an attic room which I was shown. The entrance hall is filled with portraits of Grahams. There is a large Ferneley of a meet of the Quorn outside Quenby. The portraits include a Zoffany group, a Battoni, a Hudson, a Romney. There is a wide Jacobean oak staircase. On one tread near the top a large knot of wood is shown. It resembles a horse's hoof, reputedly of the horse which planted it here before collapsing, having borne its master twenty miles home badly wounded after the Battle of Marston Moor. On the stairs a small Zoffany of the house-keeper who was to murder one of the Grahams. Upstairs an oak panelled room with double four-poster bed in which Charles I slept. Lady Graham told me that both James I and Charles I stayed in this room. In the garden are some lead figures and urns of the eighteenth century. Lady Graham had a long talk to me afterwards and said she wanted to endow the house with some private money of her own, but I was not to tell her son this.

At 4.30 I left for Newby [Hall], south of Ripon, for tea. The Comptons are living in the library, a beautiful room like the

Kenwood library, only with a flat ceiling and flat soffits to apses. Walls and soffits painted in pale terra cottas, and shades of pink and blue. The quality of the wall decorations and the stairs is splendid. Clare Beck arrived just after me for the weekend.

I left my hat behind at Womersley; also my silver shoehorn.

Saturday, 2nd February

Breakfast at nine in the library, meant by Robert Adam to be the eating-room. Delicious fried eggs and fried fish. Pitch dark and pouring with rain. At eleven the Comptons took me round the garden – rockeries, pergola walks etc. laid out by Captain Compton. Looked at the exterior of the house and the Adam stables. The brick of the house a rosy pink; the dressings of pink sandstone which have badly weathered and are shaling away. Something makes me suspect they have deteriorated, not gradually since they were first put in place, but rapidly within recent years. Taken as a whole the outside of Newby is disappointing. From the present entrance front the two projecting Adam wings look well, but seen from the eastern angles they give the house a lop-sided appearance. The servants' wing and billiard-room wing are hideous and make the house far too big and cumbersome. I am sure Wren had nothing to do with the old house for the design is provincial.

The two best rooms are undoubtedly the hall and library. The marble pavement of the hall is exquisite; so too are the white stucco trophies upon the blue walls. The inset framed pictures, the Rosa da Tivoli in particular, impart just the warmth needed. The organ-case was French-polished and varnished about forty years ago. A pity. The Roman columns at the foot of the stairs are of a sea-green tone. There is a handsome Battoni on the stairs of Mr. Weddell as a young man pointing to a recumbent Venus. The library has a fine white statuary marble chimneypiece, of which the face of the right-hand-side term has become green for some reason. The tapestry room was dark because the shutters would not open and the Boucher-Neilson tapestries are covered with cloth to keep off the light and moths. The tapestries, signed and dated, have a grey ground, not pink, like the other Adam sets. The suite of chairs is similarly upholstered. With great difficulty I managed to see the tapestries which Captain Compton showed me by lifting the covers with a long stick. The ceiling of this room is coarse and clumsy.

The famous sculpture gallery looks better in photographs. In reality the decoration is insubstantial. It has also suffered from damp and neglect during the past six years. Stucco paterae have fallen off, showing how shoddy the decoration was. Mrs C does not like the gallery at all, or the colour of the walls, a faint Pompeian red. The Barberini Venus was unveiled for my benefit. The arms and legs were added. There is a small recumbent hermaphrodite and a smashed group of a satyr rogering a female, which they showed me after some misgiving because of the indelicacy of the subject. I had expected the gallery to be more mausoleum-like, more solid. The oak floor likewise detracts from solidity. The best exhibit is the great green-veined bath with fluted domed lid.

Billiard-room 1900-ish with imitation Spanish leather (really brocatelle) walls and Tudoresque fireplaces. Perfectly beastly.

Sunday, 3rd February

I left at ten in a steady torrential downpour. The chauffeur had washed my car. The Comptons were very kind. He even lent me coupons for 4 gallons of petrol since I was running low, She is totally 1920-ish in appearance and manner, tall with dark glossy hair like Jean Masserene's. In fact she much resembles her. She has a white plastered face, with rouged cheeks and orange lips. Her artificial appearance out of doors is most extraordinary – a sort of affront to nature. I thought Mrs Beck affected. John Wilton says her affectation has become second nature. I had a late luncheon at Grantham and got home at six. After dinner went to see Rick who was painting rooms in No. 102 Cheyne Walk. Had a scratch meal with him in the kitchen of No. 97 and stayed talking till 12.30, then walked home. Felt a slight stiffness in my left cheek.

Monday, 4th February

Woke up with a stiff face. Looked in the glass and saw my face very swollen. Knew at once that I had developed mumps. A doctor called in the evening and confirmed it. At first I was

19

furious because I have so much to do. Then became resigned. London seems to be rife with fell ailments and diseases.

Saturday 8th February

Only on Tuesday did I have a temperature of 101. Have felt quite well and written letters, done N.T. work, telephoned to friends, and slept. Enjoying *Siegfried's Journey*.

I have now been incarcerated a week and had but one visitor in old Clifford Smith. I am not in the least bored for I am a natural recluse. When the sun shines at this time of year in an inviting snowdrop way I feel an urge to go out and snuff the air.

Tuesday, 19th February

Have finished my book, but have much correcting to do. Went this afternoon to see the Constables at the V & A Museum, mostly small sketches for great paintings. Then met Kathleen Kennet in the Park under Watts's statue of Energy. Sunny but cold. We walked round the Serpentine and to the Round Pond. Two old men were sailing toy ships. They followed them earnestly and savagely, poking them with sticks. K. told me that when the weather is warm she hires a rowing-boat for 6d. an hour and rows herself once round the Serpentine.

Wednesday, 20th February

Considering myself free of infection today, I lunch at Sibyl Colefax's house. Violet Trefusis looks like a basilisk, upright in carriage, and very ugly. When we rose after luncheon I noticed a circle of toast round her chair on the carpet, large pieces crescent-shaped where her teeth had bitten them. I sat next to Tony Gandarillas, grey and yellow and ill. On my right Mrs Hudson. I remembered how James shocked her at an Ordinary lately. So when she introduced politics I said I was not a Conservative, not a Liberal, not a Socialist. I thought it did not matter what government were in office, and that, if anything, I was an anarchist. I was certainly a Papist and would like to be ruled by the Pope. I heard her asking

Raimund von Hofmannsthall afterwards who I was and whether I was a lunatic.

Went to the Greek Exhibition; but all the catalogues were sold and the exhibits numbered only. The crowd was appalling, the smell overpowering.

Dined with Charles Fry [a director of Batsford's], back from the States. He drank seven whiskies and soda while I was with him between 7.30 and 10.30. He is violently pro-American and anti-English. He said he had been away eleven-and-a-half weeks and slept with forty people during that time. From what he told me he must have behaved outrageously through drink. Said the Americans are to a man anti-English (I cannot believe Charles is their single exception); that life there is life, and England so dead that people living here have no idea just how dead. In America you can get up at 3 p.m. if you wish, and lunch at 4.30 a.m. Restaurants are open day and night. I am glad I am English and live in England.

Friday, 22nd February

This afternoon slipped away from the office to see Geoffrey's [Houghton Brown] exhibition of paintings in Ebury Street. Sacred abstract art it is entitled. There was one picture of three heads, called the Holy Family, that I liked. Dear Geoffrey, he is peculiarly modest about these works. He has sold none and does not seem in the least surprised. Yet they are not derivative and have a style of their own, and deserve more recognition. Considering how Tory and reactionary his views are it is strange that he puts into his paintings, if not avant-garde, then unorthodox expression.

Johnny Churchill had a small cocktail party of people from his wife's shop. I knew none of them. J. just the same sweet ungrown-up he always will be. John Wilton dined at Brooks's and was gay and charming. One should not see one's friends too often. That is the secret.

Saturday, 23rd February

Lord Crawford came into the office this morning. Only I was on duty. He merely wanted to have a talk, but unfortunately I had a slight hangover from last night and could not make much sense. He said that my mumps had caused more interest in London than the UNO news!

Had tea with Margaret Jourdain and Ivy Compton-Burnett, but really could hardly bear it and left early. These two women do not eat. They stuff. Ivy consumed eight cakes, for I counted, and God knows what besides. Their greed, apart from the indifference if not positive beastliness of their food, has the effect of nauseating me so that I can swallow nothing. They remarked rather pointedly, 'Of course Jim never eats a good tea' – a hint that I don't give them enough to eat when they come to me. They regard a guest not eating a good tea as worse than impolite. One is not paying respect to their way of life, not observing the proprieties, as though, if they were Catholics, one entered their private chapel without genuflecting before the Blessed Sacrament.

Tuesday, 26th February

Old McKechnie, the dentist, warned me that very soon all my back teeth in both rows would have to come out [mercifully he proved wrong]: this on top of incipient baldness is the end itself.

Wednesday, 27th February

To Wildenstein's to look at the Jack Yeats pictures which are a triumph of the rainbow. Eric Newton says they are magic and as such cannot be criticised. Waves of paint stand out a quarter of an inch from the canvas. Dined with Anne Rosse and we cooked woodcock in the basement.

Thursday, 28th February

Motored with Ivan Hills and Hubert Smith to Layer Marney Towers in Essex. Went over the house. Inside there is absolutely nothing that matters save the reverse side of the terracotta window mullions and cills, which like the outside terracotta are in good repair. Climbed on to the roof and noticed two twisted stacks of rubbed brick. The house would do as an institution for there are masses of outbuildings. The owners, nice, dim people, with money and no taste.

Set off with the plasterer from the V & A Museum. It began snowing heavily as we motored out of London. At West Wycombe we looked at the ceiling of the blue drawing-room where a piece of painted blue sky has flaked off. Plasterer says this can easily be repaired. The Museum will do the work for nothing whereas the estimate they gave Grandy Jersey for Osterley came to £80.

Motored to Hartwell [House] and looked at the furniture there. Troops are still in parts of the house. Mr. Cook and Captain Hill have for some reason gutted the place. Both staircases have been taken out and makeshift substitutes put up. All the walls bare to the stone; and floors and ceilings gone. I can only suppose there has been bad dry rot. Grounds in a terrible mess, but the equestrian statue of Frederick Prince of Wales well repaired. The avenue is lovely. Went inside the octagonal church. It has a convincingly perpendicular fan-vaulted ceiling with central boss, constructed by Keene in the 1750s. Owing to the Georgian Group the roof has at last been repaired.

I reached Upton [House, Warwickshire] at 6.30 to stay the night with the Bearsteds. He and Lady B. both charming, with unassuming manners of the well-bred. Hubert Smith arrived just in time for dinner, his car having broken down.

At midnight Lord B. took me round the house. Inside there is nothing of consequence architecturally save a few early eighteenth-century chimneypieces and a beautiful Coleshill-style staircase, rearranged by Lord B. and extended. Morley Horder, architect, built on to the house in the 1920s. But heavens, the contents! There is a lot of good Chippendale-style furniture and some marvellous Chelsea china of the very best quality. It was badly packed away during the war when the house was occupied by a bank, and some on unpacking found to be damaged. The picture collection superb, as fine as any private collection in England. Many of the pictures are not yet back from the Welsh caves where they were stored with the National Gallery pictures.

Very cold, bright, sunny day, snow still lying in patches, which means more to come. This morning we walked round the garden with Lord B. and the agent. It is only the garden he is offering with the house; but he wishes to include all the works of art. So does his son who is to inherit. One side of the house is 1695, the other 1735, but Lord B. has very much enlarged it. The result is pleasing. The grounds are beautiful, a high bank with belt of trees and a steep range of terraces. I am a little doubtful about the propriety of accepting this place, and without contents the offer could not be entertained.

After luncheon drove to Stratford and visited the church where they charge 6*d.* for entry, which causes resentment. Shakespeare's grave at the altar and its inscription give a tingle down the spine. How can anyone doubt Shakespeare's existence? I had tea with Mrs. Wellstood, a friendly little woman, in her cottage next to Anne Hathaway's at Shottery. She is Secretary of the Shakespeare Trustees. There were two others to meet me. They put me through my paces and criticised the N.T., as well they might, for ineffectual publicity.

Went on to Wickhamford, arriving about seven. Mama well and fatter.

Motored to Coughton [Court] to lunch with Sir Robert Throckmorton. Nobody else present. He was disarming. He has no back to his head. He looks very young still. He spoke about Coughton with great sense and intends to live there from time to time.

Mama and I were alone in the evening. We looked through old letters which depressed us very much. They are emblems of mortality. She gave me a beautiful photograph of my grandmother.

Elsie Pethard called this morning and was overjoyed to see me. Talked nineteen to the dozen and kept repeating, 'Isn't he beautiful? Oh, I shouldn't say it, but isn't he beautiful?' For these words I kissed her affectionately when she left. She was my nursemaid when I was two, and sees me at that age today.

Picked up Ben Nicolson at Leamington station and took him to Charlecote. He found nothing of any interest among the pictures, which he dismissed out of hand. These art experts seem to have no regard for family portraits *en masse*, with their historic and social traditions. We left after an early tea for London but on climbing Edgehill ran into fog and snow. Decided to return to Charlecote but the descent was so icy and slippery that we abandoned the car and walked with my suitcase to Edgehill village. There I telephoned Upton. Fortunately, or unfortunately, the Bearsteds had left for London but Dick Samuel said we might stay the night. He welcomed us most warmly and hospitably, gave us wine and dinner and put us both in the big room I had occupied the previous night. Ben is a strange creature. He had no bath and he did not wash. He hardly addressed a word to Dick who cannot have been pleased to have us. Ben is very grubby, but very easy-going and very sweet. I don't think strangers always detect the two virtues. We left the following morning at nine. Ben did not so much as say Thank you to our Good Samaritan host.

Wednesday, 6th March

Went with John MacGregor to inspect the Roman Bath just off the Strand. More interesting than I expected, for there, sunk below the earth in a vast tank lined with Roman bricks, is a bubbling spring. The whole shamefully neglected and choked with dirt and rubbish. I dined with Grandy [Jersey] in his large Victorian-Tudor house in Wimbledon. Inside ugly with shiny mahogany wainscoting. His little touches are 'how', as Harold would say.

Thursday, 7th March

Nancy [Mitford] lunched with me at Wilton's. She is radiant because she has already made £2,000 out of her novel *The Pursuit of Love* and has high hopes of it being filmed in America, where an edition is about to come out. She told me that Tom died intestate and so his estate, quite considerable, was divided between his six sisters. When that fiend Decca was notified she cabled from America, 'Give my one-sixth share to the Communist Party'. Nancy says she is not going to act upon it. She said Michael Duff will almost certainly marry the Duchess of Kent. Peter Rodd thinks her the most beautiful woman, without exception, whom he has ever met. The Duchess very flattering to Nancy about her book.

This evening went to see Doreen, one of my dearest friends. She invariably launches herself on a wave of preciosity. After a couple of glasses of African sherry she, and in consequence I, become acclimatized, and indulge in confidences. She told me she had never been interested in sex, either subjectively or objectively. For example, she cannot bring herself to deal in her book with 'the highly sexed woman' which, she is told, Queen Victoria was. The idea bores as well as repels her.

Friday, 8th March

At luncheon to see the James Ensor collection at the National Gallery. Very interesting this old man's paintings. They are nearly all dated 1881, some even 1879, and he is still alive. I recognize that they are good, but don't much care for his clowns and skeletons wearing hats.

Michael came back from Ireland today, and I dined with him and Anne at the Dorchester in their suite. Bridget and Sachie Sitwell there. He so screws up his face when he laughs that his mouth becomes a tiny triangle.

Had a shock this evening to receive a letter from Stuart, written only a week ago, referring to Logan Pearsall Smith's death. He died after a quick heart attack, his last words being: 'I must telephone to the Pope-Hennessys'. He has made John Russell his literary executor, which will infuriate many older friends.

Sunday, 10th March

James telephoned to explain why he had not been in touch lately. For the past seven weeks he has been madly in love with a French 'cellist. His life has been a turmoil. I drove to lunch with Joan and Garrett [Moore] and there found both James and 'cellist. Both looked very alike, two little black-headed objects, dissipated, green and shagged. James had scratches over his face.

26

Monday, 11th March

Lunched with James Mann, recently appointed Surveyor of the King's Works of Art. He complained that he had so much work to do reinstating the Tower of London and the Wallace Collection that he had no time for the royal collections. He showed me Sir Edward Barry's deed of covenant which he wants the N. Trust to implement by adding a protective clause covering the heraldic glass in the hall at Ockwells. Before luncheon I went to the V & A Museum with Clifford [Smith], and Leigh Ashton took us into the downstairs basement where there are piles of dusty furniture from which to choose pieces for Montacute. I left at the museum Queen Elizabeth's reputed napkin from Charlecote which Leigh thinks may be sixteenth-century. Also the miniature of Sir Thomas Lucy which may be by Isaac Oliver.

Tuesday, 12th March

This morning the Historic Buildings Committee to my surprise, but pleasure, agreed to recommend acceptance of Upton House on account of the collections, but were very much against acceptance of Hever Castle.

Wednesday, 13th March

At 4.30 Lord Newton called. The silly man was regretting that he had offered the choicest furniture at Lyme to Manchester Art Gallery. Now that the arrangements with Stockport Corporation for the running of Lyme have gone through he realises what a mistake he has made. Of course, he said, they ought to remain in the house, which all along I had begged him to arrange. I was appalled and urged him to write to Manchester asking for them back. He said he did not know how he could. I implored him to put his pride in his pocket and do it.

Thursday, 14th March

Met Michael at Brooks's. He wanted to know whom Grandy Jersey would like the Georgian Group to nominate as an Osterley trustee: not Keeling, not Acworth I said, but I would suggest Michael himself.

Darcy Braddell the architect called and showed me his plans for converting the first floor at Polesden Lacey into flats.

Went to Sibyl's Ordinary. My respect for her gallantry and kindness has developed into true fondness. She is old now and the worldly are always pathetic. Sat next to Joan Oglander who told me that Desmond MacCarthy was trying to persuade John Russell to surrender Logan's literary executorship. Stephen Spender has said that Julia Strachey attended the reading of the will and protested aloud at the fortune having been left to J.R. Spender said it was a real Henry James sequel to Logan's life. Rose Macaulay, with whom I sat after dinner, said she saw J.R. in the London Library looking sheepish and embarrassed. I feel sorry for him. It was not his fault that Logan took a fancy to him.

Saturday, 16th March

Motored to Lacock, having taken my typescript to Batsford's. Lunched at Marlborough at my favourite inn where I was treated as an old, venerated customer. Arrived Lacock Abbey at 2.15, but Miss Talbot in bed with phlebitis. However, a friend deputised for her. Having been asked to come in order to arrange the furniture and expecting it to take the whole of this afternoon and Monday, I was a little annoyed to find there was nothing at all for me to do. Miss Talbot had already done it – and badly. Furthermore, irritated to be given her draft of the guide book to approve, whereas a year ago I at great trouble submitted my own, which was far better then hers, (incidentally based on mine). I was given tea and drove on to Bath, reaching Mrs. Knollys's house, Richmond Lodge, at 6.30.

Sunday, 17th March

Horrible rainy day. Sung Mass in Bath not very inspiring, but the church full. On to Corsham Court in time for luncheon with the Methuens in the Nash library. They believe they have let the Victorian centre part of the house to an art teaching establishment, the state rooms to be used by them only occasionally and shown to the public regularly. Paul and Norah are to live in the north wing which has ten bedrooms. At present the hospital is still in the house. After luncheon I talked to Paul until 5 o'clock tea-time about Corsham and the N.T., and gave him data for his speech to *La Demeure Historique* in Paris in May.

After tea I left Corsham at 6 o'clock. About a mile from the village on the Bath road I saw a small car facing me, up the grass bank as though run into the wall, on its wrong side. I pulled up and was met by a man frantically waving, and holding a handkerchief to his head which was covered with blood. I asked him if he had had an accident. He said he had been assaulted and robbed by two sailors to whom he had given a lift from Bath. I stopped an approaching car and asked for help. They seemed bewildered and did not wish to be involved. So I pushed the man into my car, turned round and drove hell for leather to Corsham again, holding the man's shoulder with my left hand and talking to him without cease. Drove straight to a Maternity Home, which I remembered passing in the morning, rang the bell and handed the man to two nurses, then ran down the street for a doctor. The doctor was off duty and at first reluctant to come. But I made him, while I telephoned the police. They came and took all particulars. The man was badly knocked about, but not unconscious. He had complained about his terrible pain all the way in the car and I was afraid he might be going to die. The moral is not to give lifts to more than one person at a time, and then not to let one sit behind you. For it transpired that the sailor in the back seat had biffed the man over the head while the sailor in the passenger seat opened the driver's door and pitched him out. Before doing so he had rifled his pocket of 10s.!

Monday, 18th March

Went down early to Bath to give a statement to the police station. Wandered into the Abbey, the Pump Room and round the Roman baths. The water is extremely warm and steaming. I cannot think why more use is not made of these natural springs and baths and why the people should not be allowed to bathe in them. Instead the water is filthy and full of litter. The ruins are gloomy and ill cared-for. In the Pump room drank half a glass of sulphur water from a dirty tumbler. Pump Room dirty, dingy and neglected.

Left Bath for Great Chalfield Manor. The Fullers away, but his secretary showed me where Major Fuller wanted us to have the drive mended and how they had weeded the moat. On to Trowbridge but Clifford Smith never turned up either there or at Westbury station as arranged. So I went on to Montacute where he arrived soon after me. We stayed this night and the following at The King's Arms.

Clifford and I spent the day arranging the few inadequate pieces of furniture so far collected. Did not make much of a show, the only pieces of interest being the Queen Anne chairs given by a Phelips. They originally came from Montacute. Eardley joined us in the evening, and hilarity ensued.

Eardley and I took Clifford to Yeovil station and motored to Melbury where we had a quick luncheon with Lord Ilchester, Lady I. being ill in bed. He conducted us round the house, which is huge and in a state of desolation. Lord I. said that unless he could get some more servants he would have to leave the place. Although seven-eighths of the house is unused, little attempt has been made at dust-sheeting. The rooms and furniture are consequently untidy and dreadfully dusty. I understand that Lord Stavordale will pull down the Victorian wing. We did not go inside it. Lord Ilchester's father built it in the 1880s in imitation perpendicular, well designed, well built and not at all to be despised. The library by Salvin, built in the 1870s, is very fine: simple and effective roof, book shelves of pine. Salvin impresses me more and more favourably. The 1690 wing is very beautiful. The material yellow Ham stone, glowing like honey, the columns and dressings of silvery Portland stone, as are the cornices, of which the mouldings have weathered the centuries, for they are still sharp. One contemporary long room has survived, but most of the ceilings are modern and indifferent. One 1690 ceiling, painted with gaily plumed birds, is unusual. Good and indifferent furniture. Interesting collection of family portraits.

Eardley and I visited Barrington Court which is now open once a week and in apple-pie order. Tenants make it clear they resent interference from us. We both disliked the interior, which is merely a museum of bits and pieces brought from demolished houses. The school which has vacated the house did only superficial harm.

Mrs. Knollys, with whom we are staying, is worried to a state bordering on hysteria because her cook is leaving. She is a source of much anxiety to Eardley, with whom she is very proprietary and exacting. She wishes to be kept informed of his every movement and action. This is a mistake. She lives only for him. Poor old lady, with her stately Victorian manner and manners.

Thursday, 21st March

Left Richmond Lodge early for Horton Court on the edge of the Cotswolds near Old Sodbury. House lies in a cup of hill, steeply wooded, and overlooking the Severn. It is offered us by a Miss Wills and Tony Wills, Lord Dulverton's son, is to rent it. It is a manor-house with seven or eight bedrooms. Miss Wills has spent thousands on it, too many thousands. It has a Norman hall of 1150, perfectly hideous, some interesting Henry VIII detail, notably carved arabesques; a late Gothic ambulatory (detached) with Renaissance heads of Emperors, most unusual. Nothing else inside. The outside was badly restored some sixty years ago and the stone pointed with black mortar. The walls should be harled all over. I suppose the house is acceptable on account of its archaeological interest. The situation is beautiful. The agent whom we took there was a flash-cad, whom at first I so much disliked that I could not speak to him. In the end we quite liked him.

Saturday, 23rd March

Bridget dined with me at the Ritz, I having ordered dinner for 9 o'clock. Found oysters waiting for us on our plates and had a delicious meal. Took her back to her flat and walked home in the middle of the night.

Monday, 25th March

I motored Gordon Wordsworth in my car to Barnsley Park, four miles our side of Cirencester, and arrived in time for tea. Lady Violet Henderson is Gavin Faringdon's mother and the aunt of Gordon's wife, Doreen. A very friendly woman,

31

nearly seventy, grey haired, wearing trousers. Unlike Gavin and Roddie she is unsophisticated and direct, and I would say, uncomplicated. We wandered round the outside. Park naturally pretty but the trees, elms and oaks much decayed. House fascinating, being of the Vanbrugh school, tall, compact, almost gaunt. Does not stand well. It wants a forecourt or some more striking external setting. Of beautiful yellow stone, the capitals of the pilasters, cornices and moulds sharply defined. The interior extraordinarily baroque, the hall monumental, with bold plaster reliefs, broken pediments, shell-headed alcoves, statues. Lady Violet is ignorant about houses. She has painted the iron stair balusters and the oak dado the same green as the walls. The dining-room painted egg blue is of Adam date, with screen at one end. The gilt pier-glasses between the windows belong to the house. The two semi-circular console tables with straight classical legs under them were bought by her at the Bolingbroke sale of Lydiard Tregoze. We had *foie gras* for dinner.

We called at the Wordsworth rectory at Broadwell on our return. Gordon's father greatly resembles the poet, his great-grandfather. He has the only portrait of Dorothy in old age. She is wearing a cap.

Wednesday, 27th March

Grandy Jersey and Leigh Ashton lunched at Wilton's, which cost me £4. Discussed the part the V & A is to play over Osterley. Rather a sticky business, but Grandy wished it. Then to Batsford's for first talk with Charles Fry and Mr. Batsford about the Adam book, for which they will pay me £350.

Thursday, 28th March

Went to Logan Pearsall Smith's memorial service at St. Margaret's Westminster. The Pope-Hennessy family in the front row. The Dame said to me reproachfully, 'I have been in my new flat six months and you have not yet visited me.' The lesson from Ecclesiasticus, beginning 'cast thy bread upon the waters', was read. And what did his bread bring back to Logan? Three volumes of *Trivia*, a reputation of a grammarian, and a sad, lonely and unfulfilled old age. Was struck by one passage in Jeremy Taylor's prayers, 'Accept the stupid and the fools to mercy'. How many did Logan accept? John Russell and wife sat in front of me, he with golden hair like spun treacle.

Sibyl Colefax and Eddie Marsh lunched with me at the Ritz to meet Doreen Baynes, who was the lioness. Doreen seemed happy and was very gay and entertaining. Sibyl amazed me by her memory and apt quotations. Talk was of Maurice Baring, whom Doreen saw much of in Scotland during the war, and loved. I thought Eddie was rather bored.

Friday, 29th March

Trained to Conway. There was a restaurant car again, but the breakfast was so disgusting that I didn't risk luncheon. Attended a meeting with the Town Council in 'Aberconwy'. It was not an easy meeting to start with, for they evidently think, not without reason, that the Trust ought to be more generous with funds and advice. It is a deplorable little property, a neglected and lifeless, unnecessary museum. Stayed two nights with Michael Duff at Vaynol.

Michael has staying a very nice New Zealand boy just back from Germany, by name Dick Wardell, who has intelligence and charm. He contracted pneumonia in a British hospital in Germany through sheer neglect. David Herbert also staying accompanied by his friend Joe, a Glasgow boy with thick black hair like a cedar mop and a baby face – very tiresome and argumentative. Michael can hardly be polite to him.

Thursday, 4th April

To see the collection of Sir Hickman Bacon's watercolours at Agnew's. They now belong to Mindy Bacon of Thonock. Wonderful collection but too large. Charles Brocklehurst came to the office to ask if the N.T. could offer him a job. Tea party at Doreen's. Arrived at 5.15, brilliant sunlight outside. At first I thought there must be a magic lantern show on, the room plunged in darkness, sunblinds down and curtains drawn. I groped my way across to Doreen who was officiating in a canary-coloured dress. Doreen loathes daylight and out of doors. Her annual agony is having to stay with her brother in the country for a fortnight when the servants have a holiday.

33

Talked to Lady Lovat, now a little, thin, frail old lady. She was wearing a preposterous black pixie hat, with two grey birds' feathers over her temples and a stiff veil that stuck outwards at a crooked angle. On talking about Europe and our destruction of Vienna and German cities she waxed earnest and intelligent. Betty Richards there, very middle-aged and big. I felt like Proust in the last book at the Prince de Guermante's party.

Friday, 5th April

Had to give evidence today in the robbery and assault case at Chippenham. Kind John Wilton called for me at 7.45 in his beautiful Rolls-Royce and motored me down. Weather broke and it rained incessantly. The Chippenham Police Court was Dickensian; a bare Georgian room up a steep staircase. The benches inches thick in dust. John with his broken ankle sat throughout with me. First we listened to a bigamy case. The magistrate, an old fool, might have been John Sutro mimicking. Then our case came on. The two sailors stood handcuffed in the dock. One aged twenty-one, a terrible rough type; the ringleader, aged twenty-two, very small like an eel, very pretty but very wicked, by name Tulip, who in the dock kept winking and giggling with the other, unchecked, which surprised us a lot. We were kept till 3 o'clock, without being allowed a cup of tea and just as though we were the criminals. I was bound over – or whatever it's called – to attend the Salisbury Assizes when the case is referred to them in three weeks time. The whole business a damned nuisance and waste of time.

On our return we went to Lydiard Tregoze. To enter the church one has to get the key from the house. Church has several extremely fine Bolingbroke monuments, some stained glass and rich altar rails in gilded wrought iron that might be by Tijou. A caretaker took us round the house which is empty. It has been bought by Swindon Corporation which does not know what to do with it. It has one w.c., no bathroom, no light and no heating. Until 1942 the Bolingbroke family all lived in the servants' back premises, leaving the front of the house furnished but unattended. Garden elevation typical Palladian, without a perron, the state rooms being on the ground floor. They are very fine. Central hall a high cube with rococo plasterwork. Indeed every room lavishly stuccoed.

Small chapel with recess. Remains of old red flock paper on walls. Stairs long and straight, with small balls on the handrail. Condition very poor; some ceilings down and you can see through to the roof timbers. Sad sight.

John dined at Brooks's. Told me he pays his chauffeur £8 a week.

Wednesday, 10th April

At the end of each day I think of what I have accomplished. Today I had tea with Lady Binning in Hampstead. She loves me with the passion of friendship and would lavish costly presents upon me, were I to allow it.

Thursday, 11th April

Today went with one of our new agents to St. John's Institute at Hackney, the first time I have ever visited this property. And what a wretched one! It is no more important than hundreds of other Georgian houses still left in slum areas. Very derelict after the bombing all around it. Tenanted by a number of charitable bodies. It does have one downstair room of linenfold panelling. I found it terribly depressing and longed to hurry away.

At an S.P.A.B. meeting we discussed Chelsea Old Church. As before I was alone in voting against it being rebuilt on the grounds that there is too little of it left. I was in a minority of one – decision taken to rebuild over what rubble remains and to retain absolutely those surviving fragments, but not to reproduce an exact fake. But an exact fake is what they will have to produce, can only produce.

Friday, 12th April

The prevailing anxiety is the threat to surface-mine the actual gardens of Wentworth Woodhouse, up to the back door – a disgraceful business. Shinwell, that wretched man, is bound to allow it.

Dined with Charles Fry at Rules after trying some six restaurants in Soho and not getting a table. Charles far less drunken tonight, but more sinister. He said I was in bad form, whereas I thought I was in better form than I had been for

35

days. He took me to task for not being on good terms with Jamesey. Jamesey told him last night he was very fond of me except when I was 'diabolically malicious'. Now that is the very expression which he and I have consistently used in describing Charles. This has given me something to ponder over. Did he learn it from James? Charles also told me in a flat sort of voice that I was a great snob. Now if that is not diabolical malice I don't know what is. Of course I am a snob, not a social snob but an intellectual one. I like the company of my intellectual superiors.

Saturday, 13th April

This afternoon finished off additions to my book and went to tea with Margaret Jourdain and Ivy. Did not enjoy it at all. How these women eat! And how horrible their food is! And talking of social snobs, that is what they are. Their conversation all about the most worthless society people they have recently met and admired at tea parties. Dined excellently at the Ritz with John Philipps who leaves tomorrow by air for a hospital in Switzerland. His blood pressure is too low. Didn't enjoy this either.

Sunday, 14th April

Very virtuously attended 10 o'clock Low Mass and waited till 11.30 all through the Blessing of the Palms ceremony, and got my palm in the end. Was amazed by the way elderly well-dressed Pont Street ladies jostled and fought their way to the altar just as though they were fighting to get the last packet of spam at Marks & Spencer. Palms this year are the old sort again, and not that horrid box.

After midday motored with Rick in his friend Barry Till's car to Mersham-le-Hatch, the far side of Ashford, Kent. The caretaker, an old family retainer of the Knatchbulls, took us round the house which is now empty. Troops have been in it all the war. It is much messed about. There are few decorated rooms, apart from the Doric hall and the drawing-room with semi-circular bay. In this room, over the chimneypiece, is an oval inset portrait of Robert Adam. Since Zucchi did the grisailles in the hall I think this portrait is probably by him. The architect is in his early thirties and very handsome. No one else seems to have noticed this portrait. The ceiling retains its original colours, but it and the chimneypiece are much blackened by the banked-up fires of the soldiers. It is a fine room. The dining-room is disappointing; likewise the library; bookcases are Regency. The north front is rather too gaunt, but the brickwork, a beautiful rose, is in perfect English bonding. The stone work of parapet and cornice very clean cut. There is nothing 'ersatz' about this house. The north view over the water to the chalk downs is splendid. Got home at 11 o'clock. The caretaker at Mersham made me quite sick by insisting upon showing us the amputated stump of his arm.

Monday, 15th April

Rory Cameron lunched at Brooks's. I ate a fried goose egg which also made me feel as sick as the stump did yesterday. The raw flesh colour of it is nauseating. Left Rory and walked to the Courtauld Institute. Looked at the ceiling of the library and behold! there was a small circular medallion of Adam, also by Zucchi, only ten years older than yesterday. These discoveries are rather interesting. Here Robert Adam is in company with Milton, Newton, Locke, etc., which proves that his contemporaries estimated him, or he estimated himself, highly. This portrait is a small one. Then delivered my typescript to Batsford's again. Mr Harry [Batsford] suggested my editing their new edition of the Methuen guides, which would apparently involve little work and no research.

Tuesday, 16th April

Lunched at Olga Lynn's flat – excellently. Juliet Duff arrived wearing a tall straw top-hat with wide brim, which made her look more than ever like a giant dragoon. But what an outward-giving woman she is. I sat next to Oggy [Lynn] and Mrs. Gilbert Russell. At 2.45 I went to Kenwood where I was shown over the house by the Secretary. It is not yet open to the public, but is very well kept. So too are the grounds, which the public seem to respect, not trampling the grass down or picking flowers. The notices are neat and not over-conspicuous.

To the Piccadilly Theatre, with David Lloyd, his wife and Blanche Lloyd. The latter has mellowed. I think her nice daughter-in-law has humanized her. Blanche spoke with utter contempt of the present Government, and said it was the fault of Mr. Baldwin, which I could not quite understand. The Secretary at Kenwood today also surprised me a little by saying that she considered any infringement of a law passed by this Government was justifiable. We had supper at the Savoy. Blanche so sweet, kind and tolerant that I was much moved. She used to be farouche even when supposedly enjoying herself. I remember when staying with the Lloyds at Lerici in the house they rented from the Lubbocks Blanche would swim with grim determination every morning to a rock. Noël Coward described hers as the face that launched a thousand ships, for we all dived into the sea in order to swim ahead and watch her slow breast-stroke and her fierce demeanour. On her head she carried a book, spectacles, knitting and cigarettes crammed into her bathing cap. Indeed even in pleasure Blanche used to be a forbidding woman.

Wednesday 17th April

Motored Robin Fedden to Polesden, which was looking fresh and beautiful through the sun-tossed rain.

Thursday, 18th April

Bought for Mama a present of a glass paperweight ball with water inside, which when you shake turns into a snow storm. It cost six guineas, an absurd price and I daresay when made cost 5s.

Ivy and Margaret took me to tea with Elizabeth Bowen who lives at No. 2 Clarence Terrace, Regent's Park. She is a very handsome woman only her teeth are rather yellow; she smokes a lot. She stumbles with a slight, breathless stammer over unexpected words. Speaks deliberately, with conviction, and is observant; and sharp as a razor under layers of charm. She said it was more difficult to write a very short short story than a long short story. Said that we must all fight against being state-ridden. She seldom goes out or away for weekends. Besides Ivy and Margaret, Dame Una and James were present. J came over to talk to me and said that pressure of work alone had prevented him from ringing me up. His Monckton Milnes will not be published until 1948; meanwhile he is trying to finish his book on America. Says he is quite penniless again and has no income. Has £1 to last him till next week. All said with that calculating charm which it is hard to resist. I liked Elizabeth Bowen immensely.

Mass of the Pre-Sanctified was at eleven at the Oratory. I had to leave well before the end. Before I left Geoffrey [Houghton Brown] took me round his Thurloe Square house which is in process of decoration by that horrible H. and his pals. G. wants to move himself and me there in the autumn. The prospect of moving once again appals me. To him it is the breath of life.

Called on Helen [Dashwood] at West Wycombe. She told me that a crowned head, real monarch, might rent the house this summer, and asked what we would do about public opening? Just as I have arranged to open one day a week this is annoying. At Oxford stopped at the Blackfriars church and St. Aloysius church and said a prayer in each. Ate my luncheon just beyond Woodstock. This pretty village is quite spoiled by pylons and thick wires the whole length of the street. The Marlboroughs ought to have stopped it. What are dukes for? The country is looking its very best now, every bush bursting into bud. You can hear them like pistol shots ring out. Stopped at Chipping Norton church and said another prayer.

Called on Deenie at Stow-on-the-Wold and drank coffee with her. Then on to Broadway and said a prayer in that church, making five in all – a small penance for curtailing Mass today – a kind of Stations of the Cross. And what has all this holiness amounted to? Some very reprehensible springtime desires. Devoutness and physical needs have always gone hand in hand with me. They aren't foes, but blood brethren, who refuse to be kept apart.

At Wickhamford they were in the throes of preparation for a cocktail party this evening which they held in the garden. I hardly knew a soul. A few recognizable wizened faces of pre-war good-timers. Nothing but pleasure-seeking and in-anities. They having *nothing, nothing* to communicate. The only possibly interesting person present was Pug [Sir Hastings] Ismay, who as Military Adviser to the P.M. during the war, must at least be intelligent. He was being jolly and

gay, living down I suspected. He spoke to me most warmly of
George Mallaby, towards whom I feel cool.

I motored to Birtsmorton Court – most luscious, low-lying
Worcestershire country, my very favourite – under the lee of
the Malvern hills, so long-backed, naked, nobbly and impressive. The dreadful Mr Bradley-Birt received me. House
surrounded by a moat and very romantic, were it more
genuine. The remains of the gatehouse are thirteenth-cent, the
house fifteenth- and sixteenth-cent, I judge, rather like Bad-
desley Clinton, which is of course the genuine article. But the
old boy built just after the last war a wing to the east on the
foundations of a wing destroyed by fire a hundred years
previously. He did it well outside in half-timber and rosy red
brick. Swans swim in the moat, and peacocks preen on the
walls. The moated grange (not quite) all right. The interior –
two or three rooms of interest, Elizabethan panelled parlour
with early Renaissance frieze, plain plaster ceiling. Mullions
have been inserted where sash windows were shown in the old
Country Life article. I could see no contents of quality save a
shove-halfpenny table. Most of the furniture heavy black-
stained Victorian repros of lodging-house baseness. Brass pots
and pans in plenty, table-cloths of plush and doilies. Everlast-
ing flowers in vases of plate. Pretty little church in the garden
with two monuments by White of Worcester, one signed, the
larger not so, but of a recumbent gentleman. The house is so
cluttered with dusty, frowsty things that it appears a mess in
spite of four servants, all male, perhaps because all male. Mr.
Bradley-Birt spoke almost exclusively of his friendship with
Prince Ruprecht of Bavaria and the Kaiser, of whom he has an
enormous photograph on the piano.

Called on poor old Canon Alsebrook in the Evesham hospital.
He is a wraith of what he used to be; sitting up beside his bed,
looking extremely handsome, but so ill and resigned. He
spoke slowly about the Sandys tombs in the church. How
often have I listened to this conversation over the years, almost
since he christened me? He is an educated but not wise old

man. Devoted to the classics, and taught me Latin. Treated abominably by the family who would hide when he called uninvited at the manor, because he, who knew nothing of hunting and shooting, bored them. I can see him retreating shamefacedly and disappointed from the front door down the drive. But I always loved him.

Tuesday, 23rd April

Motored to Wolverhampton and lunched with the Manders. I found Wightwick Manor more interesting than I previously realised. The Kempe stained-glass drawings in a folder more beautiful than the finished things. The Manders' enthusiasm for the Pre-Raphaelites is infectious. He is a very decent, good, thoughtful man. Left-wing. He told me he was sure socialism was right and the rich should be taxed more. But he offers an additional £5000 to the N.T. so that his house may be maintained out of tax-free money. Is that disingenuous? I think not. Lady Mander talkative and pretty ('Call me Rosalie.' 'Call me Jim').

After luncheon I took Lady Mander and her son to Moseley Old Hall. Met old Mr. Wiggin there and spent two-and-a-half hours seeing round. Mr. Wiggin is so slow, mysterious and mystic about Charles II that it is difficult to make headway.

Wednesday, 24th April

Motored to Charlecote where I lunched and spent the afternoon. Back to London. Was just in time to eat a morsel at Sibyl Colefax's Ordinary. Sat next to Ben and after dinner talked to Bogey Harris and Rose Macaulay about Lord Acton the historian. All the time I was only interested in a piece of skin on my index finger that I was trying to twist off.

Thursday, 25th April

Motored the British Legion man and attendant to Cliveden where I installed them. To West Wycombe and back to London. The opening of both these houses is going to be a great problem.

Thomas Cook advised me it would not be difficult to get a seat to Switzerland provided the visas were first obtained, the French and the Swiss. This afternoon I trained to Eastbourne where Paul Latham met me at the station. Just the same in appearance, like a bounding retriever puppy, hatless, his hair still yellow, clustering and curly. Complexion slightly sunburned. We had tea at the station buffet. I have not seen him since my disastrous visit in the summer of 1943. He was giggly and rather endearing. We dined with his old mother who is staying in Eastbourne to be near him. She is a dear, ordinary old woman of seventy-nine, adoring her son. Paul is angelic to her and I have seldom seen any son treat his mother better. She, he told me, befriended him when he was in prison, never missed writing, never reproached him, and never has done since. He says she has always been and always will be his best friend. We drank South African hock. Paul is living in a different house at Herstmonceux, on the road: not very comfortable and the ceilings very low. He is greatly improved. Far less hysterical and more reconciled. Less sex mad. Seems to take a far saner view of life. He will of course always be self-centred in that he at once takes it for granted that one is interested in whatever local or domestic matter is absorbing him at the moment.

Sunday, 28th April

Rained all day as usual. Up very late this morning because I did not get to sleep till late. I sat on Paul's bed till about 3 a.m. out of affection and a desire to console. He talked non-stop. We went to Herstmonceux Place, which is not yet de-requisitioned, and into which he intends to move next month. It is a beautiful house, not small. Paul plans to do some unfortunate things, notably alter the entrance hall. The library with exedrae is a prettily shaped room; the oval stairwell pretty too, but the troops have smashed several of the balusters. The white panels of Coade stone on the outside of the house are decorative.

Lady Latham came to luncheon. Paul has a butler who lives out. He, Paul, not the butler, pays 19*s*.6*d*. income tax and all his money is in trust, so he cannot live on his capital. It is hard for someone in his circumstances, very rich on paper with little money to spend. Went to the Castle after luncheon and walked round it. Paul has sold it to Greenwich Observatory. This was my doing for I introduced the Astronomer Royal to him three years ago when he came to ask for a house from the National Trust.

Paul says that no one has ever insulted him since he came out of prison, but I noticed that people in the Eastbourne hotel stared at him. It gives me a perverse pleasure to be seen with him. All the servants, his own or other people's, seem devoted to him. He is always doing kindnesses and giving people lifts, and making jokes. Yet he is profoundly unhappy.

This morning I bussed from Hailsham to Uckfield and was met by Mr. Basil Ionides who motored me out to Buxted Park. He is a pleasant, jolly, *bon viveur*, large and well-fed. He told me in confidence that on his wife's death her estate would be worth £2 million. We went all round the house, which was burnt out in 1940. Immediately afterwards they began reconstruction and are still continuing. They took off the top storey altogether so that from the outside the house looks grotesque. Nothing of the inside is left at all except two plaster overmantels of coats of arms and mantling. Everything else is new, or imported. There are chimneypieces from Clumber, overmantels and columns from Kingston House, Felix Hall and so on. Yet the reproduction looks flat and of poor quality. The staircase comes from the Burlington Hotel, General Wade's House. Buxted is full of good things and contains nothing that I would not like to have myself, except the famous scent bottle collection. I cannot recommend the house on its own merits. It is a travesty, a pastiche. And the Ionides do not offer any contents. The park is beautiful, but so are most English parks.

This evening went to 41 Yeoman's Row where Geoffrey Lemprière, my Australian friend, is staying. I have not seen him for seven or eight years, perhaps nine. He is exactly the same, like a startled kangaroo, and his age is only betrayed by the tight fold behind the ear, and hair growing from the lobe of

43

the ear. He is no more a ball of fire than he used to be, but thoroughly, intrinsically decent. He was in a Japanese pris-oner-of-war camp for three years and seven months and spoke of his sufferings quite cheerfully. They were starved and beaten all the time. The Japanese have no redeeming qualities of any kind – not even good looks – and are treacherous, insinuating and cruel. He says he will take me as his guest to Sweden the first week of June by air. This will be a treat.

Wednesday, 1st May

Bridget [Parsons] dined with me here. Anne's son Tony is very ill with meningitis, supposed to be of a fatal kind. At 10.30 Bridget made me accompany her to Emerald Cunard's. Neither of us was changed. We found a dinner party still at the table, all in evening dress: Lord Bruntisfield, Lady Milbank, Mary Lady Howe, the French Ambassadress and the King of Greece. Ambassadress thanked me for the synopsis of British architecture and furniture I sent her. Was presented to the King as the man who looks after all the public houses of England – Emerald always does this – and shook hands, while bowing slightly. Should one shake first, or bow first? Or simul-taneous? Then B. and I were left talking to each other and were miserable. We left as soon as we could, long before the party showed signs of breaking up.

Friday, 3rd May

Dined with Malcolm [Bullock] at the Turf. What is the matter with me that I find a staleness and futility in those of my friends whose tacit superiority is that they are sophisticated and in the swim? Lord Ilchester joined us at dinner, telling us how corrupt the police are. He instanced the case several months ago when he was fined for driving through a military zone at Wilton. It goes against the grain for me to criticise the police, naively believing all policemen to be like our dear old Sergeant Haines at Wickhamford and Badsey who spanked the boys for stealing apples and succoured old women and lame cats; and, after the Vicar, was the pillar of village society.

Alvilde dined. I called for her at Violet Woodhouse's. What a gruff, rude man Mr. W is. Took Alvilde to the White Tower and gave her a delicious dinner; then to a news reel. Think A. enjoyed it. I almost loved her this evening and kissed her affectionately on leaving her at her hotel.

At last got through to Michael Rosse on the telephone at Caernarvon. He cannot leave Anne and keep his engagement to address the Wisbech Society tomorrow. Wants me to be his substitute. Annoyed me a little by implying that it was my duty to the N.T. to provide another speaker at short notice. Not an easy thing to do when I am just off on a number of engagements in Norfolk, and on a Sunday too. The worry about this meeting upset me all day. It is a horrid, squally, cold, rainy day too. I motored after Mass to Bedford and had a look at Willington stables and dovecote – both well worth holding, and both in tolerable condition. Stopped at Houghton Mill, rather dilapidated, weather-boarded construction on river Ouse with distant church spires in the landscape. Then to Ramsey Abbey gatehouse; very ruinous and in bad state. A huge crack down the entire side fronting the road. Then across the fens, the car nearly blown off the straight bank into the drain. One, called Forty Foot Drain, I followed for nearly eight miles. Bleak and desolate as in Vita's novel. I approached what I thought was a bad fire. It proved to be dry black earth driven by the wind. There was a cottage receiving the full brunt of it. It was smothered, almost inundated by a death-like pall of dust. Had a look at Swanton Morley, where we have done nothing, and on to Bradenham [Hall] at 6.30. Alec Penrose and his wife out when I called, but returned; and I stayed the night with them. I was so tired that after two cocktails and a bottle of burgundy I hardly knew what I was doing. Nevertheless, after dinner endeavoured to concoct a speech for Alec to deliver in lieu of Michael, he being only too willing and I unwilling.

Alec talked of Christianity of which he is now an enthusiastic supporter. Says this separates him from his family who do not sympathise. Shares with me the recognition of a need to introduce Christian principles into British politics. Thinks a new Christian movement or party must be founded to counter Communism and totalitarianism. Agrees that the next war will be a civil one on a gigantic world scale, not between nations but between these two creeds or issues.

Arrived at Blickling at midday and spent afternoon there with Birkbeck [agent] and Miss O'Sullivan.

Dined at Brooks's with Professor Richardson. He said that he reads the Gospel lesson for each day of the year; that age has taught him humility; that never will there be architects until there are patrons again; that without aristocracy of the higher and lower grades there could be no beauty; that consequently it was our duty to oppose this Government at every turn. Yet there is no bitterness in this old man. He is a dear and good man.

My Historic Buildings Committee went well. Michael was present. Esher said afterwards that it was the best of all the N.T. committees. I met Roger Fulford at the bottom of St. James's and he took me to lunch at the Reform. He is as whimsical, teasing and anti-papistical as ever. I like him immensely. He is finishing a book on the Prince Consort. Says that he and John Summerson are both turning their interests from Regency to mid-Victorian. In some measure they have both set a fashion. Says I am always associated in his mind with Christopher Hobhouse and Tom Mitford, both dead.

I motored two of the British Legion attendants back from Cliveden. One of them had a wooden leg and had lost an arm. He was a very nice old fellow. Told me had been a steeple-jack and fell ninety feet from a factory chimney. His father and grandfather were jacks, and he loved it. Had climbed Salisbury spire and St. Paul's. Had a photograph of himself standing on one of the arms of the cross taken by a pal from the other arm. Four men can sit on each. Yet he fainted with fear when taken down a mine.

Thursday, 9th May

Called on Harold [Nicolson] at six. He said he would not consider the National Trust secretaryship because he was intent upon returning to politics. But advised that the status should be elevated to Director-General or some such term, and the salary raised. Said James's 'cellist friend was charming. Doreen wrote today that he was 'a wonderful being'.

Friday, 10th May

Meeting day. All the staff made to leave the room while the Secretaryship was discussed. I learned that the committee agreed to ask Peter Earle to accept; if he refused, then to advertise. My canvassing had results, so I like to think, in that the committee scotched a proposal to make the Chief Agent into the Secretary or to invite Matheson to return.

Saturday, 11th May

After luncheon I called for Keith [Miller Jones] at Sudbrooke and motored him to the Wick, Richmond Hill. Went over the house opened to members of the Georgian Group. Then to Riverside House, Twickenham. Admired the Gibbs Octagon Room and had tea with Mrs. Ionides. Margaret Jourdain came, wearing a fur wrap. Mrs. Ionides said peremptorily, 'M.J., take that thing off. You can't be cold.' M.J. had her revenge when at tea I remarked innocently, 'Dare we cut this beautiful new chocolate cake?' 'Yes,' she said, 'of course. It will be good for *her*.' She said Ivy C.-B. has finished her new novel, but none of her novels make sense. She said she knew little of Ivy's antecedents, but thought her family had lived in a *substantial* house. She had two sisters living. Her brother was killed in the 'Little War'. Ivy, she said, had no everyday common sense. For instance, she never knew in a terminus station which way the train would leave from.

We looked at the saloon in Marble Hill. John Fowler thought the brown veining was original. I am sure it is not.

Low Mass at ten. Read most of the day the history of Sweden, etc. At tea Miss Sybil Paley Ashmore came to talk about the Baileys, but was a little disappointing. She is aged sixty-nine and my second cousin. It is curious suddenly to meet someone who remembers my grandfather who died in 1889, and my grandmother in 1896. I had a photograph of the latter on my mantelpiece, and she said, 'There's Christina!' Said she had a beautiful low, Scotch voice; that all the family loved her. That our great-grandfather amassed the family fortune, that his grandson the late Lord was a millionaire, and that in between his two marriages the first baronet led a gay life and begat many illegitimate children. He was perfectly hideous, so there's hope for us all.

Colin Agnew dined. A sweet little man. He said he weighed only eight-and-a-half stone. He is like the White Rabbit in *Alice in Wonderland*.

Monday, 13th May

Alan Lennox-Boyd asked me to luncheon at Chapel Street. There were Princess Natasha Bagration and her husband Charles Johnston, an intelligent, good-looking man, in the F.O., younger than her I should say. She is very nice, with popping eyes and wide teeth. It is ten years since we met. I drank red wine and felt inebriated the rest of the day.

Wednesday, 15th May

Had a long day. Left at 8.30. Trained to Gloucester where I was met by Eardley in his Ford. We lunched at The New Inn. Then drove to Crickley Hill and walked round it. Very beautiful hilltop but we ought to have more of it, right to the edge of the escarpment. Then to Hayles Abbey. I agreed with E that perhaps after all we should surrender it to the Min. of Works. As it is, it is simply falling down and we have no funds whatever to maintain it. I got to London at ten and had a cold hot dinner – my fault – with the Moores. A French woman and M. Rocher there. He said Anglo-French relations were bad because we imported no French produce. Our Labour Government would not allow it. Joan looked tired. Her beauty shines no less, but it is of a different calibre to what it was when I first met her. It is as though a diamond had turned into a topaz, a no less dazzling jewel, but different.

Thursday, 16th May

Trained this morning to Aylesbury and was motored by Mrs James Rothschild's agent to Waddesdon Manor. What a house! An 1880 pastiche of a François Premier château. Yet it is impressive because it is on the grand scale. There is symmetry, and craftsmanship and finish. I suppose most people today would pronounce it hideous. I find it compelling. A nursery school, which was here throughout the war, has just left. It is being scrubbed and cleaned. The Rothschilds are moving back into the whole of it, which is huge. They have been living in the wing. Most of the rooms are panelled with gilded Louis XV *boiserie*. One drawing-room is lined with marble. Furniture French of the highest quality. One room stacked with pictures, taken out of their frames. Could not see them. A hundred acres of grounds offered too. Beautiful trees. In all a better Cliveden. I have written a report, by no means contemptuous, upon it.

Friday, 17th May

A terrific struggle in the Passport Office. They have endorsed my passport which I retrieved from them after being told at first – when my turn in the queue came – that it was not to be found. Then left mine and Geoff Lemprière's at the Swedish Legation for a week. Went to Albert Hall to hear Schnabel but was frankly bored by the thirty-three Beethoven waltz variations.

Saturday, 18th May

Sheila de Rützen lunched at the Ritz but I was obliged to leave in order to pack and start off for the Vyne. Arrived at 5.45. I liked the Chutes much more this time, perhaps because he treated me in a less schoolmastery, more equal-to-equal manner. It is a beautiful house and the garden looking so green and spruce. The wide lawns all mown again. The school has left

49

and they are living in the whole house because she says you cannot shut up part for the moth and general corruption. She is a childlike, almost childish woman, but fundamentally sweet. They live in a Spartan fashion, and their food is not good. Their views are too conservative and unaccommodating. I slept in the Gothic Room above the tomb chapel. We talked for hours and I think they will hand the place over. They know they must be the last of the family to inhabit the whole house and to submit themselves to its exacting demands. A younger generation which has not lived in it as children could not be expected to do the same. They have no servants living in. Four village ladies come during the week.

Sunday, 19th May

Left the Chutes at 10.30. A long sermon delivered at Newbury en route by a very saintly-faced old priest who punched us from the shoulder for not attending the Benediction. He declared that Europe was becoming apathetic to the Real Presence. It was a pity he delivered himself in a style imitative of Mr Churchill making his blood, sweat and tears speech. It hardly came off. This made me late for luncheon at Ted Lister's where I arrived at 1.20, having battled through storm and rain.

Westwood [Manor], Ted and Christo [Bulgarian servant] all looked well. Alex Moulton lunched. He and Ted very thick and see a lot of each other. This through my introduction, and I am pleased. Ted and I drove to Iford [Manor] and had a word with Mike Peto, still on his back with thrombosis, and very bad. He has had three days's injection of penicillin every four hours, deep like a bayonet wound, he says. And he becomes more frightened each time. He was lying on the terrace off the first floor overlooking the garden, even during the rain, which means most of the day, but under a ground sheet. When I saw him, the rain having stopped, he was stripped, wearing a tight pair of blue drawers and a blue silk vest without arms, which made me cold to look at him.

I drove to Bridgewater after tea and stayed alone at the Royal Clarence.

At ten met our Holnicote agent at Nether Stowey. He is the stage pork-pie hat, 'May good fellar' type. I gritted my teeth, determined to be a good fellar myself. Succeeded apparently, for he pressed me to stay with him and wife. I declined. Went all round Coleridge's cottage and decided that Biffens, care-takeress and husband, should stay. Nice people. From Nether Stowey a most beautiful drive to Arlington Court, stormy skies with golden sun, the moors purple, and views distant and clear. Could see right across the Channel to Wales and the houses there. I think Exmoor more appealing than the pent-up lowering Lake District. Arlington Court is plain to ugliness. Of a dark, hard ironstone, the old part is severe Greek Regency, featureless. Unappetising annexe built on *c.* 1875 by Miss Chichester's father. The park untidy and overrun with rabbits, the whole estate no more remarkable than the country round it. Miss Chichester very old, white haired and dropsic-al, the last of her line. Looked after by a gentle, fawn-like young man from Shaftesbury Avenue. Her museum, made by herself, is a nightmare of model ships, shells and New Zealand Maori headdresses. She lives and sleeps in her drawing-room which is made into an aviary. Birds fly over her bed and perch on a clutter of bric-à-brac and masses of flowers. In the church is a memorial tablet to Mr. John Meadows, architect from London who died in 1791. The Rectory, which Mr. Meadows may have built (if he was still alive) is a very satisfactory building, with four projecting rounded bays. It has the mini-mum of ornamentation and relies upon line and curve. A pure architectural abstraction. I was riveted. The Holnicote agent, with the most sympathetic attention, could see nothing in it at all.

Drove over Dunkery to Bradfield [Hall] and stayed the night with the Adamses.

Tuesday, 21st May

Terrible showers all day. Spent the morning with Mrs. Adams in the big house. It is horribly over-restored but the great hall and the Spanish Room are so good they make the rest worth while. The elaborate interior porch and overmantel in the latter room are superbly grotesque. She talked of Ayrrshire and our mutual relations, all of whose names begin with Glen. She told me her sister, Maud Wellington, had died as a result of 'faithful repression' by the Wellesley family, into whom she had married. Said the aristocracy was played out and that God had arranged for their economic eclipse to coincide with the decline of their morals. This house belongs to her son, Lord Waleran.

Left before tea for Montacute. Found Clifford Smith there. A lovely evening and after dinner we walked round the park, golden with buttercups. Both very depressed by the sad state of the garden, not a whit improved since our last visit. C. says that most of the furniture sent by Mrs. Trafford is the wrong lot, and not what he chose.

Wednesday, 22nd May

Motored to Salisbury to the Assizes. Was not called upon to give evidence for the two sailors pleaded guilty and were given only eighteen months on account of their youth, service and previous good record. The judge was young, about my age, and looked resplendent in his red robes. There was a subsequent case of a man who had raped his daughter, aged fourteen, which I could not wait for and was sorry to miss.

Friday, 24th May

Having spent all yesterday with Clifford arranging to the best of our ability the scanty exhibits we welcomed Sir Geoffrey Hippisley-Cox and Christopher Hussey today. They came from London and made several useful suggestions. Everyone at Montacute is so enthusiastic, the Yates family at the inn and the Shoemarks, a hereditary family of masons in the village, and all helping. At six I motored Sir G. back to London. We dined at The White Hart, Salisbury. He talked the entire way and I was distressed that my car made such a rattle. He told me that the late Sir John French, Lord Ypres, left his whole fortune to Sir Geoffrey with the direction that he should dispose of it as he thought fit. This will caused him enormous worry, trouble and expense. French was one of his greatest friends and a man to whom posterity has yet to do justice. Sir G. is very intelligent, wise and a bonhomme, without being intellectual. The best product of the squirearchy, with no sense of self-importance. Quietly dutiful, self-effacing and human.

A long day. Left at ten from King's Cross for Doncaster. Michael R met me and motored me to Wentworth Wood-house. Had time to walk round the outside and over parts of the inside. It is certainly the most enormous private house I have ever beheld. I could not find my way about the interior and never once knew in what direction I was looking from a window. Strange to think that up till 1939 one man lived in the whole of it. All the contents are put away or stacked in heaps in a few rooms, the pictures taken out of their frames. The dirt is appalling. Everything is pitch black and the boles of the trees like thunder. To my surprise the park is not being worked for surface coal systematically, but in square patches here and there. One of these patches is the walled garden. Right up to the very wall of the Vanbrugh front every tree and shrub has been uprooted, awaiting the onslaught of the bulldozers. Where the surface has been worked is waste chaos and, as Michael said, far worse than anything he saw of French battlefields after D-day. I was surprised too by the very high quality of the pre-Adam rooms and ceilings of Wentworth; by the amount of seventeenth-century work surviving; by the beautiful old wallpapers; and by the vast scale of the lay-out of the park, with ornamental temples sometimes one-and-a-half miles or more away. Lady Fitzwilliam in a pair of slacks, rather dumpy and awkward, came downstairs for a word just before we left. I fancy she is not very sensitive to the tragedy of it all.

We 'entrained' (to use a military term) back to London the same day. On our return Anne gave M. and me a sandwich dinner and a bottle of M's best white wine.

To the Albert Hall, Schnabel concert – all Beethoven con-certos. S. is indeed a wonderful pianist, sensitive and sure, strong yet not assertive. We dined at the Dorchester at 10 o'clock in Anne and Michael's suite, i.e. the Rosses, Bridget and Christopher Sykes.

Ian McCallum lunched. He has pale blue eyes, alert and unforgiving. Spent afternoon at Batsford's. They agreed to give me £50 for the second edition of the National Trust book, and there and then a cheque for £250. Mr. Harry and Charles [Fry] still want me to edit the Methuen guides and also to reduce W.H. Ward's *French Renaissance Architecture* from two volumes to one. I had tea with Lady Esher in the Es new little house in Chelsea. Lord E. huddled in a chair, wracked by lumbago and not in his usual rumbustious form. Mrs. Oglander and Miss Ethel Sands there, both very chatty.

Thursday, 30th May

Having been to Ascension Day Mass at 8 o'c I left London. Took with me glass show-cases and the Charlecote Tudor cup. Called at West Wycombe to glance at the ceilings repaired and repainted. I thought not too well done considering how the Museum men are experts. Left a small Staffordshire ornament as a present for Sarah who is to be married on Saturday. Had a word with Johnnie Dashwood in his office. He was looking smaller and more mouse-like. Then on to Churchill near Chipping Norton. Had a quick look round the cottage in which Warren Hastings is supposed to have been born. In itself it is not up to much. Nothing remains but oak stairs with twisted balusters and some William and Mary doors. On to Charlecote which looks extremely neat and tidy. Helped arrange certain rooms. Home for supper at Wickhamford.

Friday, 31st May

A really terrible day spent at Charlecote. It rained cats and dogs and was bitterly cold. The Lucys all rather overwrought. The guide books have not come and, worst of all, the British Legion attendants never turned up. They were expected today in order to learn the history of the house and be told what to do at the opening tomorrow. Not a sign of them. There being no telephone I drove to Wellesbourne and rang up the London office. Dashed back again. Left at 6.30, nothing done. Returned to Wickhamford almost ill with nerves and anxiety.

Woke at seven, finished packing, breakfasted at eight and called at 41 Yeoman's Row. Went with Geoffrey Lemprière to the Imperial Airways House and were weighed in. Drove in a bus to Northolt Aerodrome, where we drank coffee and ate a roll. Everything is efficiently done and the attendants polite. At 10.30 we got into the aeroplane. This was my first flight since I was sick looping the loop in Captain Butler's Moth over Broadway Hill in 1925. While the machine was revving up Geoffrey said I looked scared and started to read to me. This I resented, but I was scared, and would not look out of the window for quite a time. Then I took courage and first noticed what I think was Boreham Hall with its canal in Essex. England looks small, compact and very beautiful from the air. Most striking features are the fields and hedgerows, chequer-board fashion, and the number of country houses and de-mesnes. It was not a very clear day and at times we were flying blind. I had taken a pill and a luminol and did not feel ill at all. Only over Denmark was it bumpy. I do not like it when the machine drops like a stone. Jutland is flat and neat. It has straight canals and roads with regimented trees. The number of old farmhouses, all in square formation round a courtyard, uniform. Few villages, but the area thickly populated by these scattered homesteads. Reached Copenhagen at 2.15 and bus-sed to the centre of the town. Walked in the Tivoli Gardens where we had tea. All gay and bright. The sun shining. It is far warmer than in England. It took us precisely a quarter of an hour to fly on to Malmö, which is ugly from the air.

Were met by Geoff's firm's agent who walked us round the town. I was particularly struck by the modern theatre, of simplest lines, too severe and unadorned, faced with a grey-white marble. A pity that the building resolves itself into ugly brick at one extremity. The season is over so we could not enter. The shop windows are *full* of good things. In fact the air of well-being and luxury of the Hotel Kremer where we are staying is wonderful and exhilarating. The shop windows seem replete with everything one could possibly want to buy. The beauty of the boys and girls. Everyone is young. The cream complexion of the men, their blond thick hair. Women with pale blue eyes and bare arms. The standard of good looks immensely high.

We dined in the smart restaurant in the Kungspark, the waiters in trim uniforms, clean as clean can be. Speciality here the hors d'oeuvres which go on and on, accompanied by schnapps.

Monday, 3rd June

I wandered round the town all morning while Geoff and the agent had business appointments. I made notes of the buildings I visited. We lunched with a business man who spoke no English. In the afternoon we were taken by the agent, a nice little man who has lately lost his wife, to the outskirts of Malmö and shown some of the recent suburban development. Extremely impressed by the wholeness, convenience and neatness. Everything is neat here. A garden city of two-storey buildings in rows, each alternate house facing the opposite way so as to ensure privacy. Air of gaiety and happiness. We went into Allström the agent's house, a little, low, long villa, quite prettily furnished with modern birch-wood furniture in traditional eighteenth-century style, but not absurd. A lot to be said for middle-class taste and existence. Complacency breeds content.

Allström took us to dine with a rich merchant's family, by name Mueller. They live well and modishly. Were most hospitable. Meal began with cocktails, then red wine, port wine, and brandy. You must not start drinking until your hostess or host says 'skoll'. Then you wait, or else 'skoll' the other members of the family before drinking yourself. You may never 'skoll' your hostess. Whole paraphernalia a terrible bore. We dined at six, the normal time here, and caught a 9 o'clock train to Gotesburg. You must make a speech before rising from the table and on leaving the dining-room host and hostess shake hands with each guest. I had a third-class sleeper, spotlessly clean with sheets, only a little cramped for there were three of us. The trains are all electric and no dirt. Every carriage scoured by an army of officials on arrival at a large station, and fresh carafes of water provided.

Tuesday, 4th June

Gotesburg a charming town of intersecting canals. In the morning I was free to roam around. Examined the Dom, the

Museum and all the eighteenth-century houses along the canals, including the Town Hall by Tessin. Bought a few ties and handkerchiefs. We caught a 2.30 train to Stockholm. For six hours the country never varied: fairly flat, heathy, birch woods with green glades of poor grass land, and many lakes. Soil looks thin and the vegetation not as green as in England. On arrival we drove to the Stockholm City Hotel, on the sixth floor of a huge, grim, gaunt building. We had eaten a delicious dinner of grilled salmon on the train. Walked round the town till midnight, wondering open-eyed at the combination of ancient buildings, grand shop windows and brilliant lights.

Wednesday, 5th June

Sweden is a land of lilac, though less of it in Stockholm than in the south. I shall not forget the hedges of lilac, like rhododendrons, at Malmö.

Our guide this morning appeared without his mourning band and tie, and went off to buy flowers for a lady, whom we suspect he is courting. This left Geoff and me free to do shopping. The three of us lunched at the Grand Hotel in a glass shelter overlooking the Palace. In the afternoon Allström conducted us round Skansen in the boiling sun. Looked at primitive Swedish wooden houses, brought from the north and re-assembled here, complete with furniture, utensils, etc. No protection to prevent the public from stealing. They just don't steal in this country, and the stacks of chopped wood for winter fuel lining the side streets are never looted. We drank lemonade to a band. This evening Jane Denham, the Naval Attaché's daughter, dined with us; also Allström's young lady whom we pronounced bossy. We ate at the most expensive restaurant, name of which I forget, and went afterwards to the Tivoli. Went on roundabouts and swings, and I felt ill and was sick. The lights and merriment are something I never remember in England before the war.

Sunday, 9th June

There seems little point in enumerating my doings in Stockholm. Since Geoff left on Thursday I have literally not spoken a sentence to a soul. I have visited the Town Hall, the modern Hagersten Church, the new hospital, the state apartments of

57

the Royal Palace (disappointing), the Palace of Drottningholm (enchanting French formal garden and unique 1760 theatre, complete with contemporary stage equipment), the Hagaslott Pavilion (by far the best rooms I have seen; a veritable Petit Trianon), the National Museum and Northern Museum (the one picture, the other period furnishings). I have also been to the Ballet Joos and two cinemas, one film of *Henry V*. I have eaten in the best restaurants and some of the cheapest, and have bought quantities of clothes, though not as many as I would dare to buy for the risk of paying duties.

Only occasionally in the evenings have I felt lonely. Only once I bought some pleasure. Flat, stale and unprofitable it was too. Talk of cold mutton on Monday. Had there been only some nice hot mutton on Sunday. But no. Experienced little elation and no disgust. On the other hand the sun shone and I am well.

On Monday visited the new cemetery at Eskede suburb by Asplund and was greatly impressed by it. Graves neatly arranged within boskets of birch or pine, all the new tombstones simple and unexceptionable. Did not see one that was offensive. The main chapel and crematorium of white marble; magnificent bronze group within an open temple, and vertical figures aspiring skywards, made more effective by there being no roof over them. The descending ground well laid out in a kind of terrace wall, enclosing little memorial courts, or gardens. Great polished granite Cross standing silhouetted beside the temple. The view from the approach positively welcoming. The whole conception is original, underivative, modern, cheerful. Above all cheerful, as though the Swedes are putting a bold front on death, pretending that darkness is light, corruption is amendment. Death is all for the best in the best of all possible worlds. So contrary to the English approach which is a dismal belief that the trappings of death must be inartistic and rebarbative.

Left by night train, second-class sleeper to Malmö. Met a distinguished Danish count in the next sleeper who spoke of the deplorable condition of Denmark since the war, the workers not working and demanding high wages, just like present-day England.

Arrived Malmö at 7.30 just in time for plane to Copenhagen, where I had breakfast. Plane left Copenhagen at 10.45 and reached Northolt at 1.5. It was a large liner, holding forty people, and much larger than the one going out. Consequently it flew higher. Ears started cracking. The higher the more frightening, I think. For some time we were right above the clouds, white like the Alps and dazzling. Watched the shadow of the plane surrounded by an iridescent halo, like a rainbow, chasing below us. Then suddenly a hole made in the clouds and land appeared tiny far underneath. Later we descended and the weather improved. It is strange how flying through clouds shakes the plane and makes it bump. I noticed from the air how sheep and cattle eat their way systematically across a field, keeping to a line, or rather circumference. From a height there is distinct demarcation of colour between the grazed and ungrazed grass.

Wednesday, 12th June

Philip James who lunched with me said that the late Lord Keynes was a man of such superior moral power as well as intellect that in his presence you at once felt elevated to a plane that permitted only the most edifying conversation. He drew the best out of you and his modesty never allowed his intellectual superiority to be overbearing.

John Wilton and I dined at Wilton's, and I suggested our walking across St. James's Park to inspect some photographs at my office. I had not reckoned with the surging crowds of people looking at the illuminated fountains in the lake. We were nearly crushed to death. These fountains are pretty but more suited to the formality of Versailles gardens than the informality of this park.

Friday, 14th June

Meetings today. Our new Secretary, Admiral Bevir, in attendance, although George Mallaby was in the office for the last time. Admiral seems jolly, if too inclined to be facetious. Of course he has been warned by the Chairman that we are not a bureaucratic team of experts, but a dedicated group of happy-go-lucky enthusiasts, who ought not to be bossed about.

Lunched with Harold [Nicolson] at the Travellers'. Lord Crawford pressed me to stay at Haigh Hall next weekend to see his pictures in case a few might do for Montacute. He is packing up and leaving the place for good. I said how sad it must be for him. He looked desperately unhappy for a moment and replied, 'Really, it is just terrible how much I mind.'

Saturday, 15th June

At 10.30 to the Soane Museum and began looking through the Adam drawings. John Summerson came up and said, 'I have not yet studied these in any detail, but a cursory inspection is enough to convince me what a very great man Robert Adam was.' There must be twenty volumes in all and I examined two thoroughly. The coloured drawings are superb. After a quick luncheon went to Batsford's where from two till five went through the illustrations for my book. Made a selection by process of eliminating several hundreds submitted.

At six went to Doreen. She said that when she got going on her writing she became an instrument, a gigantic machine or fountain pen through which outside thoughts and ideas poured, sometimes to the extent of thoroughly alarming her, the *she* remaining such a passive, uncontrolling feature of the process.

Sunday, 16th June

Motored to Polesden Lacey for tea with Robin Fedden who in the face of every domestic adversity has already made a splendid start with the museum. I was very impressed. Midi [Gascoigne] came over afterwards, and I went to sup with her and Derick at their new house nearby. Midi told me that Timmy Buxton is dying of cancer.

Monday, 17th June

Trained with Hubert Smith to Darlington and stayed the night at The Morritt Arms at Rokeby on the Tees. After a late supper we went for a walk to Ecclestone Priory, belonging to the Ministry of Works. Did not like the heavy black pointing of the stonework which they have done there. The situation is very romantic. I disliked the ugly little wooden hut which they have erected just in front of the ruins. The Ministry lacks taste and sensitivity in spite of its academic superiority. Listened to the curlews. Hubert told me that corncrakes are practically extinct in the south.

Tuesday, 18th June

At ten Lord Barnard's agent – very nice man – motored us to Raby Castle. It was pouring torrential rain as it has done every day this season. We had a hurried look round the Castle, of which nothing inside impressed me very favourably. Most of the rooms are heavy 1840. The ball room of that date is enormous. There are vestiges of late seventeenth-century woodwork. Most of the furniture stacked away, but what I saw of it and the pictures at a hasty glance left me cold. The outside is beautiful and 'picturesque'. The park and surrounding country fine and unspoilt. The walled garden is well set out. Of the house the kitchen is the most interesting apartment. Large and square, it is still in use. It has very highly placed windows; a lantern over all and most curious walks, like aisles, through the thickness of the walls. Many old burnished coppers and moulds on shelves. Lord B. is rather severe and practical, and only attractive when he laughs, which is rarely. Lady B. is younger, good-looking, and well dressed in tweeds. A pretty young daughter barely out, and a younger boy, aged about nineteen. They gave us a delicious luncheon of mutton and éclairs filled with real cream; also the richest plum cake stuffed with fruit from New Zealand. Our journey back to London was tedious owing to the train breaking down outside Doncaster station for one-and-a-half hours.

Wednesday, 19th June

I don't think I shall be very happy with the new Secretary, our Vice-Admiral. In his facetiousness there is an underlying disdain which I don't find funny. Lord Rochdale came to see me about his tapestries, a queer, fortyish man with heavy moustache, and rather a zanyish look that people have who are senior wranglers. My telephone never ceased ringing while he was in the office, so that I became frappy, which was rather rude to him.

Charles [Fry] dined at the White Tower. As usual he made me drink. We had a red Greek wine with saffron in it. Charles bores me with his queer talk. It is insensitive of him to suppose that I want to listen to it. He is not a person to see for long. At the St. James's Club Sachie Sitwell joined us. He is going to Holland for a month with Charles and Mr. Batsford. God help him! He talked of Sweden.

Thursday, 20th June

Motored Gwynne Ramsey to Hatchlands. He is a dull, dear little man, down-trodden and shy. Goodhart-Rendel gave us, plus Christopher Gibbs, Acland and May, his agent, an excellent luncheon with sherry and port. There is a happy air about this house, something that may have hung over from the Boscawens' day. Conversation was entirely between G.-R. and me about obscure architects, funny stories about Surrey county families long ago, and his childhood. This embarrassed me a bit because the others sat silently smirking. Christopher said to me afterwards it was a typical Jim conversation. Yet I did not start it, even if I provoked it. We settled several outstanding matters concerning the opening.

To Sibyl Colefax's Ordinary which I did not enjoy. Ben Nicolson, who was present, said to me 'How many marks out of ten do you give this Ordinary?' I said, 'Two.'

Friday, 21st June

The longest day and rather beautiful. This afternoon motored to St. John's Jerusalem for tea to discuss the opening of that house. Walked round the garden with Sir Stephen Tallents, who is a wizened apple. He has the suave, civil servant manner which I don't much trust. His eldest son is a peach – a dark peach, tall and intelligent and sympathetic. As yet untainted by the formalities of Whitehall. I still find this place interesting and desirable. On the way home a torrential downpour obliged me to stop the car for I could not see through the waterfall over the windscreen.

John Wyndham had a drink with me at six to tell me that we must write a letter which he can show his uncle, Lord

Leconfield, reassuring him that he may live undisturbed at Petworth during his lifetime. The silly old man. He has been reassured over and over again. After dinner went to the Soane Museum, where John Summerson let me look through the Adam drawings at leisure. One volume of coloured arabesques are by a certain Giuseppe Monochi, whom I have not come across before. John told me that staying with the E......s was squalor indescribable. A friend of his assured him that on coming down to breakfast at what he considered a reasonable hour there was nothing to be seen on the dining-room table but a full, steaming jerry.

Saturday, 22nd June

Took midday train to Wigan and was met by Lord Crawford, hatless, grey and charming. What a nice man he is; what John Wilton calls 'grand', and comparatively young still – say forty-five. He is cultivated, civilized, urbane, polite, industrious on behalf of the arts, dutiful, a patron – in other words an anachronism in this detestable age, fighting a losing battle with no rancour, good-humouredly, agony gnawing at his heart. He took me straight to Winstanly Hall, a large house on the outskirts of Wigan, to deliver a Queen Anne portrait of a mutual ancestress of his and the owner's. While he was delivering I went at his direction to the stable yard, built in 1834 with a terracotta fountain of Father Neptune riding his horses, whose nostrils and ears spout water. Surface mining has just taken place right up to the front door, and the land has not been reinstated. It is the most appalling mess, a wilderness of dead earth in unsightly piles. All the fine trees gone. The house belongs to Squire Bankes – I was introduced to him as such. He is an old, shrivelled man, of great vitality, rather gaga now and inarticulate, a 'character' much beloved. Mrs. Bankes also well-bred and delightful. The ATS have occupied half the house. The whole place is devastation. It has broken the old man's heart and he can talk of nothing else. Yet he shows no bitterness.

The drive of Haigh Hall is entered direct from Wigan. It twirls, twists uphill through massed hedges of rhododendron and laurel. The house lies on a plateau overlooking the chimneys of Wigan, pit heads and hills beyond. It is the house of Mr. Gradgrind, but a well built classical house of 1830, actually designed by Lord C.'s great-great-grandfather, a very pleasing house of local white stone, machine cut. The lines are concise and clean. Compact and symmetrical. Lady Crawford was away, for which he apologised, but his white-haired mother there and a genteel secretary. Hardly any servants. We waited on each other. House in a state of utter muddle for all the furniture and pictures are stacked, and in process of removal. Claret for dinner. He and I talked of all sorts of things, including the N.T., until midnight over a rare rum, which is 200 years old. Very strong and we drank it as a liqueur.

Sunday, 23rd June

Lord Crawford took me round the house to look at the stacked pictures of which there are hundreds. I made a list of twenty-five that I thought might be suitable for Montacute. They included several Teniers, a Ruysdael, Ostades, van der Neer, a Pintoricchio, Reynolds of Lady Eglington at the harp, Opie of Dr. Johnson, Romney of the young Pitt, and so forth. Superb collection of pictures, and the Duccio one of the finest pictures in existence. Much of the library has already gone to Balcarres, but he showed me a First Folio Shakespeare rebound, and a Second Folio in original boards. Interior of the house is good of its date. No furniture of much consequence.

Monday, 24th June

Motored to Charlecote for the day and took with me Ramsey and George Dix who liked each other. George a sweet and guileless American, full of enthusiasm for the social life, for which one does not dislike him. The head guide whom I had arranged to meet did not turn up.

Tuesday, 25th June

Today we had a Reports Committee at which the bewildered Admiral was present. He does not know much about the National Trust and is, besides, not an intelligent man. He pierces one with a cold blue eye like a schoolmaster trying desperately to assess a new boy; only he is the new boy. At Batsford's went through illustrations with Fry and made some headway, though not a great deal. Clarissa [Churchill] dined at the White Tower. I tried a technique of rapid talk, which answered well for one hour. After that for lack of collaboration I subsided into an exhausted heap.

Wednesday, 26th June

Arthur Oswald of *Country Life* lunched. He wants to enlist my interest in a new architectural periodical he intends launching, more scholarly than *C. Life* and less precious than the *Architectural Review*. I feel that this gentle and diffident man is under-valued by his colleagues.

Eardley and I went to Salisbury together, and motored to Long Crichel where I stayed two nights. He is, as always, the dearest and best companion on expeditions.

Thursday, 27th June

We spent the day at Montacute arranging the stuff which has come since our last visit. Daylight is beginning to appear on the dusky horizon. On the way back to Long Crichel we stopped at Eastbury Park, now a country club, of which E is a member. All that is left is one wing of Vanbrugh's house, a fine piece of architecture outside, but after 200 years it still looks the fragment it is. The interior decoration *quelconque*. The Squire's son, Farquharson, runs the club. I thought he and his assistants looked rather louche.

Eddy is unwell with influenza; very low and sepulchral.

Friday, 28th June

Finished our work at Montacute and had tea with Mrs Knollys in Bath. Then called on Mr. Cook the mysterious benefactor's house in Syon Place to see two Raeburns he offers the Trust for Montacute. Before my finger was off the bell he opened the front door himself. Was not the shy, shifty little eccentric I imagined, but a tall, self-possessed man rather like Bogey Harris. Not prepossessing however; cunning I should say. His house is decorator's Georgian; his pictures likewise decorator's, mostly the English school and indifferent specimens at that. He showed us with justifiable pride the façade of the beautiful early Georgian house from Chippenham which he

65

bought when Woolworth's pulled it down. He has re-erected it not – on the whole – too badly. Eardley dropped me at Westwood [Manor]. Alex Moultin dined and on leaving, embraced Ted good-night in the drive, very charmingly, unostentatiously. I was surprised. So too was Ted, but he was delighted.

Saturday, 29th June

This afternoon Ted [Lister] and I motored to Belcombe Court, open to members of the Georgian Group. It was built by Wood of Bath and could be an enchanting house. It belongs to the architect of the new St. George's Hospital, a perky little man called Watkins whom Ted describes as 'off-gent' and his wife as 'comfortable'. They have ghastly taste, and though some of their furniture is good eighteenth-century, yet dull, their colour schemes, light fittings etc. are gruesome. There is also along the whole of one front an unsightly Edwardian conservatory which should be done away with. The octagon room with plaster octagon ceiling and mahogany writing-table built into one wall, noteworthy. The barn, they swear, is fourteenth-century. Ted thinks far later. But architects know nothing of architectural history. If they did they would build better houses. In the evening Ted made me play chess and won every game.

Sunday, 30th June

Lunched at Corsham. Immediately after luncheon Paul said, 'Let's go into the library and sleep.' By the time we followed he was curled up on the sofa under cushions, snoring loudly. He and Norah are worn out, coping with everything themselves. The hospital has gone, leaving a great mess, and the Art School has not arrived. I persuaded Paul to open Montacute on the 20th July.

Monday, 1st July

A most embarrassing press conference was held this morning. G.M. Trevelyan in the chair. The eminent man made a good introductory speech but insisted upon answering most of the questions himself. This he did haltingly and often incorrectly.

He is deaf as a post and hardly heard a word. There was an atmosphere of hostility, boredom, and criticism on the part of the Press that we were out of touch with the public.

The Stewart-Joneses had an evening party whither I went after giving John Fowler dinner. Talked to the Eshers; rather drunk, I told him that the new Secretary was a nice philistine – generous of me to add the 'nice'.

Tuesday, 2nd July

Interview at the Treasury over Ham House. After a great deal of manoeuvre I managed to insert a proviso that the N.T. should be consulted before any removal or even selection of contents was to be undertaken. The Government proposal is that they should keep the contents to be bought, and *hold* them through the V & A Museum. I agreed only if they, and not the Richmond Council, maintained them. Lady Esher had a cocktail party. Terribly hot and sweaty day. After one cocktail I dripped. How horrible. Dined at home and worked at my lecture, but at 9.30 the Dashwoods telephoned and made me go round to them. They poured out their woes re Captain Hill, that monster. I persuaded Johnnie to write a letter of complaint to Esher, and not to involve me.

Wednesday, 3rd July

I lectured to Trinity College of Music: a young, callow audience. No black-out, so the slides were barely visible. The sun streamed in and I sweated and mopped profusely. Again how horrible. I did not lecture well and think I am a bad lecturer. But afterwards the Principal told me the audience were vastly entertained by my frequent asides of under-statement and self-depreciation.

Thursday, 4th July

Cooler, thank God. Lunched with George Dix and Malcolm Bullock at the Allies Club. Then got my visa at the French Embassy. Waited one hour in a queue, until I could bear it no longer. My conscience melted away and I exercised my privilege by mentioning M. Rocher's name, and left my passport. Went with Geoffrey Houghton-Brown to the American Ballet at Covent Garden. *Les Sylphides* and two modern ballets, of which *Bluebird* one. Norah Kaye superb dancer. Eglevsky a huge, ungainly, gauche but handsome Anglo-Saxon. Technique excellent but too much Anglo-Saxon stiffness.

Friday, 5th July

Wentworth Day lunched at Brooks's. I plied him with as much propaganda as I could about country houses and donors. He is going to write on the subject for a new Beaverbrook weekly. He is a good Tory and all in sympathy with the abused landowners.

Saturday, 6th July

Motored off at one. Called in Oxford on a Mrs Price for some Jacobean hangings for Montacute. Then to Long Compton where I looked at a lych-gate. Then Charlecote. Watched and heard the guides in action. They said some awful things: 'This beautiful this and that,' pointing to some hideous furniture. Called the William and Adelaide dining-room William and Mary. I tried to put things right without hurting feelings. Felt like the headmaster, Alington, who used to creep into classrooms and listen to the poor junior beaks making fools of themselves before the boys and head. Got to Wickhamford at seven.

Sunday, 7th July

A heavenly day, hot and mid-summery. Hay smelling. Evening primroses, Canterbury bells, mock orange wafting. Lay about the garden all day with Mama in deck-chairs. The parson's daughters are a help in spite of M calling them useless, unable to cook, slow and stupid – sometimes to their faces, I fear.

Monday, 8th July

Left Wickhamford at ten and arrived 1.30 at Charlie Brocklehurst's Harebarrow Lodge, three miles north of Macclesfield. Michael Rosse had arrived the night before. After an excellent luncheon we went at 3.30 to Adlington, stopping at Prestbury to see the church. All the churchyards here have flat grave stones made into paths upon which one walks. Adlington is a very fine house. The old part sixteenth-century. Forming a court is a 1757 orange brick wing, built by Carr I should think, with a very tall portico of sandstone columns. A cupola above. Mrs. Legh, the present owner, who has inherited through countless female lines, always retaining the Legh name, has already demolished the end projecting bays so as greatly to spoil the front. She has further horrible plans to demolish the whole of this wing. The condition of the house is deplorable. A hospital has just left. Everything peeling and disintegrating. The great hall has two carved late Gothic 'speres' like the Rufford (Old Hall) ones. Above a gallery an early eighteenth-century organ-case, the organ played upon by Handel. What organ did Handel not play upon, and what bed did Queen Elizabeth not sleep in? On the walls are huge paintings, perhaps by Thornhill or Verrio. The other good room is a late seventeenth-cent. oak drawing-room on the first floor with carved limewood *à la* Grinling Gibbons. The plaster ceiling of this room completely collapsed a month ago, but has been replaced. All the bedrooms in the 1757 wing have 'Chinese' fret ceilings and wooden overmantels holding portraits. Mrs. Legh lives in a lodge by the walled gardens and is going to move into the Brewery over against the big house. She is very unimaginative. In the wilderness garden we counted six temples, all in semi-dereliction. Charlie B. gave us a lot to drink at dinner. Got to bed at midnight.

Tuesday, 9th July

Michael is a delightful companion to travel with, precise, good-tempered, equable. This morning at ten he and I left, calling at Gawsworth Hall, to look at the outside, and the church, which we entered. It has a superb roof. Visited Astbury church again, which has an even finer roof of Jacobean date. Met Pardoe at Little Moreton Hall. Still nothing done since my previous visit, which is worrying, and now the caretaker has died we are faced with a new problem. Had a farm-house lunch there and reached Wolseley Hall at three. This place, the property of Sir Edric Wolseley, has belonged to his family since the Conquest. House has a very fine Charles II staircase, but is much altered since first erected. There is however a Charles II dining-room, the panelling by Pierce but brought from another place. In all other respects the house, gothicised about 1810 and now covered with Virginia creeper, is a poor specimen. Grounds and park likewise indifferent. Whole place disintegrating. They, poor things, rather eccentric and very grubby. We preferred him. Michael was much shocked by the unmade beds and the fuzzy, unbrushed Catholic hair of our hostess. Got to London at 10 o'clock, having eaten in the car a cold collation given us by Charlie.

Wednesday, 10th July

Historic Buildings Committee this morning, after which Michael and I lunched. Called upon Doreen Baynes at six and joined Robin Cornelle at the theatre, a new performance of *Crime and Punishment*, which cast a hopeless Russian gloom, and I did not enjoy it. Considered John Gielgud tonight too mannered. Ate at Pruniers and talked to Robin C. at his house till 2 a.m.

Thursday, 11th July

Lord Bearsted called at 10 o'clock to see the Secretary and me. I did all the talking. He is prepared to endow Upton with £200,000. Patrick O'Donovan lunched. He has a fund of humour which helped me through some miserable months in the Army. Alec Penrose called at tea-time to tell me his aunt has given us £30,000 towards our Jubilee Appeal. Not a bad day for the Trust. At 10.30 went to Oliver Messel's where Anne and Michael and Harold Acton were and a number of Oliver's peculiar friends including a Singhalese captain, whom Anne called a Celanese.

Friday, 12th July

Meeting day. I thought I acquitted myself rather well. Kenneth Rae lunched and I gave him a list of buildings to see in Sweden. At 6 left in the car for Montacute where I arrived at 10 o'c, having dined in Basingstoke. I drove with both windows down, and the smell of new-mown hay and hedgerows, of eglantine and elder, was intoxicating. How I love these long, gentle, Shakespearean summer evenings.

Busy day spent entirely at Montacute. I selected wall space for every single picture and for Lord Rochdale's tapestries. Made progress but there is still much to be done by today next week, when I shall be travelling across France. I found the arrangement of this house so agreeable that I did not want to go abroad, even for a fortnight, while there was still so much to be done.

Left Montacute this morning early. The weather has changed from the torrid to the cool and showery. I drove to Taunton and went to Low Mass with sermon that seemed endless. But the priest spoke feelingly about loyalty to the Church as a bulwark against vile creeds, whatever these may be. Then to the Somerset garage, where I was met by the coachbuilder, though a Sunday. He explained that he would generally tidy up the coach-work and re-upholster the roof of my car. I left it for at least five weeks.

Bridget dined at the Ritz. We had the nastiest of meals. Drank with her till midnight and she poured out complaints about Anne, with whom a coldness has sprung up. Michael, she complained, did nothing for her as a brother, and was useless. But what on earth does she want that he does not do, I asked. There was no clear reply. Merely a low growl. Poor Bridget, she is what is called her own worst enemy. And yet so beautiful, and proud, and aloof.

Lunched with Margaret Jourdain and Ivy at their favourite restaurant, returning to drink coffee at their flat. Humphrey Whitbread joined us for coffee. A timorous, hesitant but nice man.

Spent at Montacute with Eardley and Clifford Smith putting finishing touches to the house, which will not look too bad. They are rather cross with me for leaving them the day before

the opening ceremony. It can't be helped for I booked my seat
to Switzerland at the beginning of May.

Saturday, 20th July

Up early, having packed last night and fetched some sandwiches from Brooks's which I had the foresight to order
during dinner there. At 9.30 my train left London. I had an
early luncheon on the channel boat, my last proper meal until
late next morning. Reserved a second class seat in the French
train, but the seats are narrow. I was very uncomfortable in
consequence. Calais is extremely bombed. In fact there are
hardly more than a dozen houses standing. At Lille I had some
coffee (acorn juice) at the station, but nothing to eat. Indeed
there must be very little food in France. The people look
shabby, but not so hang-dog, discontented and truculent as
the English. I was prepared to sit up all night, but the
resolution waned as I got sleepy. By bribing the nice conduc-
tor I got a sleeper which I shared, rather oddly, with a pretty,
English Mrs Miniver.

Sunday, 21st July

Arrived one-and-a-half hours late – all trains are late except in
neutral countries. The Basel customs authorities easy enough.
At the station I had a good breakfast, with boiled egg. At 2.30
reached Fribourg. Was greeted by Georges Cattaui – Egyptian
Jew turned Christian – who came running up the stairs of the
station platform. He is little changed, perhaps greyer, balder,
now nearing fifty. He leads an ascetic, holy life, having done
his seven years stint of theology at the University here. He at
once took me to the new University buildings, having rustled
up the architect to meet me. The rooms have many points to
recommend them, ingenious mechanisms, a variety of beautiful woods. But there is much that is ugly. I felt very tired at the
end of this inspection. At tea Jean de Menasch, Georges's
Dominican cousin joined us. A very intelligent and pious man.

Tonight we dined in the hotel with the University architect,
who is called Denis Honegger, and Monsieur Barraud, who is
considered Switzerland's leading artist, a handsome, bluff,
pleasant man who smokes a pipe. He speaks no English.

The smell of the lime trees is all pervasive.

I sleep profoundly and late. Georges goes to bed at 8 o'clock every evening and, rising at 6, attends Mass. These hours would not suit me. Today the sun shone. Greedily I inhaled the strong, dry, torrid southern heat, which I have not experienced for six years. I telephoned Geoffrey's agent at Interlaken about money. To my surprise he was not encouraging so I decided the best thing was to go there immediately. Reached Interlaken at luncheon time. Ate well opposite the station. Then went to the address Geoffrey gave me. Presented my introductory letter, but although they were affable the man concerned was away in Amsterdam. Was advised to send him an air mail letter and wait.

Tuesday, 23rd July

Hotter than yesterday, and cloudless, but by no means too hot. Georges and I went to look at St. Michael's church which is rococo, and the Priests' College attached, founded by St. Canisius. Georges fusses about his health more than anyone I have ever met. Must not get too hot, too cold, wears a muffler and coat, which he puts on and takes off, and talks of his ill health ceaselessly. He also asks after everyone I have ever heard of and never heard of, which is extremely irritating. While we were sitting on a bench, he lamenting his ailments, I rejoicing in my freedom from any, along came a good-looking, sprightly Englishman called Bennet, whom Georges greeted and with whom I shook hands. This man could not linger to gossip because he was in a hurry. He is Professor of English Literature here and aged eighty-five. Georges explained that he had been a pupil of Gerard Manley Hopkins at a Jesuit school. Hopkins used to read fairy stories to him and his other pupils when they became tired of lessons. He is the only person I have met who knew Hopkins personally, unless my old friend Basil Champneys did. But I rather fear he didn't.

Georges left for Berne to lunch at the French Embassy. I, pleased to be left alone, visited the three churches in the middle of the town, looked at the sixteenth-century fountain-heads, and walked across the river over the 1840 suspension bridge, which is of wood. The cables seem most insecure, and when a lorry passed over it full of people the bridge swayed like a ship in a rough sea.

Georges is a cultivated, educated man, but withal a terrible bore. He jumps from one subject to another so that conversation never sustains a level. He never allows me to speak. He is disturbed by what he likes to call my fascist sympathies and remarked tellingly that I was a Catholic rather from political than religious motives. That this was due to my reaching a phase of life where I was neither happy nor unhappy. That later I am almost bound to turn to God. So be it.

This afternoon we went to tea at a château just outside Fribourg called La Poya, belonging to the Comte and Comtesse de Grafenried Villars. It was built in 1701 by an ancestor, and is thoroughly Palladian, and no larger than a villino. The present owner added two 'tourelles' at either end in good taste. In the centre is a high square hall with rococo plaster ceiling and baroque figures in stucco over the doorways. The enrichments are picked out in gold. There are Empire rooms with pink damask walls upstairs, very pretty. Some of the eighteenth-cent. furniture is French, and all exquisite. Oh, the impeccable taste. The Countess was charming (gracious is the word) and gave us tea. There were present the Count, who talked only of *la chasse*, an Italian Marquess who is a fascist, and a daughter and son-in-law, Baron Rambaud, who did the honours and showed me round the house. Balustraded terraces descend in front of the house which has a splendid view over the town and the snow-capped mountains beyond. The trees in the park are ancient and deciduous, and the lawns green and luscious. But on close inspection the grass is very poor, full of dandelions and weeds.

Thursday, 25th July

Georges and I left at nine for Berne, staying at the Hotel Bristol. I telephoned Interlaken, but there is no news of money, and no reply from the hotel at Lugano. Georges is very poor, yet has generously paid for my meals and lent me 50 francs. I don't like owing him money.

Went to the Vuillard exhibition. Indifferent artist, a poor sort of Sickert. It is terribly hot in Berne and we wander about disconsolately, not buying anything. Cannot even afford to buy postcards.

Friday, 26th July

Still no news and no letter from Lugano. Went by myself to the bathing place in the suburbs, called KMV, which was a delirium of excitement. Young and old were there, chiefly the latter, bronzed like niggers, diving and splashing in the blue water, which is constantly changed. Every half hour a bell announces that the waves will begin, whereupon commotion is uproarious and everyone jumps into the pool, shouting. You lie on boards sunbathing and drink tea and lemonade in a gallery overlooking the pool. Never have I felt more carefree, or happier. It didn't seem to matter a scrap whether I had a halfpenny in the world. I knew that something, someone would come to my rescue. The Swiss certainly impress me as a contented people.

Saturday, 27th July

While dressing I was told that the agents were on the telephone. Would I take the 9 o'clock train to Interlaken? This I did and was given 1,000 francs advanced by M. Osterreich who had sent a telegram from Amsterdam. Got back for luncheon, rejoicing. In the afternoon went on a shopping spree, feeling like a millionaire. Bought socks and ties and silk handkerchiefs. Wrote to Georges ecstatically, refunding him. At five took a train bound for Lugano. The Grand Palace Hotel stiflingly hot. Slept very badly; restless, almost feverish, diarrhoea.

Sunday, 28th July

Feared I might be ill, but am now inclined to attribute troubles to the height, crossing the Alps. The situation of Lugano is very beautiful, surrounded by close, high mountains. The lake is in a hole. Today the sky is thundery and there is no breath of wind. Wandered in the public gardens along the lake under tall beech and chestnut trees.

Today feel very unwell with violent diarrhoea, but better this evening. I think after all it may be due to slight sunstroke. I overlooked the fact that I am getting bald on the top of my head, damn it. Have a feverish feeling about the eyes. There is not a soul in this hotel to speak to. All dagoes when not English; and when English, dentists. I have a slight headache and am not very happy. Have finished the *Last Chronicle of Barset*.

Bought some anti-diarrhoea mixture. Felt better. Saw in *The Times* that poor Timmie Buxton has died, a war victim, though of cancer of the stomach, at the age of forty-three. This has made me wonder if I am suffering from the same complaint. Went this afternoon on a tour of the lake, right round the bend, to the westernmost point.

Am still mercifully spared though had a bad night. Took photographs of the Renaissance façade of San Lorenzo early this morning, then did some shopping. Shops not as good as in Sweden: nor is the food. This afternoon crossed the lake to Campione and photographed the baroque front of the little Madonna dei Ghirli, which has flights of steps descending to the water. Campione is by some curious chance an island of Italy in Switzerland. At the south extremity is a rather noble modern Mussolini arch of white and grey striped granite. Some of the fascist architecture is good though abused by all the left-wingers. Walked to the next village, Bissone, with a street of arcaded shops and two dull churches. Then walked across the ugly dam bridge to the far side of the lake. The sun in the full glare of the day was almost too much for me. Even so the heat was dry. I felt myself burning without sweating. Happily found a train back to Lugano in time for a delicious tea. Am reading Shakespeare's sonnets with care. Poetry and architecture are my two great loves. I judge the latter more academically and less subjectively than the former. One should fight with poetry, hammering it, thrashing it with the mind if one is to appreciate it properly.

Thursday, 1st August

Although I have passed my time this week as I had intended and hoped, yet I shall be glad to leave on Sunday. Ten, or rather eleven days of complete solitude are enough. Besides, I am anxious about that accumulating pile of work at home.

Today there is some sort of *festa* and the shops are all shut. I went to church next door (Saint' Angioli) at 9.45. Mass was in progress. I stayed till the end then studied very closely the Bernardo Luini 'Passion', a splendid thing, in excellent preservation. Visited the Museum in the Villa Cacci, a good late classical building of *c.* 1840, but internal decoration poor: stucco and painted ceilings of feeble quality. Museum itself awful, neglected and absolutely lifeless, as I should hate any of mine to be. After luncheon took the steamer to Morcote. Extremely hot and muggy, there being high clouds behind which the sun is sheltering. Climbed the steep eighteenth-century stairs to the S. Sassa church, with splendid square Romanesque campanile, which I photographed.

Friday, 2nd August

Today's jaunt was to walk along a path cut out of the rock, under the roadway, along the northern arm of the lake as far as Gandia. This is an old mediaeval village, the houses tumbling over each other and intersected by labyrinthine passages in the rock. In the evening I bathed in the Lido. I do not stay in the water long, nor do I much care to exhibit my nude body to the public. The corporate diversion of bathing does not appeal. And if I see a beautiful body it merely disturbs me.

Saturday, 3rd August

My last day. Paid my bill at the hotel which amounted to just under 300 francs. I was so horrified that I did not buy the little gold toothpick I had coveted in a jeweller's window all the week. Today I took the funicular up San Salvatore. Less than twenty minutes to climb 3,000 feet. The incline to the summit is 60 in 100 inches, rather frightening. These long established funiculars do not give one confidence. A little too much haze, but the view of the lake in its entirety very lovely.

Two things never cease to astonish me: (1) the hysterical devotion Latin men and women lavish upon male babies, and the consequence that they grow up to be normal extroverts, which is not what one would expect – and (2) the English race manages to keep its end up in the world, considering how when confronted with Europeans, of no matter what class, Englishmen never fail to appear to be intellectually inferior.

I rather dread my journey home of two days and one night without a sleeper and without food on the French train, in this torrid heat.

Sunday, 4th August

Left Lugano at nine, having walked to the station in my shirt sleeves, carrying my coat, but slowly, and even so, sweating. Got to Lucerne for luncheon, and went to the exhibition of pictures and tapestries from the Ambrosiana, Milan. Marvellous collection, including some Leonardos. Bought a catalogue to give to Ben Nicolson. Situation of Lucerne less confined than Lugano's with snow-capped mountain range in the distance. Not so sublime. Wandered to the Cathedral and photographed the west end, which is Renaissance. The wooden bridge, covered in, has fifty-two painted panels of the seventeenth-century in the spandrels. The fountains here, surrounded with flowers as always in Switzerland, gay and delightful.

Got to Basle at nine. Had rather a rush boarding the train and so too little time to buy food for tomorrow. Did sit up all night.

Monday, 5th August

Two sweet little French boys, aged eight and ten, travelled in my carriage. They had beautiful manners and offered their food to the other passengers. Were intelligent and capable. They shook hands all round on parting at Dunkirk. They also had the inestimable advantage of looking clean and fresh in the early hours of the morning.

On the whole a terrible day. No food but what I had snatched at Basle. Intolerably hot and the filthiest carriage I have ever travelled in. Half the glass panes missing and wooden boards substituted. Smuts filtering through the open window. I have never been dirtier. In the lavatory no water, no looking-glass, and indescribable caca. The formalities with passports and luggage at the douane at Calais the worst encountered yet. The only high light was a delicious tea with eggs and bacon on the English boat. Still hot on the channel, but the sun has already assumed that English muslin quality; nothing full-blooded about it. I arrived home tired out at 10 p.m. Read *Jane Eyre* on the journey.

Saturday, 10th August

All this week in London has been dull. No visits because my car is not yet ready. Very busy indexing the list of properties for the annual report. Spent three evenings at the Soane Museum looking through the Robert Adam drawings. An indescribable number. The versatility of the man.

Sunday, 11th August

There is a serious gas strike. There is now no gas of any kind and grave difficulties are experienced cooking anything in London.

Tuesday, 13th August

Had a session at Batsford's with Charles Fry and Mr. Batsford. It was settled that I should add an appendix to the third edition of *The National Trust*, inclusive of new properties acquired since the first edition was published a year ago; that I should write a guide book of all N.T. buildings to be sold at six shillings, this to come out next year; and that I should write a book on the dawn of English classicism from Henry VIII's reign down to and including Inigo Jones. We furthermore made some progress with illustrations for *Adam,* and settled that Batsford's would have photographs taken of a selection of the drawings in the Soane Museum.

At dinner tonight at Brooks's I sat with Eddie Marsh who is selling many of his books, amongst them twenty presentation copies to him from Mrs. Belloc Lowndes. He complained that he had to tear out all the fly-leaf inscriptions. 'Why tear out?' I asked. 'The books will fetch more if you leave them in.' Eddie frowned, thinking my remark to be in bad taste. Then he told me how Sir James Barrie once sold a number of his books. One day a friend informed him that the shop which had purchased them was displaying them in their window and asking a high price for each copy that contained his name and a dedication. Poor Barrie was obliged to buy back all these books at a higher cost than he had received for them. Silly ass.

Thursday, 15th August

Had a drink with the Terence Maxwells. She is a daughter of Sir Austen Chamberlain. She was rather naively surprised by the high price a copy of Churchill's *Marlborough* fetched when her brother sold it recently. It was given to her father by Winston with an inscription in it.

Friday, 16th August

Ramsey and I motored to Polesden Lacey and saw how Robin [Fedden] has completed the arrangements of the museum. Robin's good manners are more continental than English and, I suspect, actuated by policy rather than warm feeling.

Saturday, 17th August

Arrived at Paddington at 9.10 for the 9.40, but the crowds were so great I could not even reach the platform. Instead waited in a queue until 11.15 for fear of missing the next train. This I caught but was in consequence late at Taunton. Went to the Museum and turned down a sundial offered us. Then collected my car at the garage. The cost was £69, less than I feared. I drove off in a great hurry to Ven, which I found deserted but for Paul Methuen who was sitting in the garden, painting the south front. Sat on the grass talking to him and drinking milk from a mug, for I had had no luncheon or tea. Then went inside the house and looked at the Chippendale armchairs and sofa, which are offered for Montacute. The house seems from outside much larger than it is. The big central hall monumental, the gallery and panelling contemporary. Nothing spectacular in the other downstairs rooms and the bedrooms indifferent. Went on to a charming manor at

Horethorne, typical Dorset Jacobean, golden and cobwebbed with silver; shell-headed niches beside the front door. Here offered two rustic 'Chippendale' chairs. On to Sandford Orcas where received most kindly by the Medlycotts and given lemonade and a peach. Got to Montacute for dinner.

Slept at Mrs. Welsh's cottage, she being away. Her two daughters looked after me. This morning bright sun. Eardley motored over with Eddy [Sackville-West] and Raymond [Mortimer]. We checked the Montacute inventory room by room. After luncheon motored to Westwood. Called on Ted who gave me tea, and continued to Lacock Abbey. Miss Talbot received me. Looked at her pictures requiring attention, which meant every one, and I made notes. Then back to London, dining at Marlborough.

Woke up from another very vivid dream about Tom Mitford who was dressing to go to a luncheon party. He was in his trousers and shirt sleeves and slung round his waist the gold key-chain he always wore, and patted his thighs in self-satisfaction. He was cracking jokes and laughing at himself in his most engaging manner.

Today I motored George Dix on a small N.T. tour. We went to West Wycombe, Helen accompanying us. After lunching at the Apple Orchard, where I bought for £35 a chest of drawers, we went to the house. Prepared to be angry, I was angry with the guides for not being at their places. They are an inefficient lot. House looking bare but clean and very beautiful. At Cliveden we walked round the grounds and went on to Hatchlands which George liked best of the three houses. We dined late at the Allies Club and there was Malcolm Bullock. Apparently he had invited me to dine and received no reply. He sat with us while we ate and came on to Brooks's where we met Randolph [Churchill] and had drinks. Randolph has a huge belly and is very grey. George could not believe him to be thirty-three and younger than us. Randolph boisterous and argumentative. Talked of Chartwell, wanting to know if there was some snag in the arrangement with the National Trust.

He abused Mrs. Greville roundly. Then we all remembered the unwritten law never to discuss women at a club, and laughed.

Spent the afternoon at the Soane Museum with Sam Carr from Batsford's. I have looked through the whole fifty-three volumes of Adam drawings and not missed any, although I could well have given more time and attention to them.

Miss Strater, my secretary, left today, with regrets on my part. A sweet girl, aged about twenty.

Left at six for Wickhamford. Stopped at West Wycombe to look at the Pepper Pots, now practically in ruins, and the Chapel Cottage, the roof of which has collapsed. Called at the house to leave a book for Mrs. Eaton and on leaving saw Helen and Johnnie [Dashwood] on the colonnade. They were alone and pressed me to dine with them for they had a duck and a bottle of burgundy. They were so friendly that I accepted. Sitting in the dining-room and looking across the table at the north view I thought I had never in my life seen a landscape more idyllic and classical – the lake below, the temple, trees and ducks. Got to Wickhamford by ten. Both parents in bed. I talked at the end of Mama's bed till past midnight.

Left Wickhamford at eleven and drove to Coughton. Had a word with Wells the old butler and Robert Throckmorton who greeted me at the door. A polite man who does not put me at ease. Then to Warwick and talked to Mr. Hollyoak, the Charlecote agent, suggesting that he might supervise the guides next year. He will submit his terms. Then talked to Quinneys about the Charlecote inventory. Then to Warwick Castle. The guide who conducted my party was an educated man. The banqueting-hall is lamentably restored. The best room is the Red Drawing Room and the adjoining gallery with Charles II ceiling. There is more to see than at Charlecote. The view over the river is romantic, but I don't think the castle from the courtyard very fine. To Charlecote for tea. Brian Lucy and William Buchan there. I like William Buchan although he is rather a precious young man. Left at 7.15 and went to *Measure for Measure* at Stratford. There are some ridiculous scenes, namely the raping of Isabella; and the convenient morality of the Duke is questionable. Bobby Harris acted Angelo, a difficult part. Some of the best acted scenes were the buffoonish ones with Elbow, and the tapster and Froth. These comic pieces seem to make a more convincing picture of Elizabethan everyday life than the serious ones.

Sunday, 25th August

I can easily understand how the very old, in despair, surrender to an easy death with a casual passing of the skeins of life to another generation to unravel. Mass at Broadway.

I fetched poor little Audrey over from Prestbury to Wickhamford for the day. She is much brighter and was very sweet to M. and P. The whole business of A. makes me miserable, and I wonder if a family has the right to cut off a member – which is what it amounts to in this case – who chooses to adopt a life which it disapproves of.

Monday, 26th August

Set off immediately after breakfast for Stourton Castle, near Stourbridge, arriving one hour after time. Was shown round by a rather cross Mrs. Grazebrook. I had never heard of this house before. Its sole merit lies in a central tower of sandstone. The red brick accretions date from the sixteenth century. On the north side the seventeenth-century casements have survived. Otherwise modern windows put in in 1860 when the house was spoilt. The central court was covered in to form a hall – the usual treatment – and the inside entirely redecorated. A few open stone fireplaces have been left, including that in the bedroom in which Cardinal Pole is supposed to have been born. A few thick brick chimney-breasts survive; all the actual chimneys Victorian. I was in no doubts that the house is unacceptable, and when asked, I told Mrs. G. so. Drove to Dudley to see Mr. Grazebrook in his office. Nice, handsome man of sixty. I repeated to him what I told Mrs. G. Find I have now reached the age when I can say these disagreeable things without causing offence. The authority of years' experience sounds pompous, but it is true.

Next stop Trentham. Had not realised before that the house was demolished in 1905, all but Barry's clock tower and the entrance porch with noble, carved, armorial escutcheons in stone, and the curved, covered colonnade, now very dilapidated and doubtless about to be removed. I prepared to take photographs and to my dismay found my camera glass broken. Very distressing.

Reached Little Moreton Hall at tea-time. The Secretary and Mrs. Bevir arrived a few minutes after. We all had tea together and he and I talked to Bailey, who was disgruntled and opposed to our projected appointment of his wife's cousin, a Dale, in his place. Later I interviewed the Dales and liked them very much. They are descendants of the Richard Dale, 'Carpeder', who 'made thies windovs by the grac of God' in the courtyard in 1559. A lovely thought.

Stayed the night at The Macclesfield Arms in the town of that name, a charming eighteenth-century inn, all newly painted outside, clean and welcoming inside. Food not at all bad. Living in the north is of higher standard than in the south. After dinner strolled in the twilight. Autumn comes earlier here, and there is a faint, misty, burnt-leaf smell in the air. The church has some good seventeenth-century wrought-iron gates with a gilded Fame blowing a trumpet in the overthrow. Someone was practising on the organ. I peeped through the vestry door and saw one of the most beautiful baroque monuments to a Viscount Savage of Rocksavage, dated 1694. The canopy supported by two columns of black touchstone, to which white marble draperies are attached. Below in the valley the trains whistle, shriek and shunt.

Tuesday, 27th August

Drove after breakfast to Lyme the wrong way, over the moors, coming down by Disley. But a beautiful morning and I did not regret it. The large house quite deserted but for one caretaker. I spent two hours going round the inside, checking the fine furniture left – enough to furnish two rooms at most – and the quantity of indifferent family portraits which will serve to decorate. I decided that the house could be used by an institution without harm befalling it, if we kept for show

84

purposes the drawing-room, stag parlour, yellow bedroom and possibly dressing-room (all adjacent), and the saloon (detached). The rest can all be sacrificed. Far the best solution would be to convert the place into flats, if we can't treat Lyme in the Montacute fashion, making Lord Newton's furniture into the nucleus of a regional collection.

I lunched at Macclesfield, called at Moreton and drove back to London, covering 200 miles from Lyme. Dined quite well at Bedford, having had tea at Uttoxeter.

Wednesday, 28th August

Lunched at the Ritz with the Braybrookes and had a useful talk about Audley End. On my return to the office wrote a long letter to the Treasury about it, asking them to help. My new secretary, Miss Kearney, started work today. She is about my age and seems charming. I am sure I shall like her very much. How lucky I am. She told me she was Irish and a Papist.

Sunday, 1st September

Lunched with Dame Una [Pope-Hennessy] in her lovely flat in Lansdown Grove. It consists of one floor of two houses thrown into one, which makes it roomy and convenient. Only her nephew, Simon Birch in the Coldstream, present. Back from Germany. She gave us lamb and apple meringue with real cream; sherry and red wine. Says that her book on Dickens is selling 500 copies a day in the States, but she can get no money from it. She is now writing about Charles Kingsley. James is in Scotland with the 'cellist.

Yesterday saw the Mildenhall silver plate in the British Museum. It is supposed to be decadent. I thought it very fine. Moreover it is absolutely unflawed. Last night K. Kennet came with me to the last performance of the American Ballet. I got two front row seats in the stalls for 18s. each. We had a cold supper at her house afterwards. She considered one dancer, Hugh Laing, in the last ballet, called *Undertow*, the best dancer she had ever seen, better even than Nijinsky.

Tonight dined at Lady d'Avigdor-Goldsmid's house, 47 Hans Place. She looks just the same, improved if anything in looks, and obviously enjoys her London widowhood. Always hated the country. Harry [d'Avigdor-Goldsmid] joined us at eight, without his wife. He won the M.C. and D.S.O. in the war and was apparently seriously wounded in the face. But he has been well mended and I saw no sign of wounds. His appearance too has improved with age. He is still bombastic, rude and snubbing to his mother, and even to me, but there is great kindliness underneath. He is very happily married and loves his two daughters. He is probably going to give up his bullion broking, for by not earning income he will be better off, he maintains. I don't understand it. I only know that if I gave up work I would starve.

My watch stopped again. I was so angry I hit it hard against the table and the winding handle fell out and disappeared. I doubt if it will ever go again. I hope not. I hope it is dead for ever. Rather perturbed this morning by receiving a letter from Lord Esher enclosing a letter to him from Christopher Hussey, complaining about the Trust not giving *Country Life* the *National Trust Guide* to publish – complaining, in fact, about me. But damn it, it is *my* book. To the Treasury and talked with Sir Alan Barlow about Audley End and Ham House.

Saw Osbert Lancaster this evening. He was rather grey, and pustular. Full of gossip about our surviving mutual friends. Says it is all a piece of Nancy's nonsense claiming that she is loved by Palewski who, he maintains, is uninterested (which is absolutely untrue); that Patrick has gone quite queer again; that Joan is divorcing and living with a man, and so on.

To Knole where met by Cuthbert Acland. The Chief Agent, for whom this appointment was made two months ago, failed to turn up. Acland was splendid. He is very bright and at our interview with Lord Sackville after luncheon dealt excellently with him. Lord S sits there, very thin, almost tiny, gaunt about the nose and with very gleaming false teeth which he picks, like Eddy. He laughs inwardly, without comment and as though in agreement with us, when we reassure him that the N.T. will do nothing without his prior sanction. Mason [Lord Sackville's agent] is always deferential to 'his lordship', is the most loyal man in the world, and abounding in humour and common sense. Going round the rooms this morning I was horrified by the piles of dust under the chairs from worm borings. The gesso furniture too is in a terrible state. All the picture labels want renewing; the silver furniture cleaning; the window mullions mending.

Friday, 6th September

Lunched alone with M.J. and Ivy C.-B. How they eat! Ivy has a curious habit, when sitting down to a meal, of splaying her legs apart and lifting her skirt above the knees. For an Edwardian spinster it is most indelicate. She attacks the food, literally with venom. They showed me how they were obliged to sprinkle broken glass all over their flower box to prevent a neighbour's cat from squatting on it and 'using the earth for its own purposes'. They pick up the glass from the curbs in the square, as though it were cigarette ends, and scoop it into newspaper to the surprise of passers-by.

Sunday, 8th September

At Mass it began to pour with equatorial vehemence just as they were praying for fine weather for the harvest. I could not stick the sermon and left. Standing in the portico [of the Oratory] waiting for the storm to abate, a wild figure dashed out of the church, cursing. It was Auberon Herbert, incensed because the priest ought to have been preaching about Poland instead of Love Thy Neighbour.

Visited Sibyl Colefax in University College Hospital, she having broken her hip. There she was in a room darkened by heaps of flowers, with one leg above the level of her head and tins of shot, pulleys and weights on strings attached to the other. She looked tiny and lost among it all, yet so gallant, and talking enthusiastically about Lawrie Johnston's garden and the Clarks always falling on their feet, etc.

Dined with the Lancasters. Drank whisky *and* red wine – a

mistake. We ate in their kitchen. Karen is so good-hearted and Osbert very amusing and invigorating. Speaking of John Summerson's triplets he said they would of course always be known as the Georgian Group.

Monday, 9th September

By train to Leamington Spa. Colin Jones motored me to Charlecote. Met Hollyoak and discussed various schemes with him and returned to London. Dined with Patrick O'Donovan in a basement in Harley Street, where he lives, off cold turkey and Irish bread and Irish butter. Eamon Fitzgerald, also with me in the Irish Guards, was there. I drank too much cheap wine and port, but the evening was most enjoyable. Patrick has strong political and religious views, but everything is a joke. The other intelligent and donnish.

Tuesday, 10th September

At six went to see the shagreen knife-boxes which came from Montacute and have been bought by a Mr Liddel-Simpson who thinks of giving them back to Montacute. They are very pretty, date about 1730.

Wednesday, 11th September

Lunched with Ian McCallum at Kettner's. Not quite enough to assuage the pangs of hunger. At 6.30 to Sheila de Rutzen's and agreed to go to Wales the weekend after next. Johnnie Philipps there with a new Bentley which goes a million miles an hour. Michael says he disgraced himself at Brighton by sliding down the banisters of a rather stuffy hotel at 8.30 a.m., stark naked, just as the bishops and schoolmaster guests with their wives were descending to breakfast.

Thursday, 12th September

Michael and I drove to West Wycombe. We looked at all the temples and outdoor frescoes with Johnnie [Dashwood]. Michael agreed that with very little money the temples could be put in order. Lunched at the Apple Orchard and drove to Cliveden. Looked at the furniture which Lord Astor intends

88

giving – what we could find of it, for it was so badly described – and walked round the grounds. Agreed the Blenheim Pavilion needed attention; also that the public ought to be allowed to enter by the Hedsor drive and leave their motors in the back drive. An agreeable and profitable day.

Friday, 13th September

Motored this morning to Gestingthorpe Hall, near Castle Hedingham. Very remote place and rather dilapidated. Poor Miss Oates, the owner, such a nice woman. She is the sister of gallant 'Titus' Oates who deliberately walked out of his tent to die in the Antarctic. She reminded me of K. Kennet by her straightforward manner, robustness and common sense. The exterior is what Sisson calls 'utility Georgian', a little altered by her father who added a pediment, and greatly added to by him at the back so that it is two-thirds larger than originally. It has a simple, stolid Squire Western hall and an astonishing Lord Chesterfield drawing-room of most refined rococo stucco ceiling and walls. She cannot afford to live there or give to the Trust. I really do not know what we can do to help her, poor woman.

I stopped at Bury St. Edmunds and looked inside Angel Corner. Although it stands well it is not good enough for a National Trust property and should never have been accepted. Stayed with the Birkbecks at Rippon Hall. What an untidy household! Very bad-mannered children who rush at the food and leave their guest unattractive mangled portions. Talked three hours with Birkbeck, whom I much like, about Blickling matters and settled a number of points.

Saturday, 14th September

Spent day at Blickling. There are eight gardeners now and the grounds are greatly tidied up. Miss O'Sullivan is slow and tired, and looks ill. Went on to Felbrigg for dinner. Wyndham Ketton-Cremer's mother staying, a sweet, white-haired old lady. Although physically flaccid he is mentally stimulating. Plenty of serious talk. House huge, but Wyndham is well looked after by his couple. He lives comfortably in the hall. No electric light, and I had to walk miles with a candle from my bedroom to the w.c. at the far end of the Stuart wing.

Lord and Lady Templewood (Sir Samuel and Lady Maud Hoare that were) came to luncheon, which we had in the Paine rococo dining-room. I sat next to her. She is a big, gauche woman, but easy enough to talk to, and a devoted wife. One is made very conscious of that. He is a small, dapper man, every inch a politician, or rather now a statesman; wearing smartly cut blue serge suit and brown suede shoes, neat shirt and blue tie: silvery hair: very youthful. Spoke of the Government with utmost contempt, particularly of Bevan. Said the Government ought to have evacuated all the military camps for use of civilians, and moved the camps into Germany. Said his book on his Embassy in Spain had proved an unqualified success and even the left-wing papers praised it. They invited me to visit Templewood whenever I liked. They are close friends and neighbours of Wyndham, whom they call Bunny. Wyndham and I went for a long walk in the woods after tea: a gorgeous evening.

Monday, 16th September

I motored to London from Felbrigg, leaving at 9.10, and had luncheon at Brooks's. Dined at Brooks's with Ben and, since I had my car, we met Harold [Nicolson] at Victoria station off the Golden Arrow. He walked briskly up to the gate almost first of the passengers, for he had no luggage at all, only two books. He is here for a week and will broadcast four times. Drove him to Pratts where he gave us two glasses of port. Too much for me. I had had one very large glass with Ben previously and several the night before at Felbrigg. Harold says that each time he eats by himself in Paris the meal costs 25s.

Tuesday, 18th September

A foul day. Poured ceaselessly. I motored Ralph Edwards to Knole and back. Never again. It is a terrible road through south London; endless, with trams all the way and, in the wet the road skiddy, as well as hideous. Ralph is extremely entertaining. He has a great sense of humour and is as clever as a monkey. Cocky, peppery and eccentric too. Has a curious rasping, staccato voice, and delicious cynicism. I like cynics. We get on well. At Knole he rushed full speed round the state rooms, but in a few hours had valued all the furniture. Mason had most efficiently prepared an inventory and was very quick jotting down the figures as Edwards rattled them off relentlessly. I followed this performance keenly and was much impressed, for it seemed he never once went wrong, except possibly in under-estimating the tapestries. He missed nothing, giving £20 to one late French table, £15,000 to the James I bed. He pronounced the furniture to be in a shocking state of disrepair, and has already put me on to an old retired craftsman from the V & A who may spend several weeks at Knole douching the furniture with Benzine-Benzol anti-worm mixture.

Took Bridget P. to the Cambridge Theatre. *Don Pasquale*, so gay and witty. Superbly done. The baritone was Stabile and Don Pasquale an Englishman, Martin Lawrence, just as good in his way.

Wednesday, 19th September

Charles Fry and Professor Richardson lunched with me. This evening I spent packing up, and moving china and breakable objects to No. 20 Thurloe Square, preparatory to the proper move tomorrow. My rooms in Thurloe Square are not yet finished which is annoying and unsettling.

Saturday, 21st September

Motored to Canterbury and lunched with Christopher Gibbs. Then on to Denton Court, the property of two unmarried sisters of uncertain age, very well-bred and old-fashioned, the Misses Willatt: one wearing skirt to within six inches of the ankles in 1918 style and a large felt hat, turned down, like Vita's. They live in this big house without servants. It is crammed with hot-house flowers and exhales the sour-sweet smell of old women's houses. Denton Court is of little interest. Is built of brick. The garden front has curvilinear gables and late seventeenth-century sash windows. Two ugly Victorian towers have been added. Tappington Hall next door is genuine seventeenth-century, picturesque and 'a wealth of old timbers', where Barham, author of *The Ingoldsby Legends*, lived. There is a fake pedigree of the Ingoldsbys framed and hung here: also fake Ingoldsby ancestral portraits. There is a Jacobean staircase; otherwise a tiresome old house.

Motored to Stoneacre, and so to Somerhill, arriving dinner time.

Sunday, 22nd September

I like dear old Harry [d'Avigdor Goldsmid] very much. Of course he is not 'dear old' in any sense. He is astringent, disputatious, political. Rosemary I can't make out. They are spending a fortune of capital on the house and horses. Harry's attitude is that the country has gone to the dogs and he may as well spend whatever capital he pleases. I did not enjoy this visit because I do not belong to their plutocratic, bullion-broking, racing, gambling set. Years ago I was very much at home here.

Monday, 23rd September

Motored to Owletts and spent the day checking the contents which belong to the N.T. Had an excellent yeoman's lunch-eon and dear Lady Baker gave me a pound of butter and an egg. The painters are still in my flat and I cannot move in until the end of the week.

Tuesday, 24th September

Paul Hyslop lunched. He is going down to Knole to devise a scheme for the partitions Lord Sackville wants to separate the public from the private visitors. I think he is a good choice as architect for he is known to and liked by Lord S as a friend of Eddy. Desmond Shawe-Taylor invited me to Covent Garden – *Barber of Seville*, which was very bad. Figaro was such a repellent, facetious old man that he ruined the performance.

Thursday, 26th September

Went to Knole again, this time George Wingfield-Digby accompanying Ralph Edwards and me. Wingfield-Digby pointed out that the best seventeenth-century carpets had silver fish in them and were in just as neglected a condition as the furniture.

Friday, 27th September

To Pendell Court for luncheon and spent the afternoon looking over this horrible house. I did not like the Bell family. The
house, originally built in 1624, has been ruined by them:
window surrounds new, plate glass inserted, and the whole
interior fudged up. Damn this ink, which is intolerable. I
cannot write tonight.

Sunday, 29th September

Today I practically finished my new flat, having worked hard
at it all the weekend. Last night was my first at No. 20 Thurloe
Square.

Jamesey dined at Brooks's. Without any reference being
made to our recent estrangement, a *rapprochement* was, I
suppose, effected. Our confidences seemed as sincere and easy
as of yore. There are certainly enchanting sides to his volatile
little character.

Thursday, 3rd October

Eddy Sackville-West lunched at Brooks's. His appearances in
London get rarer. He seemed fairly satisfied with the efforts I
am now making at Knole. He asked me for a weekend, which
surprised me. Then I found it was because he had somebody
staying whom no other friend could be persuaded to meet.

Had our Annual General Meeting at the Mansion House.
Lord Mountbatten was the chief speaker. He was in Admiral's
uniform and is, I think, the handsomest man I have ever seen.
At No. 20 Thurloe Square improvements gradually happen.

Friday, 4th October

Motored the Admiral [Bevir] to Polesden Lacey this morning.
The meeting between Robin Fedden and Hubert Smith was
awkward: awkward for Robin, who was upset, for me, who
was embarrassed, but not awkward for the Admiral or Smith,
who are both insensitive. Robin was told that he would
probably have to move from his quarters, which are the best in
the house. He should have been told this before he had made

93

them so nice. We left Robin looking distressed, and I had no opportunity to write him a note of reassurance.

At 2.30 I motored Sir Geoffrey Cox to Montacute. He talked without ceasing but is friendly and simple. We examined some Charles II chairs at Romsey and dined at The White Hart, Salisbury. Thank goodness one can arrive at an hotel again and get dinner without previous booking days beforehand. Drank whisky and port. Sir G. loves his drink. He also loves the great with whom, as Parliamentary Agent, he is constantly in touch. He works terribly hard. He told me that Hartley Shawcross was actually served with a writ for libel by Lord Kemsley the other day. This immensely embarrassed the Prime Minister who had to dictate to Shawcross the grovelling letter of apology which he subsequently issued to the press. Sir G. says Attlee *is* a clever man, namely in steering an even course between the followers of Bevan and Morrison, who detest each other and are the leaders of the two extreme sections of the Labour Party.

We stayed the night at Yeovil where we met Clifford.

Saturday, 5th October

Got to Montacute at 10.30. Rather a rush day. Chris Hussey, Bertie Abdy and Lord Aberconway all came and everyone had his own ideas and talked at variance, except Bertie. The Yateses are installed in their new flat which is very nice except that when anyone uses the w.c. every single sound can be heard, which Mrs. Yates confided to me with a blush was the reason she could not have me to stay. Meeting quite a success, in spite of Bertie's sole comment which electrified the others. He remarked that the public could not of course be admitted to the house because they smelt. There was two minutes dead silence, after which Sir Geoffrey resumed the discussion as though nothing untoward had happened. Afterwards Bertie professed to me to be very pleased with the arrangement of the house. He is so insincere and extravagant with his appreciations and depreciations that he makes little sense.

I motored Christopher home to Froyle and stayed the night with him and Betty. It was fun. She is gay as a cricket, brisk and noisy. Him I got to understand for the first time. He is not censorious or grim as I previously thought, but delightful, with a sardonic humour. How quickly one reverses one's unfavourable opinion of people when one gets to know them. They are leaving their cottage-like house, with its very good furniture, after seven years' stay, for Scotney Castle.

Sunday, 6th October

Motored to Rotherfield Park this morning: Reptonish (actually by Parkinson) house, built about 1820, but added to in the same fashion by the Scott family throughout the last century. It has octagonal towers and pinnacled turrets, a Windsor Castle round tower in stone and flint, a red brick square tower with cupola, and presents a romantic, Germanic air. The park, sloping towards the main road, is an admirable specimen of picturesque layout. There are beech avenues to the north of the house in the form of a cross, dating from the eighteenth-century. The Gerald Cokes were lunching.

We motored to tea at Stratfield Saye. Norah Lindsay staying. She says funny things. Took me aside during Gerry's solemn tour of the house and whispered, 'That's where the humble petitioners sit,' pointing to two modest chairs the far side of Gerry's writing-table. The fire seems to have caused but little damage. The house, full of fascinating and historic treasures, is being rearranged with Gerry's unerring taste.

Monday, 7th October

To Knole again with Ralph Edwards to complete his valuation. He is very entertaining with his sardonic, precise speech in a high squeaky voice, and his irascible manner. An awful old scarecrow accompanied us, called Fletcher the craftsman, looking like an undertaker. When we met Lord Sackville he dropped a great brick by saying: 'The condition of the furniture is deplorable, caused by utter neglect,' at which Lord S bridled. We tried desperately to pick the brick up. For the first time I went into the barracks, or attics, miles of long galleries, with remains of plaster ceilings and some fine Jacobean chimneypieces, under the roofs. Here the visiting retainers used to sleep.

Historic Buildings agenda very long. I thought I conducted it well. The Admiral congratulated me afterwards (how unattractively this will read). S.P.A.B. meeting after luncheon to discuss the Fountains Abbey question, very fully attended. Esher did not present the case well. I spoke too much in trying to indicate the inconsistency of the Committee's policy in advocating the rebuilding of Holland House and Chelsea Old Church, both of which had been rendered totally ruinous, but not this Abbey. I said that whereas I opposed fake restoration from the foundations I could not on principle oppose making habitable what so largely survived. The vote was succinctly 'for' and 'against'. I and Dame Una voted 'for'; we were in a minority of two. Rick told me on the telephone this evening that I had spoken wisely. He let fall that at the MacGregors' party both Forsyth and Nye (architect members) told him they would like to be offered the chance of rebuilding the Fountains ruins. Yet both spoke and voted against! As Rick said, that Committee can be made to vote in whatever way a clever chairman wants. Dined with the Methuens in their Primrose Hill studio and discussed with them clauses to be imposed upon the Bath Academy in their lease of Corsham to that body.

Thursday, 10th October

Tony Gandarillas dined. Very sweet and eccentric. I asked him how he, aged sixty-two, managed to keep his youthful figure and complexion. He said it was the 'green pipe', explaining that he smoked opium every day of his life.

Saturday, 12th October

Am staying at Wickhamford for a few days. Can hardly speak for laryngitis, so Mama keeps me in bed. I work however. In four days I have written up 25 properties for my Guide, which added to the 30 previously done, brings my total to 55 out of 80.

Papa and I motored to Gaines to tea with the Wrigleys. Kenny and Lucy Lees staying. Kenny told me that as a boy he was brought up at Lower Clarksfield outside Lees. He remembers Higher Clarksfield as a large red brick Georgian house, now long ago destroyed. He said that my great-grandfather Joseph Lees and his brothers John and James, were never educated. Their father spoilt them as children and died when they were young. They were rich. They resolutely refused to go to school. Every morning they were sent off on ponies by their mother, but when out of sight rode away to the hills for the day. They learned nothing. John hated his mother whom, when he grew up, he referred to as 'she', and to James and Joseph as 'your mother'. Kenny remembers John playing billiards with him when he was a tiny boy at Lower Clarksfield. Joseph who managed the colliery came in and said with great excitement: 'John, what do you think? I was offered £500,000 today for the colliery.' John who never interested himself in business, said nothing at all and went on chalking his cue. Coal had been discovered under their land quite by chance in the early eighteenth-century. Until then they had been small landowners, not at all important or rich. Not that they ever did become the slightest bit important or very rich.

Called for Michael at 10 o'clock at the Dorchester and motored to Womersley. Stopped at Willington in Bedfordshire and made notes of the condition of the dovecote and stables. On to Hinchingbrooke for luncheon. Rosemary's mother, Ruby Lindsay, wearing an old overall and looking what M called 'tired and streaky', greeted us. Rosemary Hinchingbrooke, wearing an untidy overall-cum-maternity-gown and sandals down at heel, which outfit likewise shocked M., also greeted us warmly. She was, as always, so welcoming, unaffected and charming. She appears to be going to have her fifth child. They have a manservant whose clothes, for sheer scruffiness, excelled any garments I have ever seen. We looked round the house, now furnished. Family portraits of high quality and interest – a Hogarth of a boy and several Georgian Montagus.

We reached Womersley for dinner. Edward Moulton-Barrett, a great-nephew of the poet, came from London. He had been stationed in the back part of the house during the war.

Motored Michael to York and spent the morning in the Treasurer's House with the local committee. On the whole a good collection of furniture, well maintained. It is stiffly arranged and the rooms are bare. The Dean took us to the Deanery to show us his collection of modern pottery which we thought very indifferent. He is a friendly, forthcoming cleric. Oliver Sheldon met us and took us to lunch at his house in Bishopsthorpe. Gave us a rare meal. Then took us over Lord Burlington's Mansion House – finer in than out, and the big double cube exquisite. All the décor in the most splendiferous mayoral taste. The Lord Mayor, a self-important man, welcomed us. The mayoral silver was spread on the table for our benefit: some lovely things, notably a 1670 chased chamber pot, two Queen Anne tankards, and a gold cup, dated 1650, valued at £5,000. Then to the Merchant Adventurers' Hall, a dull mediaeval structure, with long hall of wooden columns. Sheldon is Governor of this Company. He is a splendid fellow who runs the York Georgian Society. He would introduce M as the Earl of Rosse. Finally, to the Assembly Rooms, in a truly lamentable condition. Motored back to Bishopsthorpe, the Archbishop's Palace. Archbishop with handsome dark chaplain on the drive to meet us. He took us hurriedly round but it was too dark to see much. But a lovely house, especially the Georgian gothick hall by Atkinson 1769. The gothick façade not really pretty. Wonderful 1680 room with Wren-like ceiling and Renaissance chimneypiece which the Archbishop, injudiciouly, wants to take away in order to reveal a possible Tudor fireplace behind. M. and I expressed polite disapproval. He showed us the icons given him by the Russian bishops on his recent visit to the Soviet. Says that religion is freely practised and there is no persecution of priests. I didn't know which to marvel over more, his lack of taste or his gullibility. Yet we liked him.

Drove to Mass at Askern, taking Anne's two Irish maids who have bicycled these three miles innumerable times. They allowed me to lose my way and when I gently reprimanded them remarked that it was quite a different matter to find the way by car.

We went to tea at Nostell Priory, the Winns. Charles Winn is the present owner, his father having disinherited the elder son, now Lord St. Oswald. Winn aged about forty-five, bluff, exquisite manners in that English natural way, unlike the Frogs. It was foggy as we approached. The Paine block is too squat for its length and the Adam addition is not in scale or in proportion. We spent one-and-a-half hours looking over the inside and even then did not get as far as the Adam block, where I understand the decoration to be nineteenth-century. In the Paine block the Adam hall is superb and the Adam drawing-room a restrained variant of the music room at Home House. All these rooms still under dust-sheets and the furniture piled in heaps. Could not therefore see the famous Chippendale things. The outside of the house is *pitch* black, there being a mine only 100 yards from the house. The park large and not very beautiful. Lord and Lady Strathallan staying, both very handsome. Mrs. Winn, the third wife, appeared at tea, a friendly, pretty American. Paine's few rooms likewise fine, and distinctly rococo. This house, like Wentworth, has a number of lovely eighteenth-century wall-papers. Nothing is shabby and the place is well kept up for the Winns are rich. During the war they put away everything for safety, and all the pictures were taken out of the beautiful inset frames.

Monday, 21st October

Battery completely flat this morning and the car had to be pushed to start it. A horrid, very foggy drive from Womersley to Lyme over the hideous Peaks. We got there at twelve and met Charlie Brocklehurst. Michael most conscientiously went through every room and was vastly impressed by the house, especially the south front and courtyard. We took a lot of photographs. At 2.30 the whole Stockport Corporation arrived in a body. We amicably settled outstanding points.

Michael is so good and they were all impressed by his manner. It is essential that lightweights do not deal with people of this sort. We walked in the sun to Lyme Cage in the late afternoon; then drove to Charlie's lodge where we stayed the night.

Tuesday, 22nd October

Drove to Little Moreton Hall, arriving 9.30 with Charlie where we met Colin Jones, our area agent. The Dales, new tenants, are installed. Already certain improvements have taken place I am glad to say. Michael left at 11 for Clumber. Charlie and I arranged furniture and at 1.30 I drove to London. Arrived without misadventure at 6. Opened the door and there was Stuart Preston. He had arrived from New York yesterday.

Wednesday, 23rd October

Today Professor Richardson lunched with me. We left Brooks's arm in arm, he in a long, thick topcoat, limping now since he broke his ankle and carrying a stout, unfurled umbrella. Slowly we walked up St. James's Street. I imagined the scene to be like William IV and a Cabinet Minister, as might be described by Creevey. The Hanoverian Professor took me to his new offices, above Lenygon's shop in Old Burlington Street. The building is, appropriately, by Kent and his room furnished with incomparable old furniture and a deep Savonnerie carpet. He pointed out with pride and merriment his chair of Queen Anne date, with original covering, and then his gold-headed cane in a corner. 'I like a touch of gold in a room,' he said. He is a darling old man. 'The devil is a real person. You meet him everywhere, James,' he said seriously, shaking his head.

At 6 o'clock had a drink with Bill Astor who talked about Cliveden matters. After a couple of whiskeys I became too confidential. He said that H.S. had no brain and was a lightweight. I agreed, which I should not have done. James dined at Brooks's. His old enchanting self. Told me of his last weekend at West Horsley. Lady Crewe is, he says, the most malignant of women. Of course next week this stricture will be totally reversed.

Lunched with Midi who said she was dining with Lady Crewe when James was there. Bridget Paget, whom Midi did not know, took Midi up to her bedroom after dinner and said, 'Do you like Peggy?' who is Midi's grandfather's wife. Then she said, 'I hate her. She is inefficient and wicked. All owing to unsatisfactory love life.' Midi concluded that she was doped, but I suggested that it was merely drink.

Friday, 25th October

Lunched with Baron Ash in his rented flat to talk over Packwood affairs. He wants to see Polesden Lacey in order to get ideas for showing Packwood. Then I went to Batsford's to approve the final selection of the illustrations for *Adam* which Sam Carr has made. Sachie [Sitwell] was there and Mr. Batsford showed us amidst guffaws of asthmatic laughter a volume of Gillray cartoons of 1792, all of privies and bums and farts. Too extraordinary, but some very funny indeed. One plate called 'The Blenheim Fart' was, I admit, hilarious. We rocked, as Nancy would say.

Went to Bridget's at seven. Cynthia Jebb was with her, talking rather sweetly about a pinchbeck coronet she had bought for the top of her divan bed, as though the future of the world depended upon it.

Saturday, 26th October

To Wildenstein's to see the exhibition of Sir Harold Wernher's pictures. Not too many, thank goodness. The best I thought was one of a young man with golden beard by Cranach.

Sunday, 27th October

The ridiculous Baron Ash lunched at Brooks's and I took him down to Polesden. It was a dark, drizzly day, but the house was lit up and looked charming. Baron was vastly and genuinely impressed and said that if Packwood could be made to look like this he would be pleased indeed. I refrained from remarking that it never could owing to the inferiority of the contents.

Goodhart-Rendel lunched at Brooks's at his request. He told me he was a little distressed that the agents had decided to cut down some trees in his park contrary to his wishes. He was very nice about it but I was determined that this sort of thing must be put a stop to. The truth is that all aesthetes hate any trees being felled whereas counter-aesthetes love felling as many as they can.

Tonight went to Tony Gandarillas's house at 7.30 to find him and Daisy Fellowes drinking champagne downstairs. So I joined them. Daisy looking younger, thinner and seductive. Her facility for gaiety is infectious. We went to dine at the Savoy in her large Rolls-Royce. It has a glass roof which can be revealed by pushing aside the inner covering; also the glass partition between the back and the driver's seat gently opens or closes by a handle operated by Daisy. I sat next to Carmen Gandarillas, Tony's sad daughter, and to Georgia, whose appearance was lovely. She was wearing little velvet bows in her hair and a heavy gold wrist chain with enormous seals. Sachie and Peter Quennell dining too. Also Daisy's married French daughter, Jacqueline, who has just left a French prison for having betrayed her girl friend to the Gestapo during the war. She is very *mal vue*, and is a silly fat girl. This party such a contrast to my six o'clock talk with darling Doreen, with whom I can communicate for hours on all subjects. This time we discussed the mystery of the 'gentleman'. She said the 'lady' was no mystery. The quality of the first was indefinable, a gift of God; that of the second mundane, and merely a social acquisition.

Tuesday, 29th October

The Eshers motored me down to Polesden. They went round the museum and were delighted with it. Lord E. has approved Michael's memorandum on the proposal that we should have area representatives as well as agents. Lord E. wants to call them area artists, but Lady E. and I think that a bad name, which will cause resentment in those who are not artists. I have engineered this little scheme.

To Knole again by car. Found a new quick way through Sydenham and Bromley which takes only one hour. Mason and I completed our notes on the condition of the contents. I love working with Mason. The Admiral, Admiraless and Miss P[aterson] came down in the afternoon. I introduced the Admiral to Lord Sackville. Robin who was with me said of the A and lady: 'They are King and Queen Low-Brow.'

Cliffy and I met Colonel Horlick at Partridge's and saw eighteen of his Daniel Marot-like chairs, which are ugly yet first-rate. They are valued by Cliffy and Mr Partridge for insurance at £3,500. Colonel Horlick offered to have the seats re-covered. Mr Partridge produced a roll of exquisite green Genoa velvet and Colonel Horlick, without batting an eyelid, agreed to have them covered with this stuff at a cost of £300. The chairs will be loaned to Montacute.

Diane Abdy this evening alone. I was rather apprehensive but it went very well. She is an angel. I took her to Covent Garden to see *Coppélia*, which was gay and extremely pretty. Margaret Dale is a good dancer; Turner an ungainly man. On the whole women excel men at dancing. We dined at the Ivy. This evening cost me all told £5, including taxis.

After luncheon motored to Watlington to stay with the Eshers, arriving tea-time. They live in a small house called High Wood, which their son Lionel built for himself before the war as a weekend retreat. They have made over the large house to him and his four sons. Lionel intends to introduce his architect's office there, make flats for the staff out of the back regions and generally contrive a hive of industry. No one in the world is more delicious company than Ld. E. After dinner, and indeed before, and during, he talked incessantly. He is amazing for a man of his age. He honestly thinks the world pleasanter and more interesting than ever before, and that the new post-war life is the most exciting adventure. He sees a resurgence of interest in the arts on a wide basis, and praises this Government for being more progressive in patronising the arts than any former one in history. He dislikes Bevin and Byrnes because he believes that other less intransigent ministers, instead of wrangling with the Soviet, would foster better relations with them. He never fails to be merry and entertaining.

Sunday, 3rd November

Lord E. says he has had a wonderful and enjoyable life. He even sees a great future for the British aristocracy. He possibly overlooks the fact that his life has been a peculiarly easy one, without much hardship and without, I guess, much suffering. We went to lunch at West Wycombe, and afterwards had a conference about particular matters concerning that property, and the awful Captain Hill.

Monday, 4th November

Motored to Hartwell and went round the house. Both Eshers delighted with it, thought it lovely, and deplored what Hill had done to the interior. He is going to write to Hill expressing his concern, affably he says, and offering guidance.

Today the loveliest day I ever remember: sun almost burning and no breath of wind. I went on to Long Crendon and looked at the Court House. Then lunched excellently in H.J. Massingham's little white house. His wife did the cooking. Agreeable people, but he did not strike me as a big man, except physically. He is lame and his hands are feeble. Arthritis probably. He showed me his collection of bygones; boring things. Old milk pails and shafts of shepherds' crooks, smocks, etc. Had a look at Boarstall Tower, and on to Upton for tea.

Tuesday, 5th November

Staying with the Bearsteds. More of his pictures are back from war storage, including the Italian primitives. The whole makes a superb private collection. Lord Esher said that B.'s manner is deprecatory. It is. He speaks in a low voice. He told me that Esher as a boy at Eton was intellectually pretentious. He wrote poetry which his father published privately, and this went to his head. I can just imagine this.

An undergraduate from Oxford, named Carris, or something [David Carritt] came to look at the pictures. Lord B. warned me beforehand to be kind to him for he would probably be shy. He was by no means shy. A perky youth of eighteen dashed into the room with abounding self-confidence. Within minutes he was disputing the entries in Lord B.'s catalogue. I must say his knowledge of pictures and of everything else touched upon was astounding. I was amazed. Though polite he is too sure of himself.

Wednesday, 6th November

Diane had a party before dinner. Loelia Westminster looking very handsome in a sensible, pretty little hat, not the enormous cartwheels she sometimes sports. Diane's brother Newport and his wife. She is new, young, tall and with the bloom of youth, but nothing more.

Thursday, 7th November

To the Geffrye Museum to look at a table offered us. It was Victorian, *circa* 1850, nice but not important. The museum is housed in a long seventeenth-century range of almshouses in Shoreditch. Very remote. It was quite well arranged before the war but now has a dusty look. It is on the shown-to-the-children lines. Dined with Stuart, Ben Nicolson and Baroness Budberg who was H.G. Wells's mistress until the end. She is a Balt. Has a low, fat, intelligent chuckle. She spoke well of death. Said that H.G. had no belief in an after life, or of God. His faith, or lack of it, never wavered.

Friday, 8th November

Saw Sibyl, still in her hospital. I hate going there and then feel ashamed of myself for so nearly not going. I overheard her telephoning to a friend about Lady Anglesey's death. 'No, no, my dear, it was the left lung; you're quite wrong. She spoke to me herself only four days before she died. The children rang

me up at nine that morning, three hours after she had died.'
Sibyl, must *be in at* every death, even that of her greatest
friend.

Lunched with Midi and Colin Crewe before the Albert Hall to
hear George Chavchavadze play three concertos – a herculean
effort, for he had to rehearse all three this morning, owing to
some Trades Union condition which I could not understand,
nor, I think, could poor George. Took Midi to tea with James
and then we rushed to a party given by Princess Galitzine for
George. He looks much the same, only handsomer. John
Wilton dined. Tells me he really is renting Coleshill.

Lunched with Paul Hyslop and Raymond Mortimer, whom
do I really like? Not at all sure. Edward le Bas, with black
beard, also lunching. He is painting Raymond. Dined with
Rory at Claridge's: Alvilde, Tony, Emerald and a beautiful
French woman, circa fifty, called Norah Auric, wife of com-
poser. She rolls her lovely eyes and shows the whites, like first
quarter moons. After sitting in the lounge (what hell restaurants are) Alvilde and Tony and I went to Angus Menzies's
house, where Barbara Ward, Jimmie Smith, Lennox Berkeley
and Angus M were playing and singing. Barbara Ward would
sing in a very missish voice which no one applauded. Angus's
voice is deep and mellifluous. What a seductive creature he is.
Just slightly affected. He has glossy black hair and a Michelangelo mouth and eyes.

Motored, a rare sunny day, to near Chaldon. Car broke down.
A succession of pings would have revealed to the initiated that
a short-circuit was happening. My battery was flat. However a
taxi took me on to Tollsworth Manor, a small farmhouse
belonging to the Hylton estate which the Youth Hostels
Association wants to buy and vest in the Trust. It is of no
account at all.

Jamesey having persuaded me to give a dinner party at home to Harold Nicolson, Maurice Gendron and himself, chucked this morning because he had been invited by Clarissa Churchill to dine with the Duchess of Kent. Can't blame him. So I invited Patrick O'Donovan instead. Harold talked and talked, chiefly telling funny stories about General de Gaulle's complete lack of humour. Maurice I liked very much. He is very like James, but his dark hair curls, not waves.

Saturday, 16th November

Trained to Neath in Glamorganshire. There are restaurant cars again on the trains, though the food is poor. Was met by an old chauffeur in an old car and motored to Derwydd in Carmarthenshire, inhabited by Miss Stepney-Gulston. The outside just like a modern villa, stuccoed over. An ugly house which in England would be of no account, but here is held in some esteem. It does contain several chimneypieces and ceilings of rather remarkable post-Restoration plaster-work in crude, provincial Inigo Jones style, notably the chimneypiece of the upstairs King's Room, putti holding swags. Sheila de Rutzen came for tea and motored me to Picton [Castle]. Just she and Johnnie [Philipps, her brother], there. Good dinner at which we drank hock and a bottle of port.

Sunday, 17th November

This afternoon Johnnie motored me to Manorbier Castle which he offers to the National Trust. It is very overgrown with ivy and neglected. J. is totally irresponsible and what the older generation would call a rotter. But he can be very funny.

Monday, 18th November

Armitage motored me to Tenby this morning. We joined the Rayner-Woods at the Cobourg Hotel where I stayed the night. Spent a wretched day looking at the Tudor Merchant's House and then meeting the Mayor and Councillors of Tenby, endeavouring, without success, to induce them to be responsible for the house's upkeep. Tenby is a lovely little town and was beloved by my grandmother who paid it an annual visit when her servants were on holiday. Lying in bed I almost became reconciled to the sea, listening to its gentle susurrations.

Thursday, 21st November

Went to Brown's Hotel to tea with Colonel and Mrs. Wingfield Digby who are very worried about Sherborne Castle. However I much doubt whether it will come to anything. Their manner not conciliatory and their attitude philistine. He has the typical M.F.H. mentality but, poor man, was today curiously sleepy and, I suspect, ill.

I had a dinner party of Kathleen Kennet, Bridget and Malcolm Bullock, whose wit struck me tonight as the most trenchant and unremitting I had ever listened to.

Saturday, 23rd November

After working in the office this morning went to Agnew's exhibition, one of their all-sorts mixture. After luncheon set off for Moor Place, Much Hadham, for the weekend. This is an interesting house which was built by one Robert Mitchell, a Scot, in 1777 under the full Adam-Wyatt influence. I found the stairwell actually more Wyattish than Adamatic. Mr. Norman is a very charming host with his emphatic utterances. Mark, who is almost as handsome as his extraordinarily handsome father, lives in the house with his wife and five children. Brothers and sisters, all married, live in the village; a most united family. Surprisingly, the house has yellow lincrusta walls.

Sunday, 24th November

It poured all day without cessation. After luncheon Mr. Norman lent me a huge red and blue umbrella and showed me the village of Much Hadham which is truly remarkable for its old cottages with overhangs and substantial red brick Georgian houses. A most élitish village. We had tea at the Hall with the de la Mares. This is a lovely house, red brick again, about 1730, with rectangular entrance hall and splendid wide staircase and contemporary balusters rising in a straight flight.

Very fine doorheads and surrounds, particularly those on the first floor landing with the continuation of the cornice over the keys. De la Mare has an unrivalled collection of Japanese porcelain.

Monday, 25th November

Drove to Colchester but my car was going so badly I left it at the inn and continued to Blickling in Carew Wallace's. He is a devastatingly earnest young man. We interviewed candidates for caretakers at Blickling. Found a telegram from Aunt Dorothy and went to tea at Maud Mosley's new house at Aylsham, half a mile from Blickling. Maud M. has become white-haired, crippled with arthritis and an old woman. Aunt D. unchanged I was glad to see.

Tuesday, 26th November

Left Blickling – Wallace and I stayed at the inn – at eleven for Beccles. Looked at Leman House, in deplorable disrepair and not as interesting as I had expected. Motored to Boxted Hall and inspected a pair of late eighteenth-century library steps, the most exquisite things I have ever seen. They will do admirably for the library at Montacute. Then to Colchester where I picked up my motor, which is still going appallingly.

Thursday, 28th November

Motored the Admiral to Audley End. Every day this month without a single exception it has rained. At eleven we met Lord Braybrooke. Mrs. Hugh Dalton, the Chancellor of the Exchequer's grim-visaged wife, came over from Cambridge, bringing Hickson, secretary to the Cambridge University Extra-Mural Studies people. Went all round the house again and afterwards lunched with Lord and Lady Braybrooke at their nearby villa, and talked. I think Mrs. Dalton was a little impressed by Lord B's story of his death duties and appalling financial stringencies since his inheritance, as well as by the importance of Audley End. The purpose of this visit was to solicit her to help the Trust engage the Treasury's interest.

Ate at Brooks's with Ben Nicolson who told me how

deeply he regretted not having been more dissolute in his youth.

To Newbury with Eardley where we were met by Mr. Behrend. He took us to see his Memorial Chapel at Burghclere built in 1926 for Stanley Spencer to decorate. This Spencer did over a period of seven years. All the walls are now covered with scenes derived from his experiences in the R.A.M.C. in Salonika. As an achievement it is colossal; as a period piece highly representative. Mr. B. offers it to the Trust. It is, I submit, well worth holding.

Mrs. Hammersley had asked me to her house this evening. But it was raining and I felt too tired to go. Dined with Colin Agnew. Paul Wallraff there. We had a lot to drink, including brandy. Colin became very communicative and persistently upheld the conviction that Hitler had been homosexual.

Monday, 2nd December

Grandy Jersey lunched and we discussed Osterley, still not through yet. I suggested he should agitate his lawyers. I also persuaded him to agree to sell his picture of Upton to Lord Bearsted and let me get an independent dealer's valuation; so I asked Leggatt's to act for him.

Called on Doreen [Baynes] at six. Both agreed how much we disliked, and feared, the *New Statesman* highbrows. When I said to her that among these upstarts, snobs and iconoclasts there were one or two I tolerated as individuals she said, 'That may be, but it is the vapour that arises from them collectively that one disrelishes.' Dined with Malcolm Bullock at the Guards Club and accompanied him to the House of Commons at 10 o'clock for several divisions. I heard no speeches but from the gallery over the Speaker's chair watched the Members dividing, and thought how subfusc, undistinguished and insincere the majority of them looked.

Wednesday, 4th December

At the Estates Committee this morning felt sure that Dr. Trevelyan was the worst chairman I had ever witnessed.

Eardley said 'costive' is the adjective for this committee. At luncheon time paid my third visit to the King's Pictures. Thought the Waterloo Lawrences dull, and the Flemish pictures dull. Preferred Charles I's choice of baroque painters. I like the idyllic, pastoral blue garments worn by Bassano's classical shepherds.

Dined with the Eshers, and sat next to Jane Clark who talked of K.'s 'wealth'. When I said he ought to be made a peer she purred. She said it was only peers and their eldest sons who invariably disliked one another, instancing David Crawford's dislike of his father. I thought her rather patronising in her reference to Crawford's poverty. She told me it was my duty to press Sir Alan Barlow to get him paid a salary for his chairmanship of the N.T. She went on about his inability to meet his expenses. My other neighbour was Lady Riddell, oldish, who said she did not believe in the devil and the power of evil. Afterwards talked with Mrs. Lionel Brett, whom I at once found velvety beautiful and adorable – really someone irresistible. She talked of Watlington and their scheme for living in a flat when the rest of the house was divided into offices and flats for his, Lionel's, partners and employees. Esher says Lionel is very much cleverer than himself. This is hard to believe. K. Clark laughed at me because I had never heard of either Itma or Monteverdi. The Eshers' dinner party was in a private room at the Connaught, old-fashioned and cosy.

Thursday, 5th December

Motored this morning to Long Crendon. Visited Mrs. Barry, lady of the Manor. She had asked me tomorrow and I could only manage today. When I arrived a quarter of an hour later than I had stipulated I understood why she had been cross on the telephone, for she was dressed for hunting and was waiting for my visit to be over so that she could look for hounds. The Manor is a rather attractive, old-world and completely fake house. Slyly I asked her to lend me photographs of the house before as well as after restoration. This did not make her less cross and she pretended she had not restored it. But a great deal of timbering and several stone gothic fireplaces have obviously been inserted. The great hall is quite bogus. I do not think the N.T. ought to accept covenants over this house. The only good egg is the gate-house on the road. One drives under it. It is of stone, late gothic. She ended in being very sweet to me. I decided that the grounds were worthy of covenants in order to protect the village.

Lunched at the Apple Orchard, West Wycombe. A frightfully cold day and a leaden sky, as though predicting snow. I drove to Hughenden [Manor] at Langley-Taylor's request. The R.A.F. have gone but police still occupy the requisitioned part. They were reluctant to show me over, but ultimately consented. The rooms are empty and, except in Dizzy's library which is quite untouched, all the charming Victorian wallpapers are ruined. I saw no furniture. It is stacked away. Much redecoration is needed. Several chimneypieces are eighteenth-century ones of inlaid marble.

Friday, 6th December

Motored to Salisbury where I lunched. At Exeter I had tea and continued in the moonlight across Dartmoor, which is very beautiful at night, and terrifying – what with escaped prisoners demanding lifts and hounds of the Baskervilles baying at the moon. I reached Tavistock before seven, and had a bath. Stayed at the Bedford Hotel which was full of local diners in pink coats for a Hunt Ball in the town. The ladies I saw were very provincial and un-chic in their home-made, trailing dresses, or 'gowns'.

Saturday, 7th December

Very showery but beautiful day. After breakfast motored across the Tamar into Cornwall, up and down steep hills and descending narrow lanes till I reached Cotehele, which faces east over Calstock and the river. Were it moved just a little further southward the house would be better situated. Then it would overlook the lovely ribbon loop of the river. As it is, the situation is romantic, wild and wooded. The caretaker was away with the key, but the farmer's wife most kindly motored to fetch a daily help from Calstock who has another key. This kind and intelligent woman showed me round the house which is fully furnished. Meanwhile the old coachman, seeing my motor, came and talked. Told me that until 1939 he drove a 1911 Rolls for the late Lord Mount Edgcumbe. He expressed himself very concerned about my 'points'. He left and presently returned, wearing a topcoat with velvet collar and old-fashioned billycock, to present me with the distributor points of his old Rolls. I was charmed by him. Didn't know what to do with object presented.

Cotehele House is not striking from the outside, being squat and spread. It is actually far larger than one is led to suppose from the front, for it has two courtyards. It is uniformly old, late mediaeval with pointed windows, all of granite. The great hall is as fine as any I have seen, with curved windbraces in the roof and plastered white-washed walls, hung with armour. In the oldest wing all the rooms are panelled, walls plastered and the Stuart furniture upholstered in needlework, none later than the eighteenth century. The contents are untouched, superb. Indeed it is a superb house. Lunched at Tavistock and motored to Pixton [Park, near Dulverton], arriving for tea. Mary Herbert, my hostess, came just before dinner. Only Eddie Grant and an Austrian countess staying.

Sunday, 8th December

Pixton is a little more orderly than usual. The evacuee children have all gone of course, but the house is left rather knocked about. Mary is as majestic as ever, tall, robust, windswept, exceedingly untidy. Her tweed coat and skirt are stained and torn, and the pockets have holes in them. Her breeding and dignity are impeccable; her views are uncompromising, proud and right. Her humour is unimpaired. She is a splendid creature with a massive soul.

Today it poured in cascades from morn till eve, the north wind driving blankets across the valley. So I did not go to Holnicote, but sat indoors all day, talking to Mary and that kindly, silly Eddie Grant.

Monday, 9th December

A better day and at 9.30 drove to Holnicote. By working hard I saw within two-and-a-half hours Luccombe, Horner, Bossington, Allerford and enchanting Selworthy villages, the last up the hill. The view from its church steps superb. What a view! What a church! There is a Jacobean interior porch from the parvise, and some splendid vaulting and fifteenth-century bosses. Lunched at Taunton and reached Montacute at 2.30. Did some good work there with Eardley who joined me. We dined with the Yateses in their new flat (avoiding the w.c.) and stayed at The King's Arms.

Thursday, 12th December

Motored to Knole in Robin Fedden's car, taking Lady Smith-Dorrien of the Royal School of Needlework. Went round all the state rooms, she commenting on the fabrics and we agreeing to send two specimens, one a pillow from the King's bed, for her to repair. She will give us an estimate for having the other things done.

Dined at Lennox Gardens at Mrs. Carnegie's. This interested me historically for here was a pre-Great War upper middle-class régime in full fig. Large, ugly, late-Victorian house. We assembled in capacious drawing-room on first floor. Lots of silver in evidence, silver photograph frames, silver boxes and bric-à-brac displayed on dainty tables. Dining-room table with white brocade cloth and silver candlesticks, spoons and forks shining very bright. Butler and footman both in white ties. Circular metal suspended centre-light with Edwardian electric fitting, called, I think, an electroleer. Sixteen candles burning. Present the Petos and Mrs. Carnegie, whose last husband was Canon Carnegie, Frances Peto's father, and her first Joe Chamberlain, whom she referred to as 'Mr. Chamberlain'. Mrs C., grey, wispy-haired, tall, upright like a ramrod, dressed in black tulle, thin Edwardian waist, low V front, and long grey kid gloves. Opposite me at dinner hung a splendid portrait of her as a young woman by Millais. In the drawing-room is another of her in the early thirties by Sargent, this one full-length depicting a feather plume in her hair. In the Millais the head is close curled, showing delicate ears. Very pretty she must have been. Now be-pince-nezed, severe, correct, but oh such a delightful woman. There is a third portrait of her as a child by William Hunt, American portrait painter. There is one of Joe Chamberlain by Sargent in the dining-room. After dinner she and I talked of Millais, whom she much liked – 'he was so jolly' – and of 'Mr. Sargent' whom she liked too. I wondered how this impeccable, immaculate lady could have allowed herself to have two husbands, even though she was a widow when she married the second, the first being satisfactorily in heaven. Which would she belong to when *she* reached heaven?

Such a flavour of Edwardian London this evening conveyed to me, of hansom cabs and artificial flowers in a long, frilly vase, for a dense yellow fog enveloped us, percolating through the closed windows at the time, and the street outside chill and muffled. Mrs C. is still young in spirit and quick in uptake, with her perfect old-fashioned manners. Speaks with a low, slightly husky, Bostonian voice, very beguiling intonation.

Sunday, 15th December

M. Jourdain and I. Compton-Burnett came to tea at 5 o'clock, which we had before the fire. (I must tell Emily not to put paper mats under the cakes. She must have bought them – with the cakes?) Bought cakes today are detestable, without mats. James and Maurice came in later. They were longing for the ladies to go, and made it plain. But the ladies made it plain that they were not going to leave just to please these two young men, and stayed and stayed till 6.45. Then James and Maurice both leapt to their feet, saying goodbye. So the ladies had to leave whereas the boys stayed behind. I feared this was rather pointed. Maurice spoke not a word until they left, and then asked in his French English, 'Who are these impossible governesses?' J. explained that one of them was the foremost novelist of our time.

Monday, 16th December

Went to Osterley this morning. Perishing. Spoke sharply to the Ministry of Works man who wishes to buy a triangle of the park upon which to erect permanent Government offices. I said the Trust would not stand it for a moment.

Tuesday, 17th December

To tea at Emerald's. Robin Ironside and Lord Tavistock, whom I cut for auld-lang-syne. Horrid party though Emerald was as trilling and funny as I ever heard her. She was very emphatic about men. 'A woman of course can only love a dead

115

man. Why! live men are fickle, inconstant, vain, unreliable, ridiculous. Dead men are none of these things.'

To the ballet at Covent Garden with Sheila. *The Fairie Queene;* Purcell music; Shakespeare *Midsummer Night* recitation and singing. Singers awful and Margaret Rawlinson a poor sort of Titania. Helpmann a dignified Oberon, with very strong character, distinctive face. Scenery and dresses by Michael Ayrton as pretty as could be.

It was snowing when I left for the office. Was invited to three cocktail parties, and went to one, John Murray's, at delightful No. 50 Albemarle Street, surrounded by Byron relics. Surrounded by old faces. The party was given for Freya Stark. Why? When dozens of the other guests were just as distinguished. I was much moved by Byron's glove in a case, and the shirt worn at his wedding which had been George II's (shirt, not wedding).

Oh, the cold! Motored with the Admiral to Fairford, where we lunched. Had a quick look round Fairford Park, which is flat and dull, with nissen huts all over it. Could not see inside the house which is 1690 outside. It has plain, rambling extensions. At three we reached Buscot. Gavin Faringdon showed us the outside, all kept in apple-pie order. A lovely walled garden in a hollow. The Harold Peto path from the SE angle of the house towards the lake is impressive. The house a well contrived fake. Paul Hyslop has done very well, I think. Gavin certainly has some first-rate furniture and pictures. House well appointed and heated. The Admiral bewildered by Gavin's socialism-cum-plutocracy, as well he might be. Gavin has a youngish, ogling, rather raddled American staying, or perhaps living with him. For dinner Gerald Berners, Robert Heber-Percy and another young man came over. Rather a sticky meal because of the Admiral being out of things. Poor Admiral more bewildered than ever by the company. His incredulous eyes on stalks. His instincts offended. I did not enhance my credibility by talking too much about art and drama, about which I know little and the Admiral even less. He was well out of his depth and kept trying desperately to surface like a moribund dolphin. When the Faringdon Hall party left Gavin kept us sitting up till long past midnight in spite of poor Admiral's unrepressed yawns.

Saturday, 21st December

A terrible frost in the night. My car could not be started even by Gavin's chauffeur, who actually looks more like a Shaftesbury Avenue cissy than a skilled mechanic. For one hour it was pushed and towed by four gardeners and Gavin's smart Rolls over the icy drive, but it would not budge. So we abandoned it – points again, I suppose – and went by train to London, arriving three hours late, perished, in time for tea.

Monday, 23rd December

Had an awful time trying to do Christmas shopping. Could hardly get into a shop and when in, nothing to buy. Tried five shops for an O.E. tie for my father with no success.

Tuesday, 24th December

Caught the 9.15 to Faringdon. The crowds at Paddington were dense but the queues for each platform were kept in good control. Got to Faringdon at midday, collected car, which started, and drove to Oxford. Lunched at the Randolph vilely and then looked at a portrait by Watts of Mrs. Senior, *née* Hughes, sister of Tom Hughes, author of *Tom Brown's Schooldays*. A fine full-length, *c.* 1868. I have written to Sir Geoffrey Mander to ask if he would like it at Wightwick [Manor]. It is enormous. Arrived at Wickhamford for tea to find Deenie staying. No one else of the family.

Friday, 27th December

Papa and I drove to Brockhampton near Bromyard in the morning where we met the Admiral and Mrs. Bevir, Ruby and Christopher Holland-Martin, and Colin Jones. Lunched in the cold, cold hall and walked round the house where Colonel Lutley's personal belongings are left lying about since the day he died. Something poignant in a house which has suddenly ceased to exist with the last owner. Life arrested in old tobacco jars with the lids off, smelly old pipes, books turned face downwards on tables, the well-worn favourite chair with deep imprint of the late 'behind' and threadbare arms, and the mournful, reproachful gaze of dozens of forgotten ancestors on the walls. Estate, house and contents all left to the National Trust. The house, which has a situation of unparalleled Midlands beauty overlooking valley and woods, could be made decent by the removal of Victorian trimmings round the windows, and the installation of sash-bars. No furniture of museum quality but very nice plain utility Georgian, as genuine as the old squires who for centuries loved it. Two good Georgian bookcases. The Admiral being incredibly muddleheaded and Ruby as friendly as I am sure a swordfish can be. Christopher shocked me deeply by warning me that G., whom I had proposed for election to Brooks's, would be black-balled. What possible reason could there be other than some personal spite? No one is less offensive or more affable to all and sundry. Ruby who drove over in a luxurious Bentley produced a luncheon basket with fittings like a bar, complete with gin and whisky and coffee. Papa and I rather humbly drank our milk. The dear old butler with his sweet, sad smile, is stone deaf and speaks in a whisper. The housekeeper, dignified and courteous like the one at Chesney Wold speaks like a B.B.C. announcer. Papa and I drove down to Lower Brockhampton and examined this little black-and-white manor and gatehouse with enthusiasm. It is just the sort of house my father cares for.

1947

Doreen telephoned and I went to her at six o'clock. She told me that she has a medium who regularly visits her; that she is strictly religious and prays; that she sees visions of the departed, unfortunately too often of the people she most disliked when they were alive; that, notwithstanding, she is eagerly looking forward to death; that her medium tells her it takes the form of life being gently drawn through the fingers. She is not the least melancholy and enjoys *her* life, which is not life as enjoyed by most people. From true life she is too divorced to care whether she exists any longer in this alien world. We all feel like this but most of us cannot withdraw from it in the way she manages to do, i.e. shut herself up in her bedroom and adjoining sitting-room, with curtains tightly drawn, for days on end. I do adore Doreen.

Thursday, 2nd January

Went once again yesterday to the King's Pictures and concentrated on the Primitives which to me are as indistinguishable as one hound in a pack from another. Called on Grandy Jersey in his shop and saw his large picture of Upton that Lord Bearsted wants but won't give £600 for. I hope the shop keeps the wolf from poor Grandy's door.

Friday, 3rd January

Took the manuscript of my Nat. Trust *Guide* to Batsford's. Met Mr Harry who with no explanations put me in a taxi and drove to Marylebone station. There we met Sachie. Mr. Harry produced packets of minute negatives from his capacious pockets. They smelled very strongly of fish which he also keeps in same pockets for his cats. He spread the negatives on the platform, produced a huge magnifying glass and, while spluttering and coughing, examined them on the ground with Sachie. The two made an odd group among the hurrying passengers, Mr. B. wearing a green hat with a huge feather in it.

Cold, leaden skies. It must snow soon. Left Wickhamford for Mass in Evesham in that hideous church. On to Charlecote for one-and-a-half hours. Alianore Lucy there and Wicker, the caretaker. All is serene. Then to Packwood and lunched with Baron. We had sherry and pâté de foie gras, as good as it used to be; chicken with burgundy; omelette with quince jam and rum blazing; port wine. Baron conducted me over the house which is now in pristine condition. He showed me a Victorian lithograph of the house looking much as it does today. Saw the servants' wing adapted for the caretaker, and discussed this. B wants a disabled ex-officer, not an artistic person. We don't see eye to eye over this.

Deep snow this morning. At two Emily Empey's [my mother's beloved governess] funeral took place in Wickhamford churchyard. Disagreeable stories current about her death, which was peaceful and fairly sudden, but Mama says the village women would come into her room and discuss her before she was dead and when she may well have been conscious. On Saturday I watched Haines [our chauffeur for sixty years] and Nightingale, the sexton, digging out Molly [Empey's] grave, for Em's coffin was to rest upon her sister's. It happened that the top of Molly's coffin had quite disintegrated within eight years only, so the two have to be put side by side. The short service with *Abide with Me* and the *Nunc Dimittis* sung in a very high key to the squeaky harmonium, with Tommy Knight playing, moved me deeply. Papa, Mama and I sat in our pew, and nostalgic memories were revived. The beauty and poignancy of this little church amount to the most exquisite thing in the whole world, a sort of sacred island always at the back of my mind which I can retreat to in my thoughts wherever I may be. Mama asked me to compose a short appreciation of Em for the *Evesham Journal* which I did with a great effort this morning. She was I suppose one of the unrecognised saints of this world. After the funeral I motored back to London in the snow. Took me three-and-a-half hours only. I had to drive very cautiously. James dined with me at home.

To see Sibyl, now in her own house, but seated in a chair. I believe she hardly walks at all. The Ambassador to Spain there, very annoyed with our Government for having recalled him, entirely owing to pressure by Russia, he says. Mrs. Oglander, wearing a ridiculous, over-smart Parisian hat with vast ostrich feather now the vogue curling under her chin. She is not young or handsome enough for this extravagant bedizenment. Jamesey present, hardly spoke. Told me afterwards how much he disliked her, and Sibyl. Harold also present. Mrs. Oglander talking silly trivialities to Harold, abusing the *New Statesman* and 'Kingsley Wood', meaning thereby Kingsley Martin, foolish female. She never attends either to what she says or one says. But she is good-natured.

Thursday, 9th January

Aunt Katie's funeral at Richmond. Papa could not go and asked me to represent him. She was eighty-eight and died only because ten days ago she broke a leg. She was the last of the Lees great-aunt and -uncle generation, being my grandfather's sister and married to my grandmother's brother, who tippled. Making a great effort to attend her obsequies I nearly missed them because owing to the cold weather I could not make my car start. Just got to the church in time and left car outside the west door, right in the way, as I discovered later, of the hearse and procession. It had to be moved and I did not dare go out and claim ownership. This must have been revealed for, when the procession of four funereal Rolls-Royces drove off to the cemetery, I followed in the rear. Not an unattractive resting-place on a hill above the town. Was invited back to the old lady's house for a large tea at 2.45. A very old-fashioned sort of Forsyte Saga family gathering. Lots of rather shaming cousins claiming relationship. An un-shaming one was Henry Medd, an architect disciple of Lutyens. Best of the lot was Gladys Lees, Papa's first cousin, a very un-smart, badly dressed, lined old baggage. Distinguished in a well-bred way, clipping her g's, and totally unpretentious unlike some of the younger ones. I gave her a lift but ran out of petrol before I could get to a garage and had to turn her out. I felt a little, and not very, sad about Aunt Katie. I liked her directness.

Meetings today. Lord Esher told the committee that he thought my *Guide* excellent. It isn't of course. Had tea with Harold who has asked the Admiral to send me to the U.S.A. to lecture, and the Admiral replied, 'But I can't spare him.' Harold said a lecture tour was terribly tiring. Dined with Dame Una, James and John. How dismal and carping the Dame can be. James admits she is much on his nerves at present.

Motored to stay with Maud Russell at Mottisfont [Abbey]. Lunched en route at Winchester and went round the City Mill, our property, a dull little affair. Then to the glorious Cathedral. Particularly admired the fifteenth-century tombs of Cardinal Beaufort and William Wykeham, with fine, soaring pinnacles of stonework. This is a marvellous century for architecture, notably the nave here. What could be greater than this aspirant, congruous structure, all of a piece? Pouring with rain all day. Stopped at Sparsholt to look at Vaine Cottages, both extremely unimportant. The Trust does own some low-grade properties. Arrived Mottisfont at four. An oddly assorted party staying: Riette Lamington, who is very beautiful, with fair complexion and hair, agreeable to talk to (Cecil Beaton once called her 'prim and lecherous' to her face); an African woman; Miss Russell, an old sister-in-law; Martin Russell, Mrs R's son, dark, Jewish and clever; and Bluey Baker, a suave, smooth, elderly schoolmaster from Winchester, once an admirer of Lady Goonie Churchill, and at New College with my Uncle Milne in the nineties.

At first glance this is a beautiful old house of mellow red brick, the south front having been made symmetrical in George II's reign. The river Test running close beside it, swiftly. A pretty Georgian stable block to the west. Verdant lawns and massive old trees striding to the water's edge. Yet it is not a wholly satisfactory house and is moreover spooky. Built upon and out of the remains of a priory, the house comprises the nave of the church, the north nave wall wholly surviving. This makes me feel slightly uncomfortable. Maud Russell said that in altering floors they dug up several skeletons and reinterred them. (This she whispered to me softly in French while we were looking at a piscina in the larder in the cook's presence.) There are only three living rooms of any size in spite of Mottisfont being a large house. The dining-room is Palladian. The south-east drawing-room has a pretty rococo frieze, now picked out in gold. Mrs. R ripped out the large hall – it too was Palladian, I see from old photographs – and Rex Whistler perpetrated a ridiculous and flimsy Gothick chiaroscuro trompe-l'oeil. It is too slight and too pretty. Mrs. R has papered all the staircases and the long landing on the first floor in dull marble, rather sombre, but suitable. A curious house because the living-rooms are all on the first floor, and the offices on the ground floor, which is not a basement however.

This morning I walked through the village with Mr. Baker and along the mown grass by the river. He talked of Herbert Baker, no relation, and of Lutyens, both of whom were his friends, chiefly Lutyens. He admitted that Lutyens was always vitriolic about Baker, and Baker Christian-like and charitable about Lutyens.

The furniture in the house is all desirable but gives the impression of having been collected in a hurry. The decoration too seems unfinished. The house has the sparse tidiness of a newcomer, not the cluttered untidiness of accumulated centuries.

Tuesday, 14th January

Went to King's Cross station at 8.45 to find that the train for Gainsborough, scheduled to leave at 9.15, had been cancelled owing to the coal shortage. This put me in ill humour. Went to Brooks's. Returned to catch the 10.10 and reached Gainsborough at 3.43. Was motored to Thonock Hall. Claud Phillimore was reading in the sitting-room window, overlooking the grey and withered park. A dreary part of the world where grass never looks green and the black trees are stunted.

Mindy Bacon and his wife are delightful, progressive-minded and intelligent, with commendable sense of duty, yet not goody-goody. We had high tea. Captain Crookshank, the M.P. came in – jovial, physically sinister – and at 7.30 we attended a gruesome meeting at the Town Hall with the Town Council. The four of us men, attended by Mindy's agent, swept into a large room where some twenty-seven Councillors were seated round tables. All rose. We established ourselves beside the Chairman, who falteringly read a speech of welcome. Bacon replied, offering the Old Hall to the nation, and then a discussion ensued. The Councillors realised that somehow they must accept the Hall but were obviously embarrassed how to find the means with which to keep it up. I felt rather sorry for them confronted with this white elephant on its last legs. Quite a sticky meeting to start with, but at the finish friendly. The Bacons said the Council were a terrible lot, but Claud and I found them rather nice and fairly enlightened. I spoke from time to time when called upon to answer questions and Claud defended his architectural schemes excellently. At the end speeches were made expressing appreciation of Mindy's public spirit.

Wednesday, 15th January

Pitch dark when called by a dear old man who entered my bedroom and pulled back the heavy curtains. Rats' tails of grey fog swirled across the window panes. Tenderly this old retainer brought into the room a red blanket which he spread before the empty fire grate. Then he trundled a small tin hip-bath on to the red blanket. Then he brought a brass can of tepid water, enough to cover the bottom of the bath. The room must have been several degrees below zero. He might have been a ghost performing the customary function of a hundred years ago. But one hundred years ago there would have been a blazing fire in the grate.

Thursday, 16th January

This evening I went to Sir Ian Hamilton's ninety-fourth birthday party, given for the Gordon Boys' School. Conjuror, ventriloquist. The old gentleman sat huddled in a chair, looking extremely frail and ancient. He was rather pathetic and, I must confess, distasteful. Mama confessed to me the other day that she could not bear the physical proximity of the very old. They made her sick. She felt ashamed. I agree with her, and also feel ashamed, and sick. There was no one at No. 1

Hyde Park Gardens whom I knew, except Charlotte Bonham-Carter, always a faithful friend.

I intend next week to begin my new book.

Saturday, 18th January

Eardley and I left in my car at 10.30, a most lovely morning. We looked for an obelisk near Camberley which has been offered to the N.T. but could not find it. I stayed the weekend at Long Crichel. Paul Hyslop the other guest. Eardley, Desmond and Eddy lead a highly civilized life here. Comfortable house, pretty things, good food. All the pictures are Eardley's, and a fine collection of modern art too. After dinner Desmond read John Betjeman's poems aloud, and we all agreed they would live.

Sunday, 19th January

A most beautiful day, mild, sunny and blue. Eddy stayed indoors to write an article. We motored to Horton and walked. Admired the tiny church with Queen Anne dormers in the belfry and climbed up to Sturt's Folly which the Shaftesburys offer the N.T. A tall, triangular building of brick in English bond. All the interior gone. Only a calcined beam or two left. Shrubs growing out of the broken parapet. The central square tower is rather ugly. E. thinks it best not to accept it.

Monday, 20th January

In the morning E. and I went over Max Gate which was built by Thomas Hardy and his brother in 1885. It is perfectly hideous and shapeless. Of scarlet brick, with two ugly square angle towers. All Hardy's things were long ago removed to Dorchester Museum, so there is little connected with him of interest. Besides the house was shoddily built, with lean-to odds and ends added by him. It will be a constant expense. I shall advise the Historic Buildings Committee to sell it – it is held alienably – and keep the money for buying the birthplace, which is far worthier, one of these days.

We lunched at Judge Jeffrey's house in Dorchester and at 2.30 reached Dillington Park, a delightful Tudor house, almost entirely rebuilt about 1810 in imitation of Barrington Court by Pennethorne. It has a cosy family-house air, most sympathetic. Present owner a young Mrs. Cameron. Her mother, Mrs. Vaughan-Lee, living with her. They offer us practically anything we like for Montacute, and E. and I selected straight away a number of things, including a fine set of ribbon-back eighteenth-century dining-room chairs.

Tuesday, 21st January

I drove from Bath, where we both stayed with E.'s mother, to Brockhampton. A longer journey than I had thought. For one hour I examined the silver there. Nothing rare, but like the furniture in this house, decent country house Georgian. No gold plate or jewelry found. Drove past Ribbesford, which always makes me sad, into Shropshire. Wanted to visit Lilleshall but arrived at four o'clock and thought it too late to call on Mr. Ford. So walked round the ruined Abbey, overgrown with ivy. The whole church survives from west to east end, the huge east window intact except for the tracery. Got to Atcham at 5.30 and stayed at The Mytton and Mermaid, Clough Williams-Ellis's inn, at the gates of Attingham.

Went to Attingham after tea. Lady Berwick rather unhappy and worried about Lord B. who is in bed with a tired heart and has two nurses. I went to see him and was allowed to stay for five minutes. He looks quite a good colour but is even slower of speech than usual. She says he is quite contented and does not want to get up, a bad sign. This sweet man I shall doubtless not see again. Lady B. and I walked round the state rooms, she showing me which pieces of furniture they would like us to take for storage at Lyme.

Wednesday, 22nd January

Cut my mole shaving this morning and thought it would never stop bleeding. T.C.P. finally staunched it. Walked up the drive to Attingham at 10.15 and spent the morning jig-sawing the pictures about, trying with Lady Berwick to see how we could fit the best portraits into the drawing-room, leaving the less good ones in the dining-room which the College is to take over. It is sad for this red room is really the finest of all the rooms, with its deep Pompeian walls. She took my advice about letting the Angelica Kauffmann mythological pictures and mirrors remain in the drawing-room with the third Lord Berwick's furniture. In fact she, usually so positive, is rather pathetically ready to fall in with almost any suggestions, being, I think, in despair. She took me to the cellars and showed me the china stored there. It was made, she feels sure, for Caroline Murat, as indeed was the furniture in the drawing-room.

I motored to Wickhamford. In Kidderminster I noticed that the policemen's helmets still have the old-fashioned spikes which they had when I was a child.

Thursday, 23rd January

Dined with Malcolm Bullock at the Turf off grouse and champagne. The Duke of Devonshire joined us as we were finishing and talked for an hour. He was what is called 'lit up' but by no means drunk. Rather curiously we spoke of old Mr Holmes's association with the National Trust. The Duke said he is known as the chief bugger of the Peak – greatly to my surprise. Next morning a telegram came to the office announcing that Mr. Holmes had died at precisely the moment we were talking about him. I have before been told a story of the Duke of D. killing a man at a public meeting merely by speaking *at* him. The man became apoplectic with rage and died on the spot.

The Duke becoming rather a bore I started fidgeting to induce Malcolm to leave the dining-room and shake him off. The D. repeated the story I had heard from him before that Gerry Wellington wrote complaining that Debo Hartington had christened her son Mornington, which is one of the D. of Wellington's subsidiary titles. The D. of D. replied that she had christened him after her favourite jockey just as she had christened her daughter Emma not after any of the Cavendishes, but after her goat. He said that Princess Elizabeth had been staying with him. She is just like the young Queen Victoria with the old Queen's sagacity. She makes it very plain to the Queen that whereas she, the Queen, is a commoner, she, Princess Elizabeth, is of royal blood. After church in Eastbourne she said to the Vicar, aged seventy-five, 'Your sermon was excellent.' He bridled with pleasure. 'But,' she continued, 'you spoilt it in the last ten minutes.' The Duke says that royalty are always happy if you organise their visits and make them play games, but you must never leave it to them to make suggestions. He is devoted to Mrs. Corrigan, that ridiculous woman, famous for her malapropisms. 'My doctor said to me, if you want to avoid indigestion, you must masturbate, masturbate.'

Saturday, 25th January

Yesterday it began snowing and today doing worse things. It is so extremely cold that even with two fires and a rug over me I was cold sitting at home. I read most of the afternoon and evening. Then dined with the Glenconners in Chester Street, Regent's Park. He has a beaming, smiling face, and yet is inscrutable. Is a very clever business man, not an intellectual. Lady G. is pretty, sympathetic, and intellectual. I drove there in the snow. Dinner was to celebrate the return from the States of Cyril Connolly. Cyril had for him a good colour and behaved less like an inspired oracle, although the star of the evening. He told funny stories of his adventures in America, notably flying experiences and encounters with anti-British feelings. Cyril says our Palestine policy has alienated the American Jews in spite of England having been the asylum of European Jewry for the past ten years. The paper that corresponds with *Horizon* in the States, though far larger, has five editors, all Jews. The Jews' power is out of all proportion to their percentage of the population. Alfred Beit came in after dinner. He said that society in South Africa was less provincial than one might suppose. The English Africans are the more entertaining, the Dutch the more intellectual. The climate is unexceptionable. He invited me to stay. Said Clementine was very happy there. He has sold his Kensington Row house and lent his best pictures to the National Gallery. They are to live out there permanently. That is our loss.

Sunday, 26th January

Today snowing so hard and so cold that John Wilton did not dare motor me to Knole. Instead we lunched at Brooks's and then parted. I dined with James and Maurice who had cooked an all vegetable meal, and for some reason was in a dark humour. People look ugly when in an ill humour.

To Loelia Westminster's cocktail party at 15 Grosvenor Square, very grand flat given her by the Duke whom she divorces tomorrow, I think, for he is to marry a fourth time.

Wednesday, 29th January

Today the cold has been unbelievable. The papers say it is the coldest day for over fifty years. Wearing my snow boots and fur-lined coat I was not once warm. All my pipes, including w.c. pipes, are frozen, so a bath or a wash is out of the question. W.c. at the office frozen likewise. Throughout the country electricity has been cut off and the gas pressure is so low that it is not worth while turning the fire on. And we live in the twentieth-century. Even the basic elements of civilization are denied us. Dined with that horror Charles Fry – it is the only word for him – drunken, dissolute and destructive.

Thursday, 30th January

At the King's Pictures today the Dutch paintings literally glowed with warmth and light, like gems. Worldly but infinitely cosy and nostalgic are these little intimate pictures of everyday life, like very accurate dreams. Was especially struck by the small Rembrandt of the Wise Men with a supernatural starlight falling upon the jewels.

Saturday, 1st February

Read *The Age of Erasmus* today. Confirmed in my dislike of the man. These fifteenth- and sixteenth-century scholars were great bores, hardly less so than the 20th-century scholars who write about them. Bridget P. dined. She told me she frankly dislikes her brother for his smug, schoolmastery complacency. This remark rather upset me because I love B. and yet I had to refute the charge. She accepted my rebuke in silence.

Caught the 11.18 to Pulborough where I was met and driven through slush and snow – then pouring with icy fingers of rain – to Petworth. Lord Leconfield, now indeed slow, old and blue-faced, waddled to meet me, clad in yellow gaiters and followed by a black retriever who seems to be his only friend. He is a pathetic old man, extremely courteous and over highly bred. Today he was very friendly and not at all pompous or absurd. Seemed to think it a good idea that I should look at his furniture, wished me to see it all, and hoped I would be pleased with its condition. Said in fact he was convinced he was wise in handing over to the N.T. We lunched together (I not sent to the servants' hall). A large meal was left for us on hot stoves in a small dining-room. His kitchen is in the building over the way and his food has to pass underground. Promptly at 1.30 he summoned the nice old housekeeper and Moss, the house-carpenter, to take me round the house. All the pictures are now re-hung but the state-rooms are still under dust-sheets. Furniture in splendid condition, smelling of mansion polish and camphor. The housekeeper has one couple, the stableman and wife, who work in the house from 6.30 a.m. to midday. Lord Leconfield joined us upstairs and waddled around. We made an odd little party. He is sweet with the servants, jokes with them in his funny, ponderous way. They however curiously subservient and rather sycophantic. He explained that his mother cut down all the four-poster beds because she thought them insanitary, having once read of a dead bird being discovered in a tester.

He made me walk in the cold, steely hail outside. I don't believe he was aware of it. The back of the house, with its buttresses, is really very ugly. I left by bus at four for Pulborough, Lord L. accompanying me to bus stop. Had tea in train buffet car. Went straight to Doreen in Ovington Square. She told me I was far too modest, and that was a mistake. She is always sweet to me. Says she loves Mrs. Trefusis, an unlikely friend. She has already written half of *The Young Queen Victoria*.

Dined at Barbara Moray's. Her daughter Sarah and Mark Ogilvie-Grant there, just the four of us. The daughter is a lovely child but at the age of seventeen is racked with rheumatism and undergoing drastic treatment by injections. The cause is lack of proper food during the war. Barbara is avowedly anti-art and is irritated by all the 'culture' seeping down the classes. Thinks it rot.

Thursday, 6th February

London again blanketed with snow. I stayed at home working at my Lyme Hall guidebook. In the evening to a Catholic semi-society meeting to listen to a Franciscan friar talk on the existence of God. The evening engineered by Dick Girouard. I sat between Pam Chichester and that ape, Lady L. After supper a brains trust – Barbara Ward holding forth in her mincing little voice – which I found wildly irritating.

Friday, 7th February

John Wilton took me in his big, blue Ford car to Knole, in the snow. Bitter cold. I piloted him round the house, like a refrigerator, and the garden where no man had hitherto trod. In our snow boots we crunched over a foot of snow. The new nice housekeeper and Barbara (housemaid, not Ward) already working like Trojans in the Cartoon Gallery.

Loelia dined with me. I took her to *Lady Frederick*, the Somerset Maugham play. Not good. L. told me that the Duke, her husband, was married again this morning. I believe she was feeling rather sad for she said she did not care whether she lived or died. I expect she feels like a dethroned sovereign. She should not seek happiness through pleasure. She is too clever.

Saturday, 8th February

The jolly news today is that all fuel is to be cut off. The cold is appalling. The snow still unmelted. I went to tea at Emerald's in the Dorchester. Tony Gandarillas joined us. We talked of

French historians, the Renaissance influence upon France and England, and music. Emerald's knowledge astounds me.

This week is being a veritable nightmare. On Sunday afternoon it started to thaw and the snow mostly went. On Monday it froze again very hard, so that the slush is like slippery brick. Since Monday we have had no heating in our office apart from one electric fire. And now this is turned off from 9 till 12 and again from 2 till 4 each day. Wrapped in my fur coat with three pullovers underneath, my snowboots kept on, I am still too perished to work properly. The brain becomes atrophied. People are unanimous in blaming the Government for a hideous muddle, yet Mr. Shinwell still remains Minister of Fuel. I seldom stay in the office now but walk, dictate letters, and move away. Have twice been to the National Gallery, which is heated, to look at the Spanish Exhibition of Velasquez, Goya and El Greco. A number of poor old people sit on the benches for hours at a time, their feet wrapped in brown paper, striving to keep warm. At an Historic Buildings Committee meeting yesterday all sat in fur coats, moaning in misery, for no one could concentrate on the Agenda. Lord Esher however as cheerful as ever. He told a member of the Cabinet, 'You Labour people never let us have a dull moment.' Bridget says that if this Government goes an extreme left Government will take its place, and that she is quite ready to go to the barricades and shoot. I asked, whom? 'Well, almost anyone,' she replied. Most of the large shops are closed; those that are open have no electricity, and no light except from the odd candle. The streets are blacked out, as in war time, and millions are unemployed for industries have come to a standstill. Food is becoming very short and the situation is as critical and deadly serious as ever it was during the war. The odd thing is apparently that the Government is no more unpopular with the masses than before this *débacle*.

At 6.15 went to see Kathleen Kennet at Leinster Corner. She is in bed upstairs. I was very shocked and depressed by her condition and feel pretty sure she is dying, and that she knows it. She has pernicious anaemia and has been in bed for three weeks today, and shows no signs of improving in spite of daily injections. Before retiring to bed she had been feeling tired and lifeless, off her food and incapable of rousing herself to make plans for Switzerland in December. I wish I had been financially solvent to make them for her, for she had proposed that we should go together. Now she eats nothing but fruit. The thought of food makes her feel sick. She cannot read for longer than one hour at a time. To get out of bed to go to the bathroom tires her dreadfully. I stayed an hour and when I left she said cheerfully and without emotion: 'If I pass out as a result of this illness, I do not want my friends to mind because I have had a most wonderful innings, a wonderful life. I would rather go than linger decrepit and incurable. The best of this illness is that there is no suffering and I do not become disgusting, at least I don't think I do. I don't decay, become horrible, or smell, for instance. I just linger and gently melt away.' Poor darling, I felt dreadfully moved, yet somehow quite controlled talking to her of such a matter. I tried to make her believe that her time had not come yet, but could not deceive her. When I bent down to kiss her I noticed how soft her face had become, unlike her tough, rugged old skin. It was that of an ancient woman who lived indoors and I noticed a terrible thinness about her neck beneath her nightdress. Her eyes looked dark and shone like coals. This visit has saddened me greatly.

Tuesday, 18th February

Not a sign of thaw. Weather as bitter as ever, and I wear my fur coat and snow boots daily. Still the electricity is cut morning and afternoon. Went to a cocktail party at the Lionel Bretts. Talked to Mark Bonham-Carter, who in conversation becomes alert, whereas in repose his face is dour and disdainful.

Wednesday, 19th February

At midday quitted the office for the rest of the week. Went to Agnew's for the opening by Dr. Trevelyan of the Exhibition of Lord Spencer's pictures from Althorp. Such a crush that I could hardly see a picture, and what I saw did not greatly

npress me. Queen Mary was present and each time I wanted
o look at a picture I found myself stepping back *on to* her, and
had to sidestep. How royalty do get in the way. Nice however
to have the old lady about and to see women curtseying to her.
She looked very well in a black skin coat, little black hat, not a
toque, with blue ostrich feather. Lady Leconfield, enormously
tall with a high hat and feather, sought me out, and spoke to
me somewhat inconsequentially. I did not realise she had just
come out of a home, poor woman. Someone informed me
later.

Eardley met me at Salisbury station and motored me to
Long Crichel. Eddy S.-W. and Desmond S.-T. there. The
house very adequately heated and comfortable. Brilliant fire-
works from Desmond who is the gayest, sweetest-tempered,
most informative person in the wide world. After dinner a
curious discussion ensued about homosexuality. Eddy
showed deliberate unreason, and refused to concede a point.
He maintained that born homosexuals could never become
heterosexuals, whereas I maintained, with no intent to annoy,
that this was simply not the case. People were not necessarily
born one way or the other; that heterosexuals could become
homosexuals, and vice versa; and that there were people
capable of falling in love equally deeply with men and women.
Eddy stoutly denied the possibility of persons being ambisex-
ual, and with vehemence quoted himself as the over-riding
disproof of this notion, assuming that his case was a precedent
the world over. He adopted a highly self-pitying attitude,
became furious with Desmond and, after much high-pitched,
querulous shouting that Desmond always 'attacked' him, left
the room. Desmond meant to do nothing of the kind. Afterwards Eardley and Desmond admitted that it was impossible
to carry on discussions with Eddy. Indeed they are right. In
my hearing Eddy announced that he preferred not to arrive at
the truth than to involve himself in controversy, which made
him ill. In spite of this I have a great affection for Eddy. He told
me the next day that he knew he ought to be contented with his
lot but his chronic ill-health and difficult temperament prevented him acknowledging his good fortune. Every day, he
said, he was pursued by angst. I understand this because in
lesser measure I am too. But not, perhaps, every day.

Eardley and I motored to Montacute and arranged most of the new consignment of furniture. The house was fairly warm but the Yateses said today was the last day they could keep the boilers alight. I am beginning a cold, for I have a sore throat and am sneezing.

Yesterday it snowed so heavily that we had to abandon going to Montacute. I finally decided, after much prevarication, to put off my trip to Herefordshire next week. Came back to London in the afternoon because I detected a *gêne* hovering over Crichel, and was also rather fearful of being stricken with influenza and infecting Eddy.

Ever since my Long Crichel visit have felt so rotten with a stuffed cold that today I stayed in bed. I have chosen the first day of sun for a month to incarcerate myself in my gloomy bedroom. Midi came to tea and James dropped in to bring me an expensive illustrated book on Virginian houses which I had told him I coveted. Very sweet of him. He is naturally generous to a fault. I have been reading the diaries of Hugh Dormer with some emotion. He was a young Catholic officer in the Irish Guards whom at Dover I remember for his aloof and reticent manner which distinguished him from the others, and for his – singular and strangely moving in so young a man – devoutness. He attended Mass every day and, I noticed, always communicated. These diaries are about his courageous exploits after he left the regiment he loved for secret work behind the enemy lines, where he was dropped by parachute. He was finally killed in Normandy. What amazes me is his unshakeable faith, his 1914 ideals and conviction that he was fighting a just war and that death for his ideals would be the crowning reward of his short life.

This morning went to a very enjoyable performance – the centenary service for Ellen Terry in St. Paul's church, Covent Garden. It was cheerful, and inspiring. Very cold, yellow day in which no woman looked her best. I arrived at 11.30 and had to fight my way in, although I had a reserved seat. I was put in the front of the nave. The Sadlers Wells choir sang anthems; Edith Evans, Sybil Thorndike and Peggy Ashcroft read three Shakespeare sonnets. The lessons were read by Ralph Richardson, Leon Quartermaine and Harcourt Williams. With the exception of the last, who is a handsome elderly man, all the others looked remarkably plain, Richardson a flunkey, Quartermaine a Glasgow thug masquerading as an undertaker, E. Evans as a painted clown (male), and Thorndike as a downtrodden school-teacher. Miss Edith Craig was present and Christopher St. John, wearing a fawn teddy-bear coat, man's porkpie hat, and waving a gigantic bunch of golden daffodils at her friends behind her. The Bishop of London, a mealy-mouthed creature, gave the address.

Saturday, 1st March

I have never been colder. Huddled over a coal fire that gives out an imperceptible flutter of heat I managed to write with great speed an account of Petworth for my National Trust *Guide.*

Sunday, 2nd March

I went to the Cumberland Hotel – a typical hotel for a not very rich foreigner to choose – to meet François Carvalho and Mrs. Dalton who in the Chancellor's car followed us to Osterley. Grandy Jersey was there to receive and conduct us round the house. The visitors were greatly impressed by the quality of Adam's decoration. The state rooms are more or less arranged again and in fairly good repair, but the window frames are all deteriorating. The outside is horribly untidy owing to the brick huts built up to the house by Glyn's Bank, which still occupies most of it. On to West Wycombe. We lunched there and saw village and house – Johnnie had deliberately gone away for the day – which in contrast to Osterley is shabby and of which the quality of the decoration is less fine. Although cold it was a lovely sunny day. At 3.45 the two visitors returned to London in Mrs Dalton's car. I meant to go westwards but at Stokenchurch the car was going so badly I returned to London. At East Acton it gave out completely, so I pushed the damned thing into a garage and hired a car to transport me and all my luggage back to Thurloe Square. How I abominate cars.

Stayed in bed all morning for yesterday I felt giddy and odd at times. Rang up Mama who told me to take a train to Evesham and recuperate for a day or two.

Tuesday, 4th March

Stayed in bed reading Henry's [Green] *Back* this morning. By tea time it started snowing again and blowing a gale.

Wednesday, 5th March

All day it continued to snow. This is the worst storm in these parts ever recorded. A blizzard rages and the snow is piling up. Papa, Mama and I began after luncheon to walk to the Table Land. Bitter wind and twice my hat blew away. Outside the Idions' house and along the Badsey road were drifts six feet deep. One small car managed miraculously to pass. We sent Mama home. The two of us walked on to Badsey to Cull, the baker's to fetch some bread, which, with the milk, had not been delivered today. On the edge of the village we saw Cull's van just about to leave for Wickhamford, so we returned. At the top of the hill over Bully Brook, where a snow drift was rapidly building up, we stopped, and talked to two men. Sure enough the van came and was stuck in the drift. By dint of much pushing the four of us succeeded in extricating it.

Thursday, 6th March

Brilliant sunny day but the snow lying in huge drifts. Haines says no one remembers anything like it before. There are icicles, over three foot long, hanging from the thatch of the

cottages. I spent the morning on the roof of the pantry at the
Manor shovelling the snow off. It has even blown through the
roof of the motor-house loft and is lying in piles on the trunks.
My hunting boots were completely buried. In the middle of
the squash court was a heap of snow, two foot deep. After
luncheon I walked with the Cooks to fetch some milk from the
farm at Bower's Hill. There we saw an amusing sight – about
twenty men attaching an old cart to a tractor, they following
behind and holding the shafts and supporting the milk churns.
This curious procession, like a funeral, advanced to Badsey
and Wickhamford over snow drifts. A gang of men cleared a
passage-way along the road at Pear Tree Corner. Curiously, it
is the bits of road running from north to south which are quite
impassable. Some drifts are six feet deep. I wished I had a
camera. There is something harsh, metallic and savage about
the Vale yokels, something extremely primitive, yet un-
peasantlike, very material and earthy. Their voices are grating
and discordant. When Dick and I were children we spoke
broad Worcestershire perfectly. This afternoon they were
very good-humoured and though professing to dislike the
snow, were enjoying it. Nobody talks of anything but the
weather. I had to put off my return to London and my party
for Nancy Mitford.

Friday, 7th March

Twenty-nine degrees of frost in the night, and this morning
brilliant sun again, what Haines describes as 'a proper bobby-
dazzler'. A jeep called for me at nine and took me to Evesham
station where I marched up and down the platform waiting for
the train. It was an hour late but I got to London for luncheon.
A jeep has merits. It is not like a car, but a bluebottle, for it
darts and jumps, buzzes, turns about and practically summer-
saults from one place to another. It travels as happily over
mountains of frozen snow as over the best tarmac road.

Sunday, 9th March

Motored to Chiswick House. Claud Phillimore last night gave
me a brochure advancing his theory that the Wyatt wings
should be demolished, thus reducing the villa to Lord Burlington's original dimensions. It would be small enough to need

comparatively little renovation and upkeep. The place could then be made into a furnished house of the period. We did not go inside but walked round the garden in the snow. At last the thaw has set in with a vengeance, thank God, and the sun is out. J.F. dined with me and we discussed sex problems and how to overcome them by the most practical, mechanical and cynical means.

Tuesday, 11th March

Lunched with Ann Rothermere at Warwick House overlooking the Green Park. Very pre-war, butler and footmen, wines and desserts. A heterogeneous party consisting of Ann (hostess), Bob Boothby, Lady Crewe, James P.-H., Sibyl Colefax, the editor of the *Evening News* and me. Lady Crewe makes no attempt to be friendly or interesting and must, I am sure, be fundamentally a disagreeable woman. Occasionally she melts into a bland, cow-like smile, which has one effect – to put her neighbour ill at ease. We necessarily talked politics, and Lady Crewe began by saying she hoped the Liberals would never unite with the Conservatives, whatever else they did. Sibyl and James both agreed in deploring the present Government, yet both voted it into power. Warwick House has little architectural character, but its site, with terrace over park and proximity to St. James's Palace, is enchanting.

Wednesday, 12th March

In the morning met Charles Brocklehurst in Baker Street and looked at some scrappy pieces of Lyme Park tapestry he has taken to be cleaned by Miss Parry who works for Partridges. Her cleaning takes place in a cellar, damp, dark and low, in Dickensian gloom and squalor. Then to St. James's Street and looked at the picture of Astbury church from Little Moreton Hall, which has been cleaned; then to the Pantechnicon and saw, and approved Sir Henry Aubrey-Fletcher's chairs and settee, William & Mary, offered for Lyme. The Pantechnicon built in 1830 in neo-Grecian style is purity of architecture, with an old-fashioned air about the interior. It has Doric fluted balusters to the original ramp for horses and vans, original office screen and desk, lamps and stove. Really a lovely and satisfactory building.

After a hurried luncheon I trained to Windsor – raining again – and called at Henry II's Tower. How brash and ugly the Castle is when you get up to it. Miss Hanbury-Williams showed me three pictures she offers for Lyme. The Chapel was locked when I came out but I walked through the Cloisters and down the Hundred Steps and into Eton. At Shefford's bought six green wine glasses to add to my red selection. Bought a tie at New & Lingwood. Eton shops full of attractive clothes and quantities to buy.

On return went to Sibyl's large party in her drawing-room. Gerry Wellington, John Lehmann, Loelia Westminster, Alan Pryce-Jones, Emerald Cunard, Nancy Rodd there. John Lehmann is charming to talk to. Unlike Lady Crewe he makes himself agreeable. Christopher Sykes I find distant. Talk was of Harold Nicolson turning Socialist. Sykes said the reason was that Harold likes to consider himself 'fast'. This is absurd.

Thursday, 13th March

Johnnie lunched with me at Brooks's and said (tongue in cheek, of course) he feared Helen might not be returning at all; she neither wrote to him nor showed signs of coming back to England. He said that he had definitely taken to the bottle – 'baby' he calls it. There is nothing in these times to take to in its place.

Attended a committee meeting of the Georgian Group to discuss Chiswick House. Claud Phillimore's proposal had a lukewarm reception, perhaps rightly. We were told that young Noel-Baker was calling a committee to be held in the House of Commons to investigate the case thoroughly, and be advised by the Georgian Group.

Friday, 14th March

At the Finance Committee this morning the staff were dismissed and salaries were discussed. Mine and Martineau's were raised to £1,000, and Ramsey's to £800. Harold said to me in the afternoon, 'You should have heard the nice things I said about you. They would have made you regret the unkind things you said to me,' referring to my reproofs over his joining the Labour Party.

This evening I had Nancy, Bridget and Tony Gandarillas to

dine. At least the food tasted, as Bridget said. They all complimented me over my room [in No. 20 Thurloe Square]. Somehow I did not find the party wholly enjoyable, but Nancy, whom I love, is not always congenial, and her unkind witticisms when first-hand, are often less funny than when repeated.

Saturday, 15th March

On leaving the office at midday I wandered into the Abbey. Walked round the ambulatory and a verger got special permission for me to enter the Queen Elizabeth and Mary Queen of Scots chapel, which I much appreciated. I think the Henry VII vaulting the loveliest thing in English architecture. Nothing raised subsequently strikes the same chords of spirituality. It is the consummation of English gothic architecture. Queen Elizabeth's face must be a portrait from life. Mary's in profile, seen looking towards the light and south, is laden with tragedy. How very moving is the Abbey, especially in winter. It is the silent annals of England, more convincing than any history book, more real than any facts taught in schools.

In the afternoon I drove Rick [Stewart-Jones] and Fred Oppé to Hampton Court. Mr. Rainbow showed us over the Wolsey apartments. They are uninteresting except for the remains of the plaster ceilings of his time, with their definite Italian influence. They are now without colour. Our guide told us that the last resident, a Lady Peel, found them overpowering and induced the Office of Works to demolish half the ceiling of one room. I find it hard to believe the Office would have sanctioned such a thing within recent times. Then we went round the state apartments, most drearily arranged. They fill one with dismay. Arranged sparsely, with little taste and no imagination. It began to snow very heavily again. Rick dined with me at home and stayed till midnight. I reproved him for his sloppy abandon, physical and mental, governess that I am.

Sunday, 16th March

Mama telephoned last night warning me not to motor to Worcester today on account of the bad floods. She said that their cottage was under water and in Oxford the swans were

143

swimming into people's bedrooms, which she thought rather sweet – of the swans presumably. This disturbed me. However I motored Bridget to Kew and we lunched marvellously with Mark. The sun was out and it was warm again. Then I set off for Worcester. Parts of the road I traversed were badly flooded and I had to digress to Gerrard's Cross and join the High Wycombe road. Nothing very bad until the Cotswolds where single traffic because of the heaps of snow still on the verges. At Moreton-in-the-Marsh water was cascading through someone's house into the street. For a moment I thought I would be stuck. Then it started to rain again and a great gale arose so that I feared elm trees would fall across the car. I am now staying in Worcester in a very second-rate hotel, The Crown. There is a musty smell in my tiny bedroom under the eaves. It is so dirty that I do not like to put any of my things in the wardrobe or on the table. All wallpapers peeling. Sluts instead of servants who chatter and giggle behind the screen in the dining-room, and the proprietress in grubby black satin has a cigarette hanging out of her mouth when she speaks. God, I wish these English hotel proprietors could be forced to see what Swiss hotels are like! Food here practically uneatable.

Monday, 17th March

At ten set off for Bromyard, fourteen miles away. Crossed the Severn in Worcester but at Buildwas, two miles from Brock-hampton, I was diverted from my route by a huge tree across the road. The Teme was uncrossable. Motored by devious lanes past Abberley to Clouds Top and down to Tenbury. There just managed to cross the Teme and creep down again to Bromyard, arriving at 12.15. Decided to put up at The Hop Pole for two nights, though this is a poor class hotel. At least the people are civil and the bed is comfortable though of the feather variety. One dreads coming across hidden horrors. No bath water here either, just as there was of course none at the Crown. Lunched early at The Hop Pole and arrived Brock-hampton at 1.45. Stayed till seven. I had to leave the car at the lodge gate and walk through the snow down the drive. Old Bakewell the butler and Mrs. Hughes the housekeeper very kindly and friendly, and both disappointed that I had not come to stay. He told me a lot about the Colonel [Lutley], how he was a taskmaster of the old school, though just, good-living,

God-fearing, and a gentleman. Bakewell's wife lives in one of the lodges and yet for two years this man lived and slept in the big house in order to dress, undress and give the Colonel his bath. He had to sponge him and even clean his feet for he was so crippled with arthritis. Yet Colonel Lutley never left him anything after twelve years service and only paid him £2 a week. Bakewell spoke without resentment and was fond of the old wretch.

I went all round the house with the probate inventory, marking those items I thought might be needed at Montacute, 3 Cheyne Walk or the head office. There is no museum stuff.

Tuesday, 18th March

It poured all night and most of the morning. They say that today there is no possible means of getting to Worcester, not even through Tenbury. I hope to goodness I shall not be stuck at Bromyard for a week. Where the snow has receded and there is not a raging torrent from the high ground over the fields I saw my first snowdrops and aconites, gallantly struggling to brave a perplexing spring. Warmer today, thank God, and beautiful when the sun comes out. I feel miles and miles away from civilization here, cut off from the world. At six when I had finished my day's work I wandered round the grounds and looked at Colonel Lutley's grave. I must see that the N.T. puts up a gravestone and memorial to him. This sort of thing they are quite capable of overlooking. At least the Trust has something to be grateful to him for.

Wednesday, 19th March

I set off at ten for London. Was advised that at Tenbury the Teme was uncrossable and at Shrewsbury the Severn likewise, but that Worcester was approachable via Malvern. But I found that this was not the case and proceeded to Gloucester. Information was vouchsafed by delighted inhabitants that the river was impassable. Indeed there was a complete halt of traffic near the bridges. Rows of motors stuck in the water. Then some ruffians with a tractor, on seeing that my car was expensive-looking – as they thought – hitched me on to the tail of some lorries, swearing that nowhere was the road deeper than one-and-a-half feet. After we had started two A.A. men

145

in waders warned me that on the contrary the water would be well over the driver's seat and the car would be ruined. By this time the procession was slowly advancing. Nevertheless I induced them to stop the tractor and unhitch me. A small Morris, tied to my tail, was also unhitched. In despair I drove back to Malvern, fifteen miles. Here I was forced to abandon my car in a garage and catch an evening train to Paddington. In Worcester I saw the water in the bedrooms of all the cottages along the river. There has been nothing like these floods since 1770.

Tuesday, 20th March

Sheila took me to the first night of *The Magic Flute* at Covent Garden. Oliver Messel's scenery and costumes extremely picturesque, but the singing execrable. The whole performance too long and dragged out by cheap dialogue. In fact it was made into a pantomime.

Friday, 21st March

Jamesey, Maurice and Nigel [Nicolson] dined with me at home here. Enjoyable evening. Nigel remarked that J. and M. were like two little sparrows huddled together on a telephone wire. James said that the Andersons were staying last weekend with Lady Crewe. Sir John's is probably the best brain in England, but J. found him very unsympathetic for all his talk was political. He said the Labour Government would wear themselves out because they could not take politics easily like the Conservatives. Bridget Paget got drunk at dinner and her hair fell in the soup. Sir John Anderson was deeply shocked.

Today I received a letter from Sir Donald Somerville that G. would be blackballed. He advises me to withdraw his candidature. This has incensed me.

Saturday, 22nd March

Worked this morning at Digby Wyatt's address on foreign artists in England in the sixteenth-century. Professor Richardson lunched at Brooks's and repeated to me the speech he made yesterday at the R.I.B.A. dinner in the presence of the Archbishop of Canterbury, the French and Chinese Ambassa-

146

dors, and the Prime Minister. The speech must have been very witty. The Archbishop in replying thanked the Professor for telling him what the Almighty was thinking about current affairs. I showed the Professor Sir Donald Somerville's letter. He said he knew the reason was that G. was considered by staider members of the Election Committee to be a 'pleasurer'; and that they wouldn't have him on account of his treatment of his second wife. He added that twenty years ago such a consideration would not be taken into account, but today the aristocracy were tightening themselves up. He advised me to withdraw his name without ado, and not to resign myself. The Prof. said that after forty no man cherished illusions; that after fifty all he cherished was personal comfort and freedom from agitation. This explained why reforms were carried out by men under that age. He said that Brendan Bracken was undoubtedly Winston Churchill's son; that Dean Swift, after his marriage to Stella, discovered that both she and he were the children of Sir William Temple and his 'incestuous' marriage preyed on his mind. I know that disapproving old prude, Lord Ilchester, is at the back of the blackball affair.

Sunday, 23rd March

After lunching with Sheila I walked to see Kathleen now in the Paddington Hospital. I thought she looked better, but she is very depressed about herself. Says her hair has gone quite white, which is not true. We talked of the purpose of living. I gave her some snowdrops. When I left she said: 'When young men like you come to see me I feel that I shall get well again; that there is still a future for me.' The Gainsboroughs had asked me to tea. But I was feeling so sad I just could not go. Very bad.

Monday, 24th March

A terrible train journey to Aylsham, standing in the corridor. It poured with rain all day. At Blickling met the new caretakers and housemaid who are getting the house straight for the opening in May. In the evening went to Maud Mosley's nice little house, the Dell, where I am staying these two nights. She is very hospitable and solicitous, yet aloof. She talked a lot about the Mosleys and likes Diana at last, but dislikes what she calls her affectations.

Spent all day at Blickling. The sun shone and it was beautiful. I adore this place. Did some good work, I think, in helping Miss O'Sullivan to take some tricky decisions. Unfortunately I shall have to return in a month to put the finishing touches, for the furniture is not yet in place, and the dustsheets are still on.

Went to a revived Ordinary tonight, the first since Sibyl's restoration to health, and indeed the last I shall attend. The dinner was horrible. Nothing to drink but cider. I sat next to Ben Nicolson and a newly married daughter of Lord De La Warr, a sweet girl. The room in the Dorchester was both hideous and uncomfortable. Kenneth Rae and Ben, with whom I walked away, agreed with me that they too would never go to another.

Went to the Victoria and Albert at Leigh Ashton's invitation to a buffet luncheon party to see the French tapestries. Met Clarissa [Churchill] and we ate sandwiches together. I only saw the Louis XIV and eighteenth-century tapestries, but shall go again tomorrow, for there were no catalogues today. The twentieth-century tapestries are hideous beyond all belief. Sir Eric Maclagan said to me: 'Even if one had one of the least offensive, what would one do with it?' Bertie Abdy told me at Emerald Cunard's this evening that the rise and fall of tapestry weaving coincided with the fluctuation of economy. In what he esteemed the greatest periods, namely the seventeenth and eighteenth centuries, there were 600 different colours available. Today there are less than sixty. Lady Diana Cooper came into Emerald's for tea. She had a streaming cold. I don't care for the insolent way in which she looks through me.

I have been to the tapestry exhibition again – the formal opening day. But again there were too many people who distracted me by chat. I know nothing more symbolical of pure poetry than the lady outside her tent, 'En toi mon seul désir'. It transcends anything I have ever seen, and makes one want to cry.

Have been thinking a lot over what Professor Richardson said to me. Every man is damned by his own sins in this life at any rate, if not in the next. I am certainly damned here by my defeatism and chronic despair. The outward form my despair takes is a persistent ill-humour and an abandon to selfishness, and hardness of heart, which bespeak a shrivelled soul. I realise that in this life one should love all humanity and care for it. I do not, and so am a dissident. My ill-humour is all-besetting.

Since Friday I have felt very unwell, pains in my stomach and nausea. I hope it may be merely a form of internal chill; but at nights I imagine it to be cancer. I have for weeks past also experienced a curious burning in the legs. This I attribute to phlebitis; and a pounding of the heart, which I suppose to be angina pectoris. In short, something is the matter.

I am staying tonight at Farm Hall, Godmanchester with the Sissons, for he has offered the N.T. covenants over this house, newly bought, and grounds of twenty acres. He thinks rather too highly of Farm Hall. It is a very, very plain Hanoverian town house, built in 1746 of red brick, with no frills of any kind, a sort of Quaker house. It is too unadorned to be remarkable, but decent nevertheless. One front faces a street of the town. Across the street in a recessed retaining wall, a gate between urned piers affords a view of a small rectangular canal and the Ouse (now flooding every field) beyond. The other front faces an ancient lime avenue, also axial with the front door and canal. Unfortunately the house is not strictly symmetrical on the garden front and was never so, I fancy. Inside there are large rooms, very cold. With my chill I was perished. We sat over a green log fire, the rain battering down outside. Sisson will of course finish decorating very well, but at present the interior is shabby, empty, rather dirty and stinks of cats. The upstairs is filled with odd families which make a noise.

The A.W. Lawrences came to tea at three and stayed till 6.45. He is T.E.L.'s brother, remarkably young-looking, rather earnest, and cracks jokes which are unfunny. He looks at one in that penetrating way that was Matheson's, which I so much dislike. I suppose I have secrets to probe. After they left Sisson and I motored to Hinchingbrooke, the Hs being away, and walked round the outside, examining Sisson's demolitions of the Victorian wing. He has made vast improvements. We agreed that the destroyed wing needed a wall in its place and that the tower should not be totally destroyed, but its top taken off, made lower, so as not to look so thin as it does at present. I was slightly irritated by Sisson's pedantry, and suffered from the cold and discomfort of his house. He now takes snuff in such quantities that the end of his nose and his upper lip are dark orange. So is his handkerchief after incessant blowings.

Monday, 31st March

Loelia took me to the Albert Hall, the two Menuhins playing. Hall far too big for a piano and violin. Then I gave her dinner at Boulestins. We both, without meaning to, cut Mr. Tufnell of Langleys who was sitting at the next table. When I realised what I had done I ran after him to explain. He was quite nice, but said he thought it the rudest, most deliberate insult he had ever received. I am not sure I am glad I ran after him.

Tuesday, 1st April

Went to Knole this afternoon. The state rooms look marvellous and Mason is delighted with the housekeeper and her three women. Everything here promises to run successfully and the women are as happy as larks and proud of the place and their work. The silver in the King's Room all cleaned and shining as though awaiting its royal visitor.

Dined at Cecil Beaton's in Pelham Place. His house in flamboyant Edwardian taste. The three women guests were, I suppose, the three prettiest old-young women in London – Anne Rothermere in sparkling white, a long dress, Diane Abdy and Elizabeth Hofmannsthal, the last by far the most striking of the three. I think she is about the most beautiful woman I have ever seen. I sat next to her and her husband for there was one man too many. Esmond Rothermere was cross and rather pompous; he was suffering from sciatica. Hofmannsthal is a bore, shouting in broken English. He told a terrible story of Lord Anglesey's death which was entirely due to the doctor's negligence and stupidity. Lord A was perfectly well but because he had nothing to do for two weeks decided to have a simple operation for prostate gland. They put the wrong tubes into him and simply left him to be tortured to death. Cecil was very charming and dulcet. He is a cunning man. His power of observation is acute, and like a gimlet he twists out the inmost dust of the person his steely eye is fixed upon.

Wednesday, 2nd April

Had a good-humoured reply from G. agreeing to withdraw his candidature for Brooks's, but expressing surprise and regret. I shall never feel the same towards Brooks's for this behaviour; shall never forget or forgive.

Took a train to Tenterden and attended the funeral of Edith Craig at Smallhythe. She had been cremated and there was no coffin or urn that I could see. The service was arranged in excellent taste just as Ellen Terry's memorial was. I was impressed by it. The two old women were very upset. I promised to go down and see them in a week's time. Somerset de Chair who was present told me he intended to rent Blickling, come what may. I worked hard in the train, did a long report on the Knole contents and corrected guidebook proofs.

All Easter it was perishingly cold, with relentless rain. Harry Ashwin motored me to Charlecote for tea. I stayed the night with the Lucys. The bedrooms at Charlecote are cosy and Victorian: flowered wallpapers, washstand with pretty flowered china, maplewood furniture, four-poster bed with old chintz hangings, a fire in the grate. Bath with polished wooden rim, brass taps and brass spray on end of a long pipe; deep red, thick, comfortable bath mat.

Thursday, 10th April

Dined with the Johnnie Churchills. It is odd seeing Johnnie so conventionally established in a tidy and well-appointed house. This is entirely his wife, Mary's, beneficent doing. Sarah Churchill was there and I sat next to her. She is beautiful and attractive; physically unlike her father, Winston, and prettier than her sister Diana Sandys. Johnnie described to me his father's death and the keen interest which his uncle Winston took in his brother's illness. He kept telephoning and giving elaborate directions to doctors and nurses as though commanding a battle, using Churchillian phrases like, 'Backs to the Wall!' and 'Certainly Jack must fight to the finish.' On Jack's death he worked himself up to a tremendous emotional pitch and literally shed, or, as Johnnie described it, rained tears around the room. He gave elaborate instructions as to the hymns to be sung at the funeral, quoting dozens of them by heart. Then, Johnnie said, on the very night of his brother's death he read to Johnnie sixty pages of his first book on the South African War, as though to console him, ending with the words, 'I wish I had the power of writing as well as that today.'

Friday, 11th April

A most beautiful day, sunny, clear, balmy. I walked from Queen Anne's Gate to Paddington after six o'clock and all Londoners were singing or whistling with joy over escape from an appalling winter. Spent quarter of an hour with dear Kathleen [Kennet] who is much iller. She looks very tired, her face is softer and her voice perceptibly slower. She admits she is no better and wonders what is the point of surviving, since she can never recover and must always have injections for pernicious anaemia and take insulin for diabetes. Says she has no desire for sweet things. I was mightily depressed by her appearance and languor. As I left I thought the rarity of this woman lies in the fact that I can talk to her as to myself. She is part of me; she understands. She sees the light. She is a darling, although in the past I have in my beastly way been irritated by her. I asked myself as I walked, was my distress selfish. Was it my loss I was lamenting?

Sunday, 13th April

Again a lovely day, clear, yet hazy with heat. There are few birds, sadly enough, left to sing, and only chestnuts in bud. No leaves on the trees yet, though the earth is red as terra cotta. Yesterday Rick motored me to Malvern in his Chevrolet van. A most unfortunate expedition for I allowed my irritation with him to get the better of me and gave vent to odious ill nature. I had breakfast ready for him at eight; he came at nine.

152

At Brockhampton I warned him not to motor down to the old house. He did so and got bogged.

I drove down to Kent, singing all the way as loudly as I could, unheard. Passed Knole and lunched at Tenterden. At 2 o'clock called at Smallhythe. The two poor old women remaining were very pathetic. Miss Atwood, eighty-two, is the more spry and affable. Miss St. John, very lame, was wearing brown corduroy trousers, stretched tight over an enormous bum, a yellow scarf round her neck, a magenta beret on her grey hair, shirt and tie. The other one wore a shirt and tie too and is called Tony by her friends; Miss St. J. is called Chris. They showed me over the property and explained its problems. In the Ferry Cottage lives a terrifying woman, Mrs S— who helps them with housework. She wears grey flannel trousers, tight shirt and tie and beret, and is grubby and masculine. She is called Bruce, and refers to Miss St. John as 'Mr Chris'. Really I felt like Alice in Wonderland. I went to tea with darling Vita at Sissinghurst. We discussed Knole. She could not explain how the upholstered Jacobean furniture had survived the eighteenth century. Poor Ben was upstairs with influenza – he sleeps above the dining-room – and before I left Vita came down with his thermometer in her hand. It registered 104 and she was clearly a little alarmed. I went away thinking that the Nicolson family was the most united, luckiest, and happiest I knew. I thought Vita was going to kiss me goodbye. But from shyness I withdrew, supposing that I did not know her well enough. Vita's brick tower rises gaunt and solemn reflected through the back window of the car as one drives away, along the lane.

Had a very long day. Started off in the car at 10 o'c for Caernarvon. When I reached Stafford learned that I had just missed the train to Crewe, so continued by road, and there caught the 4.55, arriving Caernarvon for a late dinner. Met Armitage and walked round the town at dusk. Examined the Castle walls, particularly the grotesques, gargoyles and birds of stone perched upon the ramparts. The Royal Hotel not too bad but nothing to write home about.

Up here the pussy willows out, also lent lilies and rhododendrons, for it is mild. In the morning Armitage and I met Mr. Evans, the printer and Secretary of the Local Committee of the Segontium Museum. Disappointed to find no improvements yet in hand, and the place a shambles. Builders apparently about to come at any time. Took a train to Conway where we lunched. Found to our dismay that about half of the contents of 'Aberconwy' do not belong to the N.T. at all, but to the Council and Museum of Wales. Armitage rather brightly tackled the local antique dealer who may agree to rent this dismal house and move his shop into it. I bought from him a pair of Pontefract bowls on stems for 21s. which is exceedingly cheap. At four left for Crewe, got into my car and drove to Atcham. Stayed the night at The Mytton and Mermaid.

Called on Lady Berwick at 10.30 and rapidly gave her a valuation of those pieces of furniture she is sending to Sotheby's for sale. Then she again offered me her Victorian nursery scrap-screen, which this time I agreed to accept, but on a payment of 10s. 'So,' she said, 'nobody can now say that you accept gifts and bribes from your friends,' which I thought very sweet and generous of her. At 11.30 I was at Lilleshall. Thank goodness the owner, Mr. Ford, was away, and with the agent and his assistant I was able to make a quick scrutiny of two hours. House quite hideous and large, now full of Barnardo children who swarmed like ants round my motor and wrote their names on the dust of the bonnet with their beastly little fingers. I don't know what we could do with this house but the grounds of 600 acres are without question, beautiful. If the Committee refuse it Mr Ford will raise a stink. If they accept, the house will always be an embarrassment.

Called at Letocetum which is a lamentable, tumbledown property. The sheds over the Roman remains have collapsed: the exhibits consist of dusty, broken bits of Roman pottery.

The whole place unkempt and uncared for. I would like to blow it up. Then on to Packwood which I walked round with nice Weaver, the gardener, who was really pleased to see me. Now it *is* well cared for. At The King's Head, Aylesbury, drank a heavenly glass of doubtless base port wine and got home after 10 o'c.

Saturday, 19th April

Helen Dashwood dined at the Ritz after my taking her to *Odd Man Out*, a James Mason film (good) and was charming and meltingly sweet. Also looking very pretty in a new Paris hat – not the absurd sort. She expects to be a grandmother any day.

Sunday, 20th April

I motored Charlie Brocklehurst to Montacute. We ate a picnic luncheon which Emily provided. Very good it was too. Filthy weather all this trip and a great gale raging. Charlie made some excellent suggestions which I carried out. We got the gardeners to fetch and carry and re-hang the Pintoricchio in the dining-room where it looked superb. After tea went to Melbury where I stayed the next two nights with the Ilchesters. Charlie stayed with the Stavordales at Evershot. Lady Ilchester is adorable; about seventy, with a blue face and few teeth. Extremely welcoming, she at once puts you at ease. Makes one feel one is a great success. Also is very funny and full of gossip. Drink flowed and John Fox kept plying my glass. Lady I. did not spare hers and a daughter who was staying, was very drunk indeed. After dinner she sat swaying over an old photograph album making no sense at all.

Lady I. told me that her mother Lady Londonderry was a bosom friend of Lady Blanche Hosier, mother of Mrs. Winston Churchill. Lady Blanche confided in Lady Londonderry at Aix just before Mrs. Winston was born that the child's father was Lord Redesdale, her brother-in-law and my Tom's grandfather. This makes Tom and Randolph first cousins as well as second.

I returned from Montacute to London on Tuesday very late, for I was invited by Sibyl Colefax to her box at the opera. I hastily changed and dashed off to Covent Garden in the car. With my bows right across Piccadilly Circus, the car stopped dead, having run completely out of petrol. It was a bad dream come true. Traffic piled up, hooting behind me. I got out, walked up to three policemen on the pavement and begged for help. They pushed and shunted the car to the kerb. Then I walked to three garages before one would sell me petrol in a tin. I missed the first act of *Rosenkavalier*, an all-English production, the libretto translation by Alan Pryce-Jones and scenery and décor by Robin Ironside – conventional rococo drawing-room style.

Thursday, 24th April

Joshua Rowley lunched at Brooks's. He is Mindy Bacon's nephew and very like him in looks and manner. Has a quiet, gentle demeanour and sweet expression. He is frightfully keen to become keeper of Packwood and is going to see it next Tuesday.

Friday, 25th April

I lunched with Trenchard Cox at the Athenaeum. He has asked me to stay in Birmingham in June in order to show me Aston Hall which he is resurrecting. A lively, intelligent man with a dry sense of humour. I had tea with Emerald who soon went off to the theatre. She was looking very pretty and in good form. I walked away with Helen Dashwood and Robin Ironside into the sun, across the Park. Charles Fry dined. He promised that Batsford's would pay for my holiday in Rome this autumn and gave me a fine book of coloured re-productions of the U.S.A. National Gallery pictures, which was kind. But he made me drink contrary to my determina-tion to do nothing of the sort, and boasted of his sexual prowess in a way that sickened me. Terrible man, the worst and most depraved I know.

Monday, 28th April

Went to see Kathleen K. still in the Paddington hospital; and took her Ciano's *Diary* which she was delighted to have. She looks terribly tired and definitely older. Complains of fainting and then falling into deep sleeps. There is no sign of improve-ment. She said she hoped to pass out quietly in her sleep, if she cannot recover, and is going to ask Bill and her doctor to arrange it, if they are convinced there can be no recovery, which I now very gravely doubt. 'What is the point of life the moment one cannot live it in a full-blooded manner?' she asked. I left and walked home across the Park sick at heart and again impressed by the realisation that this woman is dear to me because with her I need never dissemble – which is a very rare thing – in mind or spirit; with her there is no call for flattery or insincerity; with her there are no barriers of any kind. Yet I can't determine precisely wherein the intimacy between us lies. This evening, having given me a selection of photographs of Peter's portrait drawings to look through, she remarked: 'You are of course only interested in those of the male. The young women bore you.' 'Oh,' but I said, 'so do the young men very often.'

Tuesday, 29th April

Set off this morning for Norfolk. Lunched at Saffron Walden – a poetic, medieval tapestry, wild-flower name – and looked at the Trust's Sun Inn. Then had the idea of calling on Lord Braybrooke who seemed glad to see me and said he was at the end of his tether. He asked whether we would suggest to the Treasury that they might anticipate his death now by taking Audley End in part payment of estate duties. I don't think they will somehow. Stopped at Cambridge just to visit King's Chapel screen and stalls. I suppose they are the finest specimens of Renaissance work in England. The beauty of this building stirs my very vitals into song. They are cleaning the interior. Men on scaffolding are scouring with simple soap and water the stonework right up to the roof – a vast undertaking and most effective. None of the glass is put back yet. Then stopped at Ely Cathedral and examined Bishop West's chapel, most interesting for its classical detail, notably the vaulting superimposed upon the Gothic. Arrived at Bradenham in time for dinner. Alec Penrose has been ill with blood pressure, but looks well and younger than before, having shaved off his moustache. Frances is very friendly and intelligent, with an attractive languorous, yet determined, manner.

To Blickling for the day. Fearfully cold. The ubiquitous, cutting wind persists. I am glad I came. Nothing much has been done. Wallace King's man was waiting for instructions about the posts and ropes. I had to direct him. Also did some rearranging, and put out china, etc. Miss O'Sullivan has no clue how to arrange. She is also understandably reluctant to have any furniture shifted to a different position from where it stood in Lord Lothian's day.

Thursday, 1st May

It is May Day and pouring and blowing icily. Stopped at Cawston Church to gaze my fill at the fourteenth-century roof and painted panels of saints on the screen. At Blickling made my peace with the caretakers and Miss O'Sullivan who is always nice to me. Alec came over and had some useful suggestions for arranging furniture. The rooms now filled do not look any more beautiful because the furniture is on the whole poor. The house was today open for the first time, and only twenty people came. So we need not have fussed ourselves. Alec's second boy lunched. Difficult – and Alec behaved towards him just as my father used to behave towards me. I suppose it is always the parents' fault.

After tea I motored to Holbecks at Hadleigh and stayed the night with Joshua Rowley. He lives well. I like him very much. He gave me a lot to drink. Already has blue veins pencilling his cheeks. I can't make him out. Why on earth should he want to bury himself in Packwood, in the Midlands, near Birmingham?

Friday, 2nd May

Today my left eyelid has jiggered and throbbed, clear sign of having had too much to drink, for Alec gave me a lot of wine too. After a late breakfast we drove to Stoke-by-Nayland. All this property belongs to the Rowleys, made over to Joshua by his father. We looked at Tendring Hall, the Rowley seat, now occupied by German prisoners and in a sad way. Built by Soane it is severe, if not dull, of yellow brick; but the situation a fine one. At noon I returned alone to London.

Motored to lunch with Goodhart-Rendel at Hatchlands. His
mind bubbles over with information. He never stops talking,
imparting knowledge, but so inarticulately. His step-father,
Cooper, was present. He looks like a dormouse that is trying
to retreat into his tea-pot and to put, in vain, the lid down upon
himself so as to escape drowning in G.-R.'s spate of conversation. I was conducted round the village and the grounds
and had a most enjoyable day. G.-R. is very upset by the
N.T.'s ridiculous injunctions to cut down the trees at Fuller's
Farm. I am entirely in sympathy with G.-R. and think it
intolerable of the mangel-wurzels to dare dictate to him.

Robin Fedden motored Langley-Taylor and me to Hughenden after lunching at Brooks's. We both thought L.-T. intolerably vulgar and trumpet-blowing. Robin observed at once
that we would never get a look-in at Hughenden, and therefore it would be best as well as easiest to leave the whole
arrangement of the house to him. It is after all his discovery,
his waif. Our misgiving was lest too many rooms would be
shown with too few contents to fill them. Robin is a sweet
fellow and wrote me such a nice letter of gratitude on the
completion of his first year at Polesden Lacey.

The office puts me into constant rages. The Admiral's incom-
petence is really reprehensible. How a man like this could be
given responsibility for the welfare of a fleet I do not understand. He omitted to forewarn me of the Reports Committee
this morning. He went to the Treasury about Audley End
without having read my note to him about Lord Braybrooke's
message. He ignores my advice about the Hatchlands trees.
   At midday I left for Cornwall. The luxurious train journey
dispersed my choler, restored my humour, which is bad and
uncertain. Read Ciano's *Diary* which fascinates me. Mussolini
was a bore, a philistine, and played with human lives as with
dice. I reached Gunnislake at 7.30 and Cotehele at 8 for dinner.
Lord Mount Edgcumbe is in bed with a temperature, but his

Countess, a little, gentle, sweet and pathetic old lady, was about. Their story is a tragic one. They inherited during the war, and their only son was killed at Dunkirk. They are now packing up to leave Cotehele which since the thirteenth-century has been in their family. I am given a bedroom at the top of the entrance gate-tower, approached by a twisting stone staircase, and in isolation.

Thursday, 8th May

Slept ill: lightning during the night which flashed through my casements and lit up the great tower and the courtyard. I worked all day in the state-rooms, listing those contents which the N.T. would like and a few things to be got rid of. Also noted the condition of the tapestries and furniture, which is bad indeed, rent and worm-eaten. Lady Mount Edgcumbe asked me whether I thought this and that good or bad, as she put it, so as to keep or sell. I tried to help to the best of my ability. Most of the contents are very good indeed, if only they were not so sadly perished. These state-rooms are of the class of the Knole ones and this house is a miniature Knole of the West. It is so remote that I do not suppose great numbers will visit it. I hope not. There are two rather bedint, virginal sisters staying to help the poor Mount Edgcumbes pack. At first their vapid giggling annoyed me, because I don't find Cotehele a joke, but now I quite like them. Lady Mount E.'s cairn puppy has eaten a chunk out of the Turkey-work Queen Anne settee, and she thinks it rather naughty, that's all. There are a butler and some charming servants, all of the old school. The splendid Mt. E.s, having lost their son and heir are taking to live with them their unknown heir and his wife, who are New Zealanders.

Friday, 9th May

At 10 o'c Eardley joined me and I spent the morning – pitch dark and pouring with rain – showing him the house and shifting certain pieces of heavy furniture, which I had per-suaded the family to reject, away from the state-rooms. At midday we left for Tavistock where we lunched. On to Buckland Abbey which we looked at from the outside and pronounced ugly and dull, a sort of square pele with desultory

wing tacked on – actually the crossing and nave of the church –
but thought the surroundings with distant Tamar very lovely.
Had tea at Kingsbridge, and then to Lady Clementine War-
ing's, the Moult, Salcombe. It is more fun being with Eardley
than anyone in the world. Lady C. took us to Overbecks and
the museum which contains more shockingly hideous things
than is possible to conceive. E was loud in his denunciations
which, I saw, were annoying Lady C. So I tried to cheer up
Miss Christian, the woman who in exchange for a free cottage
is acting curatrix and was accompanying us. We agreed the
butterfly collection might be quite a good one. It is strange that
Lady C., whose own taste is sophisticated, should not be
aware of the horrors of Overbecks. She talks so much that one
becomes exhausted. She is bossy and a little dictatorial; yet
intelligent, enthusiastic, forthright, tireless and very kind.
Although she frightens me I like her on the whole, but I think
E does not. After dinner heard from her the whole saga of Mr
Overbeck's love of boys, his collection of drawings of boys
and his having been involved in a police case, but acquitted.
Poor old thing.

Saturday, 10th May

Wonderful day. The Sharpitor and Moult gardens, sloping
down to the sea with no road between, remind me of the
French riviera. The blossom of magnolias, young trees and
shrubs against the blue sea was exquisite. In the morning we
motored to Saltram. This was kind of Lady C. because I had
said I was interested in Adam houses. We were received by
Captain 'Monty' Parker, tall, handsome brother of Lord
Morley, aged about seventy. He is an old-fashioned man-
about-town, Burlington Bertie sort. He never gets up before
eleven and does nothing all day but booze. Lives here with his
brother (away today), both of them bachelors. Had already
been boozing before we arrived and, having ushered us into
the hall, clad in immaculate white ducks, sat by mistake in the
coal scuttle.
This large house, with white painted stucco front, is not
very impressive – outside. But cosy. The whole bay of the
south wing has had its stucco removed for repairs from war
damage when Plymouth was bombed. The park is pretty and
today at its best. I saw no fine views of Plymouth Sound and

161

Mount Edgcumbe, but on the contrary one vista of chimneys and gasometers. The hall and majority of rooms – the library is Regency – are pre-Adam. Only the saloon and dining-room are genuine Adam, and marvellous of their sort. The saloon with its coved ceiling, a double cube, pleased me enormously. The enormous Axminster carpet was designed by Adam to match the ceiling. The walls are of striped blue silk, faded to gold. Walls of the velvet room are red, which is superb. There are numerous Reynolds portraits, for the painter was born at Plympton and patronised by the Parkers. The family seems rich. Keeble is being employed to repair the great damage caused by dry-rot. The rooms in the east wing are all under dust-sheets, and several walls have had to be stripped to the bare brickwork.

We took Lady Clementine back to the Moult, lunched there, and motored off, to comb some antique shops in Totnes. Had tea at Montacute which is looking fine. E. left me and I took a train from Yeovil to London.

Monday, 12th May

Kathleen [Kennet] said this evening that the effort of keeping alive was ghastly. They make her sit up in her room because she is no worse. But she is no better.

Tuesday, 13th May

To see Lord Wimborne at Wimborne House (Arlington Street) which he says he is leaving soon. He cannot prevent motors parking in his courtyard. He asked many questions about giving Ashby St. Ledgers to the Trust. I went to a party given by Sheila [de Rützen]. The Archduke Robert there like a tall stick, with an agreeable but unintelligent face.

Wednesday, 14th May

Meeting at the House of Commons presided over by Noel-Baker, who has the face of a young angel. He spoke very ably, but it was a terrible meeting, without a purpose. I asked if the meeting could be formulated into a committee, to which other experts might be co-opted, thereby hinting that some of the dead wood present might be eliminated.

Before the Executive Committee Lord Crawford hinted that he might take his pictures away from Montacute for the Travellers' Club. I implored him not to, and made a sudden, earnest appeal, telling him how they made Montacute what it now is. 'There you are,' he said to Harold Nicolson, 'that is precisely how he wheedles things out of the old ladies.'

Michael and I drove to Strawberry Hill after six. Wyndham Ketton-Cremer was shyly reading quite a good paper from the chair about Walpole. Professor Richardson spoke after him. Later we were allowed to walk round the house which is kept up better today than when I last visited ten years ago. The Gallery is decidedly pretty; so is the Round Room with the Adam fireplace and ceiling, the only Adam Gothick work I have so far seen. The library could be pretty if painted white and gold instead of brown and gold. We were shown Horace's chapel in the garden, now sadly decaying, the floor fallen in; but a very delicate ceiling of Gothick pendants.

Bridget and I motored to Drayton House for the day, it being open for members of the Georgian Group. We lunched leisurely en route and found ourselves at a wrong Drayton, a village beyond Rockingham, and had to retrace our steps fifteen or twenty miles. It was well worth the trouble.

Drayton is an exceptionally fine house, more cheerful than Knole which it resembles in some respects, for the spirit of Lady Betty Germain still prevails in both houses. What pleased me most were the Duchess of Norfolk's gates, the ironwork generally, the Talman front, the Grinling Gibbons table in the King's Dining-Room, the tapestries, the great bed of green needlework and velvet, the Webb chimneypiece, the silver-mounted table and silver mirror. The dining-room is in a rather thin Adam style. So is the drawing-room ceiling. What pleased in the garden were the balustrading, the lead urns, the lime avenues and, above all, the secluded luxuriant country around. Bridget and I met Mrs. Stopford-Sackville, the new wife, upstairs. She showed us Lady Betty's two rococo panels of Soho tapestry in her own bedroom. We stopped at Lowick church, with its octagonal tower and numerous weathervanes, to look at the mediaeval glass and the alabaster Greene monuments. Had a late tea at the inn in Kimbolton by the Castle entrance gates, designed by Adam, dullish work however. We joined the Sachie Sitwells for dinner at an expensive restaurant, Baldwin's, in Dover Street.

Sunday, 18th May

A quiet day to myself. So cold I lit a fire. Went to Mass, read for my new book and visited the National Gallery. The face of the Velasquez Philip IV, about which there has been so much recent dispute, does look a bit white and thin, but I don't know that it is not now as the artist left it. I think people regret the patina of age that pictures, like buildings, acquire. I thought the colours of the cleaned *Chapeau de Paille* looked rather crude. Probably the picture was more pleasing before cleaning, but again I don't think this an argument in favour of letting 'em remain dirty. I think the wholesale onslaught on the Bankside Power Station proposal is stick-in-the-mud nonsense also. What I do object to is the Government's high-handed manner of announcing the *fait accompli*. It is irritating and smacks of totalitarianism. Probably the power station will be a great work of art.

Tuesday, 20th May

Took Miss Kearney to Knole this afternoon. She certainly is the least talkative woman I have ever known. I agreed with Mason at once to raise the wages of our Knole staff who are a little dissatisfied that they receive so few tips because of the large crowds. Saw Lord Sackville who wants the N.T. to take the North Wing off his shoulders. The public amuse themselves by carving their names on the oak door of the gatehouse on days when they are not admitted to the state-rooms.

The Rosses had a cocktail party in their Park Street house. Talked to Lord Bath about Longleat. He is a handsome and youthful man, with eyes like coals and little white teeth neatly arranged. When he speaks eyes and teeth glisten so that he looks like a fanatic.

Motored Eardley to Somerset. We reached Stourhead at 3 o'c.
By that time the sun had penetrated the mist, and was gauzy
and humid. The air about lake and grounds of a conservatory
consistency. Never do I remember such Claude-like, idyllic
beauty here. See Stourhead and die. Rhododendrons and
azaleas full out. No ponticums, but pink and deep red rhododendrons – not so good – and loveliest of all, the virginal
snow white ones, almost too white to be true. Azaleas mostly
orange and brimstone. These clothe the banks of the lake. The
beech are at their best. We walked leisurely round the lake and
amused ourselves in the grot trying to remember Pope's four
lines correctly by heart, and forgetting, and running back to
memorize. The temples are not in bad order, the Temple of
Flora and the Pantheon being particularly well kept. We had
tea at the inn at Stourton; then walked rapidly round the first
floor of the house, reserving our detailed survey for tomorrow. We were staggered by the amount of first-rate furniture
and pictures. There is more than enough upstairs to fill the
whole *piano nobile*.

I stay at Long Crichel. Both Eddy and Desmond at home; full
of affection and gaiety. I greatly enjoy being here. We went off
this morning to Stourhead, taking Eddy. He made us stop at
Shaftesbury where he and I each bought a pair of blue policeman's trousers which we saw in a shop window going for
12s.6d. each and five coupons. When I tried mine on in the
evening they were so stiff they stood up by themselves as
though made of three-ply wood, and are quite unwearable.
Eddy said the Stourhead gardens were his idea of paradise. We
all walked round them once again, discussing how they should
be supervised by one person with a landscape eye. We went
into the basement and attic floors of the house. They are unfit
for human habitation. More and more excellent things reveal
themselves in the ground floor rooms. After tea at Long
Crichel I motor back to London, picking up a picture for Lyme
lent by Lord Newton at Timsbury Manor, a red brick 1880
house he has just bought and where he has reassembled his
exquisite Lyme furniture.

Lunched at the pub at Aylesbury. Was sitting beside a young man who told me he worked at advanced photography with rocket manufacturers. He said there was an Interplanetary Society of six or seven persons, some women, who expect shortly to travel to the moon. They will not be able to return but they will signal back their discoveries, and when their oxygen gives out they will die. Stopped at Charlecote where I had tea. The rooms look quite well, but there are not many visitors. I begin to think visitors will not come here in vast numbers. Got to Wickhamford for supper.

To Whitsun Mass at Evesham. In the gallery a choir of German prisoners singing, and one read the Gospel and Epistle in German – an excellent idea. Papa and I then went to Hidcote and saw Lawrie Johnston who is old and ill. I walked round the village and assessed the 200-acre property and garden. Cannot see how with five gardeners the N.T. could hope to maintain the garden with no endowment.

A lovely day. Deenie came in the morning and I drove her and Mama to Brockhampton. They loved old Bakewell and Mrs Hughes and thought how nice it would be to engage them both. We brought a picnic luncheon and ate it in the hall. Mrs Hill ('Stinkie') met me there in the afternoon and discussed various matters, what to throw away and what to keep. I gave her a small chair – not mine to give away – which she coveted. Mrs. Hill is, for someone of eighty-five, spry. She ate three pieces of cake. M. and Deenie thought her hard-boiled because she did not bewail the fate of Brockhampton, they being too inclined to sentimentalise over Brockhampton, whereas they never knew the Lutleys who were of course Mrs. Hill's intimate friends.

Left Wickhamford at ten for Coughton Court. Dear Lady Throckmorton welcomed me. A cousin of hers, Miss Hanbury-Williams, staying. Lady T. says she will be seventy next year. She looks remarkably well and strong. I love her quick intelligence. She lives in the whole south wing of Coughton, Sir Robert in the north wing when he is down. Place looks improved and no longer impoverished. We discussed many things. She told me how much she liked Baron Ash and, in a knowing way, how much she disliked Bradley-Birt.

Drove on to Dudley. Looked round the castle in order to study the parts built by Sir William Sharington in 1550. They are much decayed. The Castle grounds are a zoo, teeming with animals and people. A ghastly place. I saw what I wanted and hurried away, sickened by humanity in the gross. The people of the Midlands are incredibly primitive. Then to Wightwick Manor. The Manders conducted me round and dispensed tea. They were kind. I like Rosalie who is highly educated (a woman's college product) and cultivated, which is not the same thing as the first. He is a quiet and wise man. Got to Charlie Brocklehurst's Harebarrow Lodge for dinner.

We had a rather wonderful but exhausting day. At the end of it were both absolutely whacked. We got to Lyme at eleven. It was scorching hot. The house full of Corporation electricians, painters and carpenters lying around doing nothing. Charlie was very upset because the Parks Superintendent had the windows painted a pale shit colour without consulting him or even telling him that they intended painting them. He raised a stink and made them repaint the lot a darker shade – all he could do. Both of us very indignant about this. We ran up and down the house deciding where furniture is to go and pictures to be hung. This took hours of time.

On the way back to Harebarrow we visited Bramall, now bought by the Corporation, a much restored black and white house, formerly the Bromley-Davenports'. Quite well maintained outside and in. Conducted round by a vociferous guide who pointed out all the beauties effected by a Mr. Nevile in the 1880s when first bought from the Davenports. Charlie's house is tiny and so congested you can barely move in it. Much sherry and port drinking.

Today went to Styal village which we liked. It is interesting as an example of an early cotton industrial community, with eighteenth-century mill, master's house, manager's house, apprentices' house and artisans' red brick cottages. Then lunched at Little Moreton Hall which is greatly improved; then visited Mow Cop and Maggoty's Wood. Very hot and thundery day. Called on the Archdeacon at Astbury and saw round his beautiful Georgian house which he is converting into two and ruining in the process by ripping out all the Georgian fireplaces. It is the most extraordinary thing how holiness and hideousness are compatible. For dinner came Mrs Legh of Adlington and her daughter just married to an American and about to join her husband in Chicago. At 10 o'c we all motored to Alderley Edge and walked along the Edge till caught in a thunderstorm, then drove back through the grounds of Hare Hill, Charlie's place let to the blind for the war. An ugly, shapeless house in pretty situation, the park walks rampaging with rhododendrons and sweet smelling azaleas. I never remember another spring for such galaxies of these plants, or for buttercups. The fields are golden.

Charlie and I motored separately to Attingham from Harebarrow, which took us two hours. We found Attingham a scene of Russian tragedy. Lady Berwick was hollow-eyed and miserable. Once or twice I thought she was in tears. They are fast selling contents and clearing out of the house for the College. They will withdraw into the small east wing. Lord Berwick was wheeled up to us in a chair. He is a shrunken, almost inhuman bundle incapable of moving hand or limb. He speaks lower and slower, and is most piteous. She thinks he may die at any moment. Two nurses are in perpetual attendance and I suspect make the B.s poorer than ever, and this worries her terribly. Charlie looked at the china and bibelots which he thought wonderful but was able only to select a few things for Lyme. He packed them into his car. Lady B.

lunched with us at the Inn, poor woman. After tea Charlie and I parted. I drove to Wickhamford, laden with the posts of Caroline Murat's bed which the Berwicks are selling at Sotheby's.

Sat in the garden at Wickhamford correcting proofs. So hot that I had to be in the shade. Papa went dog-racing at Gloucester. An extraordinary diverson. Mama spent the day watching birds fly in and out of the house, she telling me which each one was, and its habits. When tired of this she looked at caterpillars climbing threads to the tops of trees and wondering, questioning how and why they did it. One of her most endearing qualities is adoration of nature and creatures.

Heat at its height today. I love it, but it is stifling. Everyone else complains. Lunched at the Ritz with Major [Jack] Abbey who gave me a delicious white wine which made me drip like a tap. He invited me in order to grumble about Langley-Taylor whom he hates, and says if we have trouble with him over Hughenden, he will weigh in and help us. After all his father bought Hughenden for the nation, not L.-T. I had a dinner party of Billa Harrod, Puss Milnes-Gaskell and Leigh Ashton. It was so hot that we sat with the windows and door open in a direct draught. Leigh, being very fat, sweated profusely. Food the best I have had here yet: chicken in aspic, strawberries and cream. I am a bad host however, and inattentive. Leigh took us to his Museum across the way where he showed us the Elizabethan miniature collection just opened. They are beautifully displayed behind glass. He is a splendid showman. The V & A was all lit up for us alone, and attendants there in their uniforms. Billa stayed and talked until one o'c, for sleep is out of the question in this heat.

The weather has broken and the English summer of one week is over. At Sothebys looked at the settee and two chairs of the famous Dundas suite from Moor Park, designed by Adam in the early 1760s. They had been re-covered in cut velvet and I thought the quality of the wood carving none too delicate.

Thursday, 5th June

In the office arranging a tour of the south-west of England in early August for Harold, Vita and myself, which will be fun. Ruby Holland-Martin came to the office to discuss Brock-hampton's future, the decision reached being to let Lower Brockhampton to the Youth Hostels.

Friday, 6th June

At Batsford's going through the Adam book illustrations with Sam Carr. He showed me the jacket of my book, taken from an Adam wall design in the St. James's Club. Very pretty. It will be the best part of the book. For £7.10.0. I bought six blue Bristol tumblers this evening with money I haven't got. Now I have blue, green and red for my dinner table.

Saturday, 7th June

Poured all morning. Went to the Hilliard exhibition and saw the last of the French tapestries. Motored Dick Girouard to Claydon after luncheon. We discussed private schools and discovered that we were both at Lockers Park, he rather before me, nearly thirty years ago. So we diverged at Hemel Hemp-stead and visited the place, which in every respect seemed precisely the same as it was when I left it in 1921, only smaller. There was the very same lilac bush where Matthew my brother-in-law, Peter Coats and I played and made our sanc-tum. I think the prevailing emotion in those days was fear, and a need for escape.

Claydon most disappointing outside; quite remarkable in-side. I have never seen such rococo work elsewhere in Eng-land. Gothick Room and above all Chinese Room the most extravagant stucco- and woodwork imaginable outside Bavaria. The latter room has a Chinese screen recess with nodding mandarins, canopy and bells. Ugly really, but fantas-tic. Drove Dick as far as Warwick and continued to Birming-ham to stay with the Trenchard Coxes.

This morning Dr. Mary Woodall, Trenchard's keeper (he is not a lunatic) motored us to Aston Hall which is beautifully furnished, better, I thought, than Montacute. All done within one-and-a-half years, like M, and in excellent taste. A minimum of posts and ropes, and better ones than ours. In the afternoon to the Art Gallery which Trenchard took me round, showing me the pre-Raphaelite exhibition which is fascinating. He is charming and kind to all, beloved, I guess, by his staff, and she has the same qualities. A *gemütlich* couple. Lord Crawford has just been staying with them and told T.C. that if England were combed no one could be found more suitable for my particular post than myself. I blush, while writing this, with pleasure.

Monday, 9th June

Left the Coxes early for Castle Bromwich Hall and looked at the work in progress. The house much battered about in the war. Then called at Packwood and saw J. Rowley. Lunched at Alcester and arrived at Flaxley Abbey at 3.15. This a very poor house in spite of one gothic refectory and Abbot's guest room with cuspated windbrace roof. Then Matson House, and motored back to London, arriving 11 o'c.

Tuesday, 10th June

Motored Michael and [Angus] Acworth to Chiswick House this morning. With [John] Macgregor, the architect we looked carefully over the rooms. The condition is very bad indeed, but not irreparable. The quality of the Wyatt wings far better than I had supposed, so I hesitated to advocate pulling them down unless the only likelihood of money forthcoming for the repair of the Burlington block were by sacrificing them. Bridget dined with me at the White Tower.

Saturday, 14th June

Harold said yesterday at the General Purposes Committee, 'Jim is as sensitive about Charlecote as Lord Tennyson was about *Maud*,' when Esher teased me again about this property, saying, 'You may repair the balustrade in any way you like. It is such a terrible house.' All this week I have been very irritable, having given up smoking. I hope within a month no longer to be tormented.

Lyme Park was opened today, but I did not attend, having done my share, I feel, in compiling the guidebook and arranging the contents. Instead this evening I attended the Polesden Lacey harpsichord concert, taking Rick and Helen Dashwood who, though nice to me, grumbled aloud. The supper was indeed poor, not enough to eat or drink, and 17s.6d. per head is quite expensive. Poor Lord Berwick has now died, and I sent her a telegram and letter. A dear, sweet, and very eccentric man.

Monday, 16th June

Motored after luncheon to Brockhampton, stopping at Wickhamford at 6 o'c. After dining in Worcester, at The Hop Pole, a horrid inn, arrived in the cool of the evening. How beautiful this place is. I walked down to Lower Brockhampton just before dark, the trees dead quiet, not even whispering, and the undergrowth steaming. Two enormous black and white bulls gave me a fright by noiselessly poking their great faces over a gate and peering at me in a meditative manner. This evening the whole tragedy of England impressed itself upon me. This small, not very important seat in the heart of our secluded country, is now deprived of its last squire. A whole social system has broken down. What will replace it beyond government by the masses, uncultivated, rancorous, savage, philistine, the enemies of all things beautiful? How I detest democracy. More and more I believe in benevolent autocracy.

Tuesday, 17th June

Up early. Visited the chapel, making notes. At eleven Eardley came and then the van to take things to Montacute, chiefly books. Thus do we despoil the Lutley's ancient heritage. The three van men all came into the house smoking. No manners. Bakewell was sweet to them. A delicious old creature. He does not seem to repine. It was a heavenly day. I motored back in the afternoon, calling on Mama, and consuming a piece of cake and some milk. Arrived in London simultaneously with my father who is to stay three nights here, he having my room, I sleeping in Geoffrey's at the very top of the house, in G.'s absence. I gave a dinner party of Lady de Vesci, Bridget Parsons, Charlie Brocklehurst and my father, five being the largest number I have yet had round my small table. It was a good meal and they all said they enjoyed it. We had lobster to begin with. Papa stayed behind and the four of us went to the Georgian Group reception at the Soane Museum. Thousands of people I knew. I was so tired that I could not sleep in Geoffrey's room.

Wednesday, 18th June

To the exhibition of the Great Duke of Wellington's silver plate, porcelain and pictures at the V & A. The quality of the silver gilt seems poor when you look into it; much of the design coarse. Yet fascinating. The plate too realistic to be great art surely. Of all the objects the diamond that had belonged to the Duke of Marlborough and was given by the Prince Regent to the Iron Duke was the beautifullest. Professor Geoffrey Webb called this morning to tell me he has succeeded Clapham as Editor of the Royal Commission's volumes and to exhort me to provide proper catalogues of the National Trust's collections.

Thursday, 19th June

I left Papa who is going to Ascot today and staying on here tonight. At 10.30 I picked up Michael Rosse and motored to Norfolk. We lunched at Bury St. Edmund's. A lovely hot day. Our first call was Yarmouth where we studied the Trust's building, No. 4 South Quay. We both came to the same conclusion that the N.T. should press for the preservation of the facades of the whole block of which No. 4 is a part; that it would not matter sacrificing the rear portion, so much of which has been devastated by bombing; that the Elizabethan rooms of our house must at all costs be preserved; and that new buildings must not show above the skyline of the Quay when looked at from the river. We suspect that much of the wainscot of the dining-room is made up. We continued to Burnham Market where we had a drink with Silvia Combe. We stayed the night at the Moorings Hotel, opposite Scolt Head, and dined at Holkham.

I would definitely put Holkham among the first twenty great houses of England. With its collections it forms one very great work of art indeed. Lord Leicester is a charming and cultivated man. There were, besides Michael and me, Silvia, Lord L. and his son, Tommy Coke, a nice, weak person, and my contemporary. Delicious dinner of cold venison eaten in the low-ceilinged, long room on the ground floor between the family and the strangers' wings. I sat next to Lord Leicester who said how disappointed he was that the family entail prevented him handing over Holkham. His last words to me were: 'If you can find any means whereby the Trust can take over this house and its contents, I shall be prepared to leave it, should my not staying on make the transfer easier.' After dinner we walked all round the house. The high quality of the architecture and contents takes the breath away. The planning too is astonishingly convenient. There are four complete wings detached from the centre block. Yet when inside the house you get the impression that there are no breaks and the five entities make one house, huge though it be. You get vistas from one wing through the centre block into another wing, conveying a surprising effect of grandeur. The other impression made upon me was the marmoreal, classical simplicity of unadorned wall spaces contrasting with the rich ornamentation of ceilings and doorways and fireplaces. The sculpture gallery in particular struck me in this way – so pure, correct, and serene. We spent some little time at the end of the tour in the library where I was chiefly interested in the detailed account book kept by the first Lord Leicester who amassed his collections before the age of twenty-five. Lady Leicester is away, staying in Silvia's house, with a nervous breakdown brought about by anxiety and the worry of keeping up Holkham with practically no servants. What these wretched landowners have to go through! Yet Holkham is superbly kept up, all the steel grates, for instance, shining brightly, the work of one devoted daily.

Friday, 20th June

This morning we visited the Mill at Burnham Overy and were shocked by its condition. We drove on to Blickling. Michael pleased by excellent condition of the house inside and the garden, but not by the house outside, or the temples. Looked at the Swanton Morley property on our way to Bradenham. Motored to Wisbech where Michael addressed that Society and spoke very well. He has a good delivery and a good vocabulary. I was impressed. We returned to Bradenham at 11.30 and only within the last three miles did I need to put on my side-lights. I love the extreme limits of days and nights. Now the chirpings of midnight delight the ear.

Saturday, 21st June

This motoring – today's is the third 200-mile drive – nearly kills me. By the end of the day I feel sick with tiredness. Yet each night I have slept well which makes amends. We left Bradenham at 10.30 and reached St. Osyth's Priory at one o'c. General Kincaid-Smith the owner, a bad seventy-seven, is slow and at times quite inarticulate, but an old dear. He gave us an old man's luncheon, ending with plum cake and port wine, a funny midsummer's day meal. The house inside is uniformly drab, but outside very remarkable, being chiefly of chequer-work grey and brown stone. There is an entrance gateway of flint, knapped within panels formed of dressed stone with quatrefoil heads. The garden is attractive. It is walled, with occasional views of the gatehouse, the octagonal tower with cupola and vane, and the large tower. We were conducted round the outside slowly, painfully. How the old do tire one. The General offers the property and investments to yield £1000 per annum. There are 350 acres of *in*fertile ground, 'with walls and towers girdled round'.

Tuesday, 24th June

To see poor Kathleen K., still in hospital although she has been taken in a chair by car to visit her exhibition of sculpture. It exhausted her. Her voice is noticeably feebler. I foolishly brought her a large book of U.S.A. works of art. At once I saw that it was too big and heavy for her to lift, but she said she would manage somehow to get it propped up. She told me not to *give* it to her for soon she would be in her grave. I am afraid she is much weaker. I did not stay long. Dined with Johnnie Churchill and wife, but was thinking of K.

Saw the Dulwich Gallery pictures at the National Gallery. How lovely are the Nicolas Poussins, those idyllic yet passionless blues and greens. What a world one enters of piping and bleating.

Motored from Long Crichel to Montacute with Eardley. We worked like blacks carrying carpets and books brought from Brockhampton. Happy beasts of burden we were. It was great fun. In consequence we made the library the best room in the house, the polished brown spines the colour of fresh conkers looming through the gilded trellis of the shelves; and the very special light which filters through the heraldic glass, splodges of azure and gules and vert on the Savonerie carpet.

Sibyl Colefax stays tonight at Long Crichel. She has just returned from Italy where she went and whence she travelled by herself. She actually spent Tuesday night sitting in the waiting-room of Milan station because she had lost a visa or something. This is gallantry as well as muddle.

I motored away early and called upon Sir Walter Jenner at Lytes Cary, near Kingsdon, an old late gothic manor-house to be left to the Nat. Trust by him. He is eighty-seven this year. He received me lying in a four-poster bed and wearing a night-cap with a bobble. A gloomy house, but with a fine open hall with braced rafters and carved frieze. Sir Walter has added a whole wing and made the house too large, out of scale. Christopher Hussey at Montacute later said it was a good example of the development of taste, Sir Walter's 'William and Mary' additions, done in the first decade of this century, and not what we would do today. The south front with chapel is very unspoilt and delightful. Got to Montacute at luncheon time. Sir Geoffrey Cox, Lord Aberconway and Hussey came to the meeting. We agreed to sack Scotts', the gardening firm, and to employ our own gardeners. The three of them very pleased with the house. Wilson, the head adviser to the Royal Horticultural Society, came down. He and Lord A. conferred.

I motored Lord A. and Sir G. back to London in under four hours. Lord A. refused to stop en route for dinner.

Sunday, 29th June

At Brooks's at luncheon sat with Eddy, up for his second broadcast on Knole. So I asked him to dine. Jamesey came too and we enjoyed ourselves. Eddy said the sort of people he was disposed to dislike were those who seemed to him second-rate editions of himself, and those who excelled in certain professions (i.e. museum experts) in which he could have excelled if he had tried.

James and I walked to Ladbroke Grove to listen-in to Eddy. On the way J. told me how two weeks ago he found himself engaged to Ann Ebury and how to his infinite relief he just managed to scrape out of it. She was very determined and even threatened to adopt Ann Pope-Hennessy as her pen name. Eddy's voice came very clearly over the air: just a little plaintive but without affectation or over-emphasis. Moreover it was poetical.

Tuesday, 1st July

Took a morning train to Appledore in Sussex and walked to the village in warm, drizzling rain which made the hedgerows and hay smell like amber. Perhaps my renunciation of cigarettes has restored my sense of smell, or made it acuter. Miss Johnston's furniture was of no account. A wasted visit, except that I read and slept in the train. It was a rest after motoring. The rhythm of carriage wheels over the track induces delicious fantasies sacred and profane. Sometimes I am in the arms of God, and sometimes of Satan, as a priest once described one of the loveliest lovers I ever enjoyed. There is romance in the queer, flat marshland in these parts, where the sea has receded within history and left low, flat pasture and elevated, straight roads.

Wednesday, 2nd July

Tony Wills, Lord Dulverton's eldest, wrote today telling me that for over a year he has been installed at Horton Court, our property, left us by Miss Wills a year ago, without our ever knowing it! He has asked me to dine at Boodles. He is about thirty-one, slight, fair, with a prominent nose between twinkling eyes. The eyes melt into smiles in a benevolent but cautious manner. He tells me he has three children. We talked about the Pilgrim Trust. He is thinking of persuading his father to endow a similar Wills trust.

Thursday, 3rd July

I motored to Great Hampden, arriving 11.30. Was met by Parker-Jervis and Lord [Bertie] Buckinghamshire, aged about forty-one, whom I now remember at Eton as Hobart. He is single, reserved, and rather charming, ugly, with a turned-up nose and moustache. He seems very much older than me I am pleased to say. I liked him for his forthrightness and excellent manners. He offers Hampden House and about 100 acres to the Trust. The house is let to a girls' school who pay a rent of £800 a year. It is really not first-rate. The property was granted to the Hampdens by Edward the Confessor. The house dates from every period, from King John even, having two arches of his reign. The great hall with roof was brought from an old barn on the estate, the late seventeenth-century balustrade being original to the gallery. A suite of rooms in the south wing decorated *c.* 1740 in Palladian style is handsome, but, if not ruined, spoilt by use as girls' class-rooms. The staircase is Jacobean and painted with arcaded panels on the dado to give a perspective effect. The south facade is symmetrical with escutcheons in stone on the roof. The windows tame Vanbrughian. The demesne now much gone to seed. I think it is a borderline case. John Hampden of course lived and died here.

Lunched most excellently at The Hampden Arms, a tiny pub. Under the inn's name is inscribed on a board, 'The Earl of Buckinghamshire licenced to sell beer and tobacco'. I reached Fenton House by four and had tea with Lady Binning, who was rather fatter than hitherto, a little deafer and very 'malade imaginaire'. She is an odd woman, ridiculous and very nice. We strolled and sat about the garden which is one of the prettiest in London. She now thinks she should make more provision for maintenance of the garden. Then I had a drink with Terence Maxwell who, as one of Mrs. Greville's trustees, complained about the N.T.'s waiving all responsibility for the upkeep of Mrs. G.'s father's and husband's graves in

Bookham churchyard. He begged me to investigate the matter. I think this is the least we can do after accepting such a great benefaction as Polesden and Charles Street. This evening the Maxwells' house was burgled while they were in bed. Terence chased the burglar downstairs. Diana telephoned the police who arrived in one-and-a-half minutes and caught him hiding behind a door.

Friday, 4th July

Went to Covent Garden to see the last performance of Oliver [Messel]'s production of *The Magic Flute*. It was the Rosses' party, Mrs. Messel, Oliver and his court there. Afterwards we dined at the Savoy, and watched the dancing. I disliked this part of the evening, drinking all the time and being bored stiff. Anne looked pretty as a picture, wearing a dress and lace shawl in Winterhalter style.

Saturday, 5th July

The Georgian Group had a meeting at Somerset House, preceded by a talk by John Summerson in St. Mary-le-Strand church, hideously decorated. Then a tour round the principal apartments of Somerset House, much cut up by offices and likewise hideously decorated. The door-locks with royal crowns and medallions of George III on key-escutcheons most beautifully chased. Clifford Smith introduced me to Banister Fletcher, that great man, aged only seventy-five. He said the vaulting by Chambers over the Strand entrance was the best work of its kind in Europe; and I had never noticed it before in my life.

Bridget and I motored to Polesden Lacey for the second concert. This time it was horrible: beastly little quaint and dainty airs, and an affected soprano warbling. Supper filthy. My car emitted appalling fumes from the back where a floor board had become detached. Bridget calls the car the Belsen Gas Van.

Monday, 7th July

To the theatre – *Annie Get Your Gun* – with Bridget and Lady de Vesci; other guests being Countess Borromeo and her son

Carlo. She is Lady de V.'s first cousin, their mothers being sisters and daughters of the Duke of Newcastle. We sat in a box. Bridget and I called for the Borromeos and motored them to the theatre. After the first interval Lady de V., accompanied by Mark Ogilvie-Grant, swept in, in one regal gesture, embraced Countess Borromeo first on one, then the other cheek, and took her front seat as of right. It was a sudden movement, full of grace and dignity, such as I imagine the Empress Eugénie practised. I enjoyed the performance more than the first time. We dined at the Savoy – Alsatian wine – and I motored them home. Then took Mark to Kew. We walked in his garden, smelling the strong lilies and sipping brandy. I warmed to him. How easy, cosy, sympathetic he is, like all my old friends of that generation.

Tuesday, 8th July

Had my hair cut and look shorn and v. ugly. However I feel in good form and none the worse for last night's lateness and drink. I feel unaccountably social and gay – so unlike me. I am in a 'swimgloat'* and don't want to be out of it so long as the season lasts. There is still a flavour of season in London, even now, with all the exhibitions and theatres in full swing. I called for Sibyl and motored her to Wyndham's theatre where she was given two stalls by Binkie Beaumont for *Deep are the Roots*. Sibyl climbs nimbly into my car which at least has leg room (although she hardly has any legs to speak of), and then scurries through the crowds, head down. I follow behind keeping a protective finger upon her rounded back, rather like bowling a hoop. Our seats were behind the Eshers. It was a most enjoyable play, beautifully acted. Deals with the Negro problem in the Southern States. Sibyl took me to Binkie B's party in Lord North Street afterwards. All the cast came in. I talked to the Negro and his mother who were sweet and as earnest off the stage as on. Both looked darker and more natural than on stage where, I suppose, they were lightened so as to engage our sympathies. The Carisbrookes were there and I was caught by him in a corner where he talked for hours about Mrs. Greville. He said she never minded about people's

*An expression used by the Souls and taught me by Logan Pearsall-Smith.

morals or what they did. That was their concern. He said he was cross with someone or other because that person had expressed disapproval of Ivor Novello's 'nancy manner'. Oh gosh! Lady Carisbrooke is thin and pretty; also rather tired and embittered. They both pressed me to luncheon at Kew next Sunday, or rather he pressed and she politely acquiesced. Then I went up to Noël Coward and said to him, 'You and I have two great friends, both dead, in common. George Lloyd and Mrs. Cooper, Aunt Eva.' He recalled who I was and made me promise I would ring him up when he returned from the States and we would dine and have a long talk about both of them. His white teeth flash when he smiles, but his smile is unconvincing. He is a very ugly man with rather bloated, sagging, red cheeks and hollow eyes. He has moreover a thin, flat behind which implies shallowness of character.

Thursday, 10th July

Anne [Rosse] telephoned at 7.30 asking me to dine, so weakly I accepted, and went. Michael's mother, Countess Borromeo and son Carlo, there. All Borromeo sons are called Carlo after the Saint. When Michael and Anne went to the Plunkett ball, to which I did not go, we stayed behind and talked of Fascist Italy. The Borromeos have little opinion of the King of Italy who, they argue, should have abdicated as soon as Mussolini fell, and then Prince Umberto would have stood a chance of remaining. She said a neo-Fascist party is forming itself in Italy today.

Friday, 11th July

Walked with Lord Esher across the Park. We lunched together. He said Lord Crawford told him that Mrs. Dalton reminded him of a certain rabbit-trap which was so cruel it had to be discarded. He, Esher, whenever he saw her thought of the wolf dressed up as Red Riding-Hood's grandmother. At Brooks's we sat at John Christie's table. Christie said it was time that bad productions ceased to be commercially profitable. Esher said that good productions were not allowed to have long runs because they were sponsored by the Government, and so were not supposed to make a return. He said to me afterwards that, whereas undoubtedly Christie had great genius, he was impossible to work with. No team spirit. If he, Esher, were made chairman of the Covent Garden trustees, he would appoint Christie because he was the only Englishman to have a practical understanding of opera, and then give him absolute control.

After dinner I helped Rick arrange No. 3 Cheyne Walk into the late hours of tomorrow morning.

Saturday, 12th July

Motored Michael Rosse to Knole. Fedden joined us late in the morning, haggard and white with a hang-over. My puritanical reaction was distaste. Bridget assured me that she found him wet. He certainly is not this, I retorted. We witnessed the crowds arriving at the house and talked to the women guides. The arrangements seem to be working smoothly. They get 400 to 500 visitors every Saturday.

I dined with Colin Agnew and motored a guest back to Cardinal's Wharf on the right bank of the river. A most romantic view of the river with moonlight on the swirling surface and St. Paul's silhouetted against the northern sky, the dome seeming spherical rather than circular in the semi-darkness.

Sunday, 13th July

Lunched with the Carisbrookes. Drove to Mark's house and walked across Kew Green to the King's Cottage where they live. It is a shapeless house with little character. Just the Carisbrookes, Mark and a fat, middle-aged woman in gloves, a sort of fortune-teller. Lord C. dispensed very strong martinis before luncheon (which was excellent) running around, helping us to potatoes like any little waiter. He was immaculately dressed in a well-pressed check suit, padded shoulders, and jangling with gold bracelets and rings. He reminded me of an old, spruce hen, cackling and scratching the dust in a chicken-run – really, a typical old queen. He jabbers away, yet is not altogether stupid; has good taste, and is sophisticated. Lady Carisbrooke is very sweet and has a langorous charm. We talked about brain. She said it was possible for a man to lose a third of his physical brain and yet for his mind to be unimpaired. We conjectured from this that the mind was not a

182

physical attribute nor even dependent upon a physical structure for its being. It might in consequence well be immortal.
After luncheon Lord C. took me all round the house, even into
the cellars and attics, complaining how inadequate was the
house, which the King has given him. He showed me portraits
of his mother, Princess Beatrice, and his sister, Queen Ena of
Spain. No talk however of the present royal family or the
young betrothed couple, for which good marks. He said that
Queen Alexandra was the most beautiful woman he had ever
seen. All her limbs were of a like excellence to her face.
However he did vouchsafe that Queen Mary hates wearing
black. He likes bringing the topic of conversation to venereal
disease and unnatural vice; and he chases one into a corner and
talks so close that one expects him to pounce at any moment.
'And if one resisted,' Mark said, 'would it be *lèse-majesté*?'

Thursday, 17th July

Mama has stayed with me this week. She came on Monday
and left today. I think she enjoyed herself, and I am very sorry
that I was not nicer to her. I am sadly aware of Eddy's remark
that one is irritated most by those people who share one's own
faults to an enhanced degree; and by faults I mean venial
failings, because my mother has none of my major failings.
Sheila de R. thought her attractive and her figure that of a girl.

Friday, 18th July

Dined last night at Wilton's with John Fowler and Hardy
Amies, a good-looking dress designer, who is thirty-eight,
but so youthful in face and figure as to be mistaken for
twenty-eight. Today I motored to Petworth, calling for Robin
Fedden at Polesden. We stopped at Juniper Hall to see the
'Adam' room buried in that otherwise frightful house. The
plaster panel reliefs of the Four Seasons on the walls are of
excellent quality.

Sunday, 20th July

Worked quite hard this weekend and was happy in consequence.
This afternoon I motored James and the 'cellist's fiancée to

Greenwich. Saw over the Queen's House, which escaped the bombs but shows signs of suffering from concussion. The rest of the Palace is sad and inaccessible. A tennis court in the centre open courtyard and canvas hangings. We agreed the people looked drab, infinitely boorish, bored and dirty. James said that of course they are all on the downward grade. People *are* hell! J. and the fiancée came back for tea. I dined in and read more.

Monday, 21st July

Dear Alan Pryce-Jones lunched, but I was a frost. His brilliance simply enhances my dimness. He says he is to become editor of the *Times Literary Supplement*, and hopes to make it cover pictures, music and drama. He wants long reviews to be signed by the contributors. If he succeeds the *T.L.S.* will become the most important cultural organ in England. He says James has failed to change the *Spectator* reviews for the better.

Called on Doreen Baynes. She admitted that at times James hurt her grievously by his thoughtlessness. But she said, 'I do not reproach him, for in return for my patience he gives me his youth.' Then I called for Alvilde Chaplin and took her to Paez Subercaseaux's where we dined. I enjoyed this party, and would have enjoyed it more could I have left earlier. Instead we sat till midnight. Even so I was the first to rise and leave. The Robertis from the Italian Embassy present, and Madame Auric and Robin Ironside. Contessa Roberti, an American, is quite pretty but dresses her hair in that hideous skinned fashion, rolled at the sides and on top. Alvilde agreed with me that it was a mistake. A. looking very handsome in black.

Tuesday, 22nd July

Mrs. Hugh Dalton called for me at the office punctually at 11.30 in a large Daimler limousine, driven by the Chancellor's becoming and respectful chauffeur. With her a French boy, Marc Viénot. We drove to Queen's Gate and picked up the Iraqi Ambassadress, Princess Zeid, whose husband is uncle of the present King, and their daughter. The Princess is middle-aged, rather big with handsome, beaming lacquer face and two pairs of eyebrows: her natural brows still freely visible and the pair pencilled over them forming Moorish arches. She has dark, frizzly hair in curls kept together precariously under a web of hairpins. Fat, friendly, and an artist. The daughter, who is on holiday from a college in the States where she has led an independent sort of existence, has ugly oriental lips, like Georges Cattaui's, and spots. But she is an exceedingly well educated girl. We motored to Sevenoaks where we lunched. At luncheon the girl told me that when she returns to Iraq she will have to retire into purdah, and this prospect appals her. No wonder.

At The Royal Oak I forestalled criticism by offering Mrs Dalton some bread, already placed on the table, by saying, 'Come along. We are breaking the law but next year we won't have this golden opportunity.' She made a wry face, and took a piece. The two Iraqis made intellectual observations throughout the visit and, I think, enjoyed themselves hugely. The Princess pointed out that the carnation and tulip embroidered on the Elizabethan chairs at Knole were of Arabian origin; likewise the Jacobean strapwork ceilings. The early rugs impressed her favourably. On the way home the daughter sang songs from *Annie Get Your Gun*. She is what you might call a forward miss for she takes on whatever subject is broached; and the arts and English literature are her passion. She is going to have a rude shock when she gets back to the harem.

Today I understood the qualities of Mrs. Dalton without liking her. She is very intelligent indeed. She has a clear, practical mind. Her interest in culture is sincere. Her sense of historic tradition is genuine and I believe that she does not mean to break with it. Yet one cannot forget the diabolical venom poured out by the husband whom she undoubtedly loves and reveres. How this man can care for tradition, as he protests, is beyond my comprehension. Mrs. Dalton has, needless to say, no charm whatever, and she petrifies.

Wednesday, 23rd July

Lady Crewe came up to me at the Allies Club and asked me to speak on her behalf to the Ministry of Planning. She says she opened the local newspaper last week to read that West Horsley was to be made a satellite town and a main road was to be driven through her garden. But her house would be saved by serving as the centrepiece of a round-about. I went to Tony Gandarillas's party, meeting Lord and Lady Greville as I left and talking about Ronnie whom she worships. I did not enjoy this party. I should not go to these parties if I do not enjoy them. Unfortunately I do not know for sure that I won't in advance.

Thursday, 24th July

Oh Lord, I lunched at Wilton's with Oggy Lynn, whom to meet like this I do like. She is shaped like a small egg and it is far easier to talk to her when she is sitting down, provided one is too. Tony Pawson and Madam Auric there. Conversation was frivolous, Parisian and about dress designers. Oggy sensed that I was out of my depth, for which I gave her good marks for kindness. She exudes sympathy and understanding. She says the Government are going to exact a capital levy in the autumn.

At the Rosses, saying goodbye to them, in came Bridget and Sachie. Sachie confirms the gloomy prognostication about the impending capital levy. I hurried away to change into another suit for dinner with the Lennox-Boyds. Found Alan and Patsy drinking champagne with Prince Bernhard of the Netherlands. The latter is better looking than his photographs imply. Has a good complexion and figure, and not the Harold Lloyd face I imagined. He was dressed in a black tie with sparkling diamond links in his soft white cuffs. Was speaking volubly in slightly American English, and intelligently about the Dutch Indonesian situation. He shakes one's hand in a firm, 'manly' grip. Alan was so tired after the Baths' ball and a House of Commons sitting until 7 a.m. today that he fell asleep after dinner. I discreetly left at 10.45

Friday, 25th July

At breakfast I opened a letter from Wayland Hilton Young saying his mother's state had rapidly worsened in the last few days and was now very grave. He went on: 'She is not well enough to understand that I have written to you, but if she were, I think she would be glad that you should know.' Nothing further. I was miserable but of course not surprised. Remorseful too because I was thinking only last night that I must ring up and go to see her again, dreading to be told she was not well enough. I telephoned Keith who had been trying to get me at my office. He said that Kathleen died early this morning.

I motored to Cranbury Park, the other side of Winchester, by appointment. It was the best thing I could do. A glorious day and very hot. I was alone with my thoughts. I wept as I drove along. Not since Tom's death do I remember weeping for the loss of a friend.

I reached Cranbury Park at 1.15 to be told that Mrs. Tankerville Chamberlayne was in London. She had forgotten all about my visit, and I was cross. I went off to lunch at an hotel, returned at 2.30, and insisted on seeing Miss T. C., her sister-in-law. This curious woman, looking like a cook and speaking like one, showed me the ground floor rooms, at first suspiciously, then more agreeably. The outside of this house of scarlet brick is good imitation Georgian and I suppose *c.* 1840. A few of the rooms, notably hall with barrel ceiling and the ballroom, are magnificent, perhaps by Wyatt. I noticed a lot of good furniture and Romneys of Lady Hamilton, and large oils by Thomson of the same date. I spent exactly an hour there. Then drove to Winchester. For the first time in my life I saw the school and Herbert Baker's cloisters which excite such undiscriminating admiration. I do not think they are a master-piece, but rather chichi plagiarism. The large expanses of mown lawn are very beautiful. I had tea and attended divine service in the Cathedral. Looked at Bishop Gardner's Chantry Chapel, 1555, with its classical work. Interesting for Queen Mary was still on the throne and the Catholic Italians – or could they be Spaniards? presumably worked this. Drove on slowly to Montacute, dining at Shaftesbury under the bogus Chevy Chase sideboard. I thought of K. and how she might have admired it, and I would have been angry with her.

I don't yet know at what hour K. died this morning, but I suddenly woke up about 4.45 and remained awake for three-quarters of an hour. It is most unusual for me to do this once I have fallen asleep. I experienced a strange heaviness and depression.

Grief is an odd emotion. How much of it is self-indulgence? Today I have been very cheerful. Yesterday I was genuinely sad and yet never felt more tormented by sex. Perhaps the two conflicts have some association. I left Montacute at 10.30, having slept at Mrs. Welsh's cottage in the village – comfortable enough in the summer. Got to Westwood for luncheon.

Ted Lister is no older and, surprisingly, less deaf. Norah Methuen brought Austin Hall, the architect, to tea. In going round the house he slipped on a loose rug in the porch room and fell, crash, in a horizontal position on the floor. I saw the whole accident happen and thought he must have broken his back, but not at all. He is a handsome, healthy man of about sixty. He told us at tea that Lutyens was the greatest architect of the past 100 years; that Gerry Wellesley and Goodhart-Rendel never rose to greatness because, being rich men, they did not trouble to learn. I don't altogether agree with this. Hall said they were both better interior decorators than Lutyens, Baker or Giles Scott. The old professional architects are always contemptuous of amateurs.

Ted and I dined at Greenhill with John Leslie. John talked about K. Kennet's obituary and remarked how curiously phrased was one passage. Now I had read the obituary this afternoon. I wrote it at K.'s instigation ten years ago and on reading it today was appalled, for *The Times* have cut it by half and mangled it. In truth I admit it was badly written by me in the first instance.

The weather is sublime. It is toasting hot. Ted does not get up till after twelve when we have 'brunch'. It is an experience to stay in this extraordinary ancient house like a museum, with Christo the Bulgarian who does everything down to managing Ted, the quirkiest old Conservative ever known. 'Stinking Government!' is the phrase for ever on his lips. Alex Moulton came to dine, reserved, intelligent, yet curiously young and unsophisticated. He is re-introducing the steam motor-car into general use, so Ted claims. We sat in the garden in shirt sleeves till after midnight, under the stars, gossiping and laughing. These are life's moments. Suddenly Alex rose to his feet, embraced his host, jumped into his car, and was gone. Ted fumbled for the silver chamber-candlesticks, lit them and we separated for the night.

Monday, 28th July

I drove to Wickhamford, had a quick luncheon and fetched my Vi-spring mattress from the manor, which was sold last week. I did not want to go into the house again yet could not avoid doing so because my father came with me to help carry the mattress. Luckily the new owners were out. I tried not to look but could not help noticing how beautiful the garden was in spite of the fearful desolation. A horrible land-girl, cigarette dangling from lower lip, showed us where the mattress was in the hall. I hurried away to Brockhampton for the night.

Wednesday, 30th July

Lunched today at Sibyl Colefax's. Other guests were the Eshers, the Chancellor of the Exchequer and Mrs. Dalton, Malcolm Sargent, Barbara Ward, Binkie Beaumont and the Chancellor's P.P.S., a smug young Labour M.P., by name Christopher Mayhew, I think. I being the least important guest sat between Binkie Beaumont, to whom I have little to say and for whom I have little sympathy, and the young M.P., whom I cordially disliked. Consequently was not entirely happy until the end of the meal when conversation became general and spirited. I overheard Barbara Ward say in her genteel little manner to the Chancellor that a capital levy was quite workable, and just the ticket. How dare she on such an occasion! She was at great pains to sell the idea to Dalton and demonstrate how it could be done. Mr. Dalton fulfilled all my pre-conceived ideas of him. He is affable, bombastic and diabolically clever. I am sure he is also dishonest and evil. He is a big, tall man, bald with pointed skull – Mephistophelean. He has an insinuating, ingratiating manner. He thumped the table when speaking about the editor of the *Economist*, saying: 'He persistently misrepresents all my endeavours and I damned well won't be interfered with. He will get nothing out of me and [curiously enough] he won't get anything out of me socially.' Speaking of the Land Fund he said, 'Fifty million pounds are to me what a halfpenny is to a millionaire. I can

189

spend what I like internally. Money spent in the country bears no relation to money spent outside it.' He flattered himself that he had spent money on patronage of the arts and amenities and jeered at Snowden, his predecessor, for having declined the offer from the Duke of Montrose's executors of Glencoe, which Snowden described as 'waste land. What use could it be to the Exchequer?' He said how surprised he was that, when his proposed gift of lands to the National Trust was made at the Annual Meeting of the Trust last year through Lord Esher, it was greeted by the members in stony silence. Had Lord Esher announced that some millionaire had made a fraction of such an offer, it would have evoked loud applause. So I piped up: 'I quite understand, Mr. Chancellor. Why should the announcement be greeted with applause when the members learnt that *you* were prepared to make the National Trust a present of their own money and lands?' At this Mr. D. rubbed his hands and guffawed with hideous laughter. Malcolm Sargent and Beaumont then severally complained to the Chancellor that Board of Trade regulations prevented foreign artists being employed here, with the consequence that the standard of opera and theatre must remain low. Dalton very obligingly asked us all to brief him with our complaints. After the meal he came up and thanked me for acting cicerone to his beastly wife. My neighbour Mayhew, the young M.P., infuriated me by his condescending manner, denying that there was any financial crisis. It was all a newspaper ramp. He asked me if I was 'one of us.' I replied, 'By this I infer that you ask, am I a Socialist. Look again.' Then he said, 'You are a Tory?' 'No,' I said, 'I am far too right wing.' 'Just a reactionary then?' he said. 'Yes, against your Government.'

Thursday, 31st July

I motored to Quidenham in Norfolk for the day; through Breckland, which is intriguing no-man's land. Michael Rosse hates it. I looked at the outside of Euston and photographed it. Since I created a bad impression the only time I ever met Lady Albemarle I put myself out to please, and think I succeeded. She and Lord A. were both charming and begged me to stay as long as I wished. It is a stern house, not of great importance. Almost entirely rebuilt in 1815 by an architect called Latham, in fine rose-red brick with neat pointing. Pictures, portraits and furniture good, notably large mahogany Regency side-boards with stout brass rings and mountings. Lady A. is pretty and intelligent. He very distinguished. She told me how she became a Papist after her marriage, and so did her daughter, a lively, pretty amusing girl. I liked her a lot. Then Lord A.'s youngest son by his first wife was converted to the con-sternation of the Keppel family. Doubtless they detest Lady A. She is head of the W.V.S. I left after tea, they all waving me off at the door. It was a happy summer outing.

Friday, 1st August

Had a conference in the City about Osterley. Grandy there. I find I am apt to dictate at the meetings I attend now; a sign of confidence, perhaps over-confidence. Motored after tea to Packwood, arriving late for dinner. Joshua Rowley only just recovering from scalding his leg badly. I thought Packwood had lost its garnished appearance. Joshua pointed out how ugly the flower border scheme is; all the flowers are yellow which must indicate some odd trait in Baron Ash's character. Joshua still mystifies me. Why does he want to be isolated in this lonely place?

Saturday, 2nd August

Got to Charlecote at 10.30 and met Dr. Shaw and the brewing expert who says the brew-house here is complete, rare and important. I went round the house listening to the guides who all said their piece well. It is impossible to prevent them lapsing into occasional inanities. I wonder how much the substance of what they say matters. On my return to London I visited Sulgrave Manor. It is the best arranged and best kept of any show house I have been to. For this Clifford Smith is re-sponsible. The old man does have his good points.

At dinner at Brooks's got into conversation with a young man, Ian Anstruther, just returned from Washington where he was secretary to Lord Inverchapel, whom he greatly admires. He is shocked by this country and says for the first time in its history the upper classes are not wanted. A nice, old-fashioned young man. 'To be a gentleman today,' he says, 'is a disadvan-tage.'

Geoffrey [Houghton Brown] lunched to meet Ivy and Margaret. Ivy told a sudden, irrelevant story of their war days in a cottage near Newbury: how they kept poultry from York-*sheer*. One died. The others were so little moved by its death that they walked on it. They then looked at Geoffrey's furniture upstairs, and his bed by Jacob. When Margaret does not think a piece of furniture good she says, 'I would get rid of that if I were you.'

I got to West Wycombe after one o'c just before Harold Nicolson and Vita Sackville-West arrived. We lunched at the Apple Orchard and walked round the village; drove up to the church on the hill and looked at the Mausoleum. Then to the house. Helen [Dashwood] welcomed us. She was pretty but tired, and seemed sad. Johnnie has already moved into Chips Manor and Helen is obviously reluctant to follow. W.W. is tottering on its last legs. Harold made little effort to be forthcoming. We left at four, drove through the Hambleden Valley. The Nicolsons have a habit I like of driving up to houses. This we did at Fawley Court. The house has been refaced with very ugly scarlet brick. We had tea at The Red Lion Henley, Vita drinking water. Then on to Newbury. I pointed out the gates of Shaw House, so up that drive we went. Walked round the house which we greatly admired, only deploring the Crittall windows and corridor annexe stuck on to the back. Then to the Sandham Memorial Chapel, which they did not much like and thought should not have been accepted. Stayed at the Chequers Hotel, Newbury. We pool our money and I am made treasurer and pay the bills. Vita went to bed early and H sat up reading a book on Lenin for a review. At dinner we guessed what awful impositions Attlee would announce tomorrow. Harold admits that he foresees no solution to the predicament we are in, and his reason for becoming a socialist is that socialism is inevitable. By joining he feels he may help by tempering it; by remaining outside he can do nothing. He says the sad thing is that no one dislikes the lower orders more than he does. Vita keeps saying how hungry she is. It is true that in hotels one does not get enough to eat.

At 8.30 walking to buy a newspaper I met Vita who said she had just sent a telegram to Ben whose birthday it is today. I said, 'Oh, and not to me? for it is mine too.' So she bought me some lavender-water as a present. A very full day. We drove to Avebury and diverged to see the isolated gate-piers in the field at Hampstead Marshall, for they move me strangely. Then to see Inkpen Rectory. The gardener let us in for the owner was away. H. and V. were delighted with the little formal Le Nôtre layout and H made drawings of it in his pocket-book. We drove up to Littlecote and the gardener said Sir E. Wills was away, so we walked round this house. Large; I did not like the orangery additions to the main front. The place was purring with gardeners. Long herbaceous borders, vast lawns admirably kept, but very much the rich man's garden, tastelessly laid out. I liked the bit where the Kennet tributary flows through a narrow lawny enclave. Emboldened by these adventures we overreached ourselves and met our Waterloo at Ramsbury Manor. Vita drove straight up the drive and stopped before the front door. We admired the house when, lo! the owner, Sir Francis Burdett, wearing yachting jacket, with bibulous face and the very incarnation of Colonel Blimp, descended the steps. He was waving a newspaper. Vita said, 'Shall we drive off?' but it was too late. Colonel Blimp angrily asked us what we wanted. Vita said we had made a mistake and turned to me. I said, 'Littlecote'. After an uncomfortable half-minute we left. Harold squared his shoulders and sat dumb and miserable, trying not to be seen. At Avebury we looked at the stones and went into the museum, very well arranged, and saw the manor and church from the outside. Lunched at Marlborough and drove through Amesbury to Dinton. Were shown over Little Clarendon by Miss Engleheart and pursued by the old mother, aged ninety-two and without memory. The daughter was so sweet to her, and so humble and nice that Vita was much impressed. We walked round Hyde's House and the chauffeur told us about Mr. Philipps's will faked by a strange valet in the hotel at Mentone where he died. The valet added a codicil purporting to leave all Mr. Philipps' property to him. Went to

Dinton House and were given tea by the Y.W.C.A. lady warden. The Nicolsons did not much care for this house, nor Hyde's, preferring Little Clarendon of the three. Piggle Dene sarsen stones property they thought ill-kempt and a discredit to the Trust.

We finally drove to Wilton to have a drink with David Herbert in his strange little garden temple, the front decorated with lavish stone carving. Here we were told that Attlee's news was not at all drastic or disagreeable. From there to Long Crichel, arriving 7.30. Eddy greeted us, Eardley and Desmond being abroad. After dinner a long, interesting conversation after listening to a resumé of Attlee's speech at 9 o'c. Again Harold talked of his political belief that only the Labour Party can save us from the terrible situation we are in. He says all the factories are controlled by Communist shop stewards.

Thursday, 7th August

Extremely tired today. At twelve we left with Eddy for Amesbury where V and H parted from us to lunch with Stephen Tennant. E. and I walked into Amesbury Park which is still full of soldiers who have destroyed the entrance gates and one of John Webb's gate-piers. Park overgrown and desolate. House Victorian; the portico impressive. On the Nicolsons returning we drove to Stourhead. While the others walked round the lake I went to the house and talked to Rennie Hoare. He doesn't know what he wants and is already shifting our things about. When they met him V. and H. thought him sinister. They did not like the house.

Friday, 8th August

Harold worked till eleven when we left. We agreed that Eddy had been the perfect host. Drove to Ven and straight up the drive to the house in Vita's usual abrupt fashion that upsets Harold and now alarms me. There was a woman at the door whom I asked if Sir Hubert Medlycott were about. I thought she was the housekeeper. She took me all round the garden to look for him and failing to find him disclosed that she was the tenant. So I explained who we were and asked if we might see the garden by ourselves. She readily consented and showed us inside the house as well. Then we drove to Montacute where we lunched and walked round the garden, V and H telling me what flowers to plant in the forecourt borders. They were not as enthusiastic over the interior as I had hoped. Harold had to write his *Spectator* article so V. and I left him alone in one of the empty rooms. We drove to Ilchester where I bought a Lowestoft jug from an antique dealer. Had tea at an inn; and on to North Cadbury Court. I prevented Vita driving up to the front door. She does this thing not as a tripper but as an eighteenth-century aristocrat who has a right. We went to the church, and she walked straight from the churchyard into the garden. I rang the bell and Sir Somebody, the owner, a nice old buffer, appeared, munching his tea. He let us in. The entrance front is grey-cold stone, last Elizabethan; the garden front Regency with central semi-circular bay and iron balcony, a surprising contrast. The front hall was done by Avray Tipping very well. A Regency ball-room behind. Drove past Maperton which turned out not to be the house we expected, and quite dull. Vita drove straight through the gate and round the sweep in her inimitable manner. Then back to Montacute, where I am staying in the bedroom Eardley arranged for the public. The Nicolsons stay in Yeovil.

Saturday, 9th August

This morning brought the first signs of autumn. Montacute was silvery with faint dew in the early light. H. and V. called at 9.45 and walked round the outside. They were much moved by the silent beauty of the house. We drove straight to Stoke-sub-Ham and looked at the Little Priory. To my surprise they thought this might prove a worthy property. The little 'great hall' can undoubtedly be made very attractive. Then to Barrington Court which they also found beautiful; and were struck by the Lyles' modern buildings and layout. The gardens have got back to their pre-war standard, the borders ablaze, and only six gardeners. The Lyles, who were away, are living in the red brick wing, the Court proper being empty. At one o'c we reached Knightstones, one mile south of Ottery St. Mary, belonging to Colonel Reggie Cooper, a funny old thing who was at school with Harold, is round as humpty-dumpty, and wears an eyeglass. He bought this house just before the war. It is a plain, granity, Cornish-looking house with carved 'Jacobean' barge-boards, *c.* 1820.

He has made a pretty little garden with fountains, and has sumptuous farm buildings for his Guernsey cows. There is a large great hall with open roof and wide frieze with dolphins. He gave us a superlative luncheon of chicken Maryland with fried bananas, mangoes, junket and Devonshire cream. Cocktails and white wine. He is thinking of re-buying Cothay and wants us to see it on Monday. Then on to Killerton where we had tea with Sir Richard and Lady Acland. We all disliked this property, the garden, the ugly shrubs, the house, the ménage, the dogmatic owners, and two little plain boys. She drove us round the estate after tea. In the house is established the Workers' Transport Company, people smelling of disinfectant, a working woman singing out of tune. We saw no point in this property which is no more beautiful than the surrounding country. The Adam ceilings and marble fireplaces, if they are by Adam, are thin and poor. The Aclands live in a part of the house.

We stayed at the Royal Clarence Hotel, Exeter, and walked through the Cathedral. Fine roof. I liked a tablet in the north aisle to a young organist, dated 1586, the carved marble organ-case of remarkably modern design.

Sunday, 10th August

We had an extra hour's sleep and I went to Mass at eight behind the Cathedral. The priest scolded the congregation fiercely for coming in late. At Forde House Vita bought a silhouette picture for Eddy. Then to Bradley Manor which the Ns thought shockingly neglected: the entrance unkempt, fields a forest of thistles and the paths choked with weeds. Mrs. Woolner's husband, an ungracious, ugly man, showed us round rapidly. The house swarming with babies. We then continued to Saltash Ferry, having driven miles out of our way because Harold ventured upon map-reading which was disastrous. He has no geography sense whatever. We crossed the Tamar in the ferry and drove round Saltash to Trematon Castle. Lunched there with the Claud Russells (*fraises des bois*). All of us disappointed with this plain Regency house within the curtilage of an old castle, where the Black Prince is said to have lodged. The view towards Devonport and *Vanguard* moored there, impressive. Sir Claud is a bit of a stick, distinguished and aloof like most Russells, so Harold says. He enunciates each vowel like Mr. Gladstone masticating. She, half Greek, is pretty but whiney. Thence to Cotehele where the Mount Edgcumbes were assembled to greet us and give us tea. The Ns slightly disappointed with this house too, V. finding it inferior (which it is) to Knole. But that is no disparagement in my eyes. I stayed alone at the Bedford, Tavistock, the Ns going to H.'s brother for the night.

Today gloriously sunny and hot. The Nicolsons do not really care for classical buildings, only liking the Gothic or Elizabethan. Harold is wonderfully untidy. Dust, ash all over his hat and clothes. Vita wears one terra cotta dress, very shiny and long in the skirt, and brown espadrilles, yet is always distinguished and 'grande dame'. We all agreed the Mount Edgcumbes were charming with the most unaffected good manners – 'because they are gentlemen,' Vita added.

At 9.15 I heard Mr. Attlee's speech broadcast in my hotel. In the crowded lounge it was received in grim silence. When over not a soul spoke or made a single comment. Instead, he and she went on with their reading, so typically English. A sign of native phlegm or stupid indifference, who can tell?

Monday, 11th August

Yesterday I felt quite ill. Today better, perhaps because we leave this relaxing climate. At ten the others called for me. I took Vita to a shop I had found and for two guineas bought her a small bag she liked, made of *ersatz* leather. Then we drove over Dartmoor in steamy heat. A cloudless horizon. The police warned us that two convicts had escaped from Broadmoor. This thrilled us. Some of the ponies on the moor have become piebald. At Bradfield [Hall] we drove to the front door. I found Mrs Adams in the garden wearing a large straw hat, beneficent and *jolie-laide*. She showed us the principal rooms and the Ns thought that, although over-restored, the house was worth the Trust holding. Having lunched at a wayside café we eventually found Cothay down devious lanes. I had always heard so much praise of this house that I was disappointed. Since Colonel Cooper's day Sir F. Cook has done atrocious things to it, viz: taking off the crenellation from the gatehouse, chopping the great room into a series of little ones, putting in a hideous window on the garden side and making ridiculous ogival door-heads in the great hall. The beautiful garden laid out by Col. Cooper has sadly gone to seed, but could be reinstated. A great deal of over-restoration has happened inside and out. Inside the only good features left are the great hall and the frescoes.

From Cothay we drove to Coleridge Cottage, Nether Stowey, which interested Harold. Here we met the Agent. Then to East Quantoxhead which from the outside looks like Princetown, Vita said. To her chagrin H. and I were pusillanimous, and refused to go in. The vulgarity of Glastonbury so disappointed and disgusted H. who expected it to be like Tintern Abbey that he would not look at the ruins. We reached Wells for dinner and stayed at The Swan. After dinner we walked to the Bishop's Palace, the Cathedral and Vicar's Close. We were shocked to find the Bishop's moat a clutter of waste paper. From a distance we thought it was white water lilies.

Tuesday, 12th August

Left The Swan Inn where we had been treated with kindness. The food in this and all the hotels however is infamous. We looked at Tor Hill in good trim. Drove to Nunney and admired the Castle. It is a darling. Struck by the batter of the drum towers. Batter always conveys strength. Then to Mells, spending some time in the church and churchyard. Moved by the sad end of the Horner family with the death of Edward in the first war, and impressed by his equestrian statue by Munnings, the Eric Gill lettering, and the inscription of Raymond Asquith's tablet on the plain wall within the tower. We felt that this family had had something to contribute to life and art until the end. I did not admire Lutyens's tomb for the McKennas although nothing he did is ignoble. Drove on to Lacock and lunched at the Red Lion, badly. Then went round the monastic remains of the Abbey with a guide who was good. Remarked on the unkempt condition of the cloister garth, and the cobwebs and untidiness of the walks. Miss Talbot showed us round the house. The Ns were pleased with Lacock, though not with its condition. Then to Great Chalfield where the Fullers showed us round the Manor. Place very spick and span. Then to Corsham to tea with Norah Methuen, Paul being away painting. She took infinite pains and was most kind. Vita never drinks tea and has lemon squash and soda water whenever she can. The ceilings of the state rooms have all been re-whitened by Holborough of Tetbury and the damask curtains in the Saloon and covers of the Chippendale chairs beautifully repaired by Norah's own fingers. She has covered them with a fine net, dyed the same red as the damask beneath. The Nicolsons did not even pretend to be interested in these eighteenth-century rooms.

At Bath we stay at the Lansdown Grove Hotel, very comfortably. After dinner walked up the hill to call on Mrs. Knollys, whose complaints and too evident possessiveness of Eardley horrified V.

Wednesday, 13th August

We were treated with almost nauseating respect by the proprietress of this hotel who thanked the Nicolsons for their patronage and even me for my 'graciousness in saying I had slept well'. Harold is childishly embarrassed by this sort of remark; hates it and blushes with rage.

This morning we sauntered in Bath and were revolted by the drabness of the Pump Room where there should have been gay music and inviting coffee and biscuits. Instead no efforts made of any kind. The Ns pronounced the sulphur water horrid. Vita liked the Circus best of all the Bath sites. After luncheon we drove past Solsbury Hill to Dyrham and looked at the church. Then called on Lady Islington who showed us the house. She was very active and bustling. A 'Soul', she is outspoken, amusing, hard and thoroughly Edwardian. I quite see how Stuart is fascinated by her. She is leaving Dyrham because the Blathwayts are returning. She says she hates them and is going to take away everything that she put into the house, even the baths. She said casting an eye at me, 'He looks disapproving. Is he hostile?' Next we drove to Iron Acton, and Thornbury and Berkeley Castles, which last H. and V. raved about. Me it does not move. I like castles to have emphasis, verticality which this dumpy structure lacks. Then to Horton Court for tea with the Wills who did not seem prepared for us. They are a sweet couple and were both bewildered. The N.s were not greatly taken with this house. Then after several misadventures in the Stroud Valley we reached Nether Lypiatt at 7.45, and quickly saw over. Mrs. Woodhouse away, dying in Brighton. I think this is one of, if not *the* most covetable

house in England. It combines the classical with the picturesque. The garden layout is perfect. We dined in Stroud late but
rather well, for a change, and stayed tonight at The New Inn
Gloucester. After ten when the non-residents left, we sat
drinking in the courtyard under the stars. At eleven Vita began
to write an article for the *Observer*.

Thursday, 14th August

The New *is* pretty. The galleries are overhung with weeping
creeper, and the walls behind the galleries have been successfully painted a deep, bold red. Vita, having finished her article,
was down for breakfast before me. Harold likewise had read
books for his reviews before breakfast. We all put the Cathedral very high on our list – the stout round piers are asking
to be embraced. Some of the Jacobean monuments are
painted. We liked the lady leaning on her arm in the Lady
Chapel with her blue eyes, and the incomparably beautiful
effigy of Edward II. Oh, why do they not remove the opaque
Milanese glass from the cloisters? We set off for Hayles Abbey
and Harold was appalled by the condition of this property.
Then to Stanway where Vita demanded to see the house. We
walked straight through the house to the garden beyond.
Stanton we saw and Chipping Campden where we had the
nastiest of all luncheons at the smart hotel. It being one of the
hottest days we were given hot soup from a tin, stringy steaks,
uncooked vegetables, trifle. Of all this V. and I hardly ate
anything, neither of us indeed having eaten much at Gloucester, not being inclined to face the sausages. At 2.30 we arrived
at Hidcote. To our dismay we saw the table laid for four.
Lawrie Johnston had expected us and said rather tartly that he
had provided a succulent meal. This blow was almost more
than we could bear. Vita was given innumerable cuttings,
Lawrie J having relented. Garden pronounced lovely. We
arrived at Charlecote at four. I warned the Ns that Brian
Fairfax-Lucy was a dress reformer. Behold, he appeared in a
pair of tight little white shorts, white sandshoes, a white satin
shirt open at the neck, and a blue ribbon tied in a bow at his
navel. The Ns decided that of all the people we had so far met
the Lucys were the nicest. They considered the gardens here a
disgrace. At six we listened to the repeat broadcast about the
National Trust which we had missed on Sunday. The best part

was the feature about Charlecote and Brian's admirable speech, he sitting with us in the room listening. This is curious and to me still a bit uncanny.

We stayed at The Falcon Inn, Stratford-on-Avon, a good olde-worlde hostelry and went to the Merchant of Venice which was atrocious. Beatrix Lehmann a poor Portia, Shylock not too bad, but the young men all mannered and chi-chi, the décor shoddy modern.

So hot under the eaves that I slept badly. Vita was asked for her autograph on leaving the hotel. We drove to Packwood. The weather overcast and almost drizzling. On arrival the sun came out and the day turned into the hottest of all. The Ns rather liked this place and its contents and admired the scrupulous way it is kept up. They liked Joshua Rowley but thought he looked unhealthy. They shook hands and talked to Weaver the gardener, who said he was a wireless fan of Harold's. V. and I scolded Harold afterwards for not relishing this reference. They greatly admired the way Weaver arranged the flowers and decided that, so long as we could afford the bedding out and had so good a gardener, we should leave the garden as it is. We lunched at Banbury and spent the last money from the pool. Looked at Boarstall Tower and Long Crendon. At Slough I was dropped, and we said goodbye. They were sweet and kind in saying I had been a good guide. I kissed Vita on the cheek. I have grown to love her. She is an adorable woman. I have enjoyed this tour immensely.

Found a charming letter at home from Peter Scott telling me about the way Kathleen's remains were dealt with. She was cremated and the three of them took the ashes and scattered them, Lord K. reading Wordsworth. The sun was bright. There were few people bathing from the beach. This was at Sandwich. It was a pagan, idyllic and appropriate ceremony, just what she would have liked.

Stayed at home for the weekend happily, working on a review for the *Spectator*. Saw James this evening. He tells me he is in love with a paragon of a girl aged twenty-two. I am not sure that I believe him, but I daresay he may marry quite soon, but disastrously. This is my jolly little forecast. Then Henry Reed dined with me at Brooks's. His too fulsome praise of my book of which he has read the proofs, makes me question his intelligence.

Tuesday, 19th August

Travel agents telephoned that they have booked me a seat in an aeroplane to Milan on the 25th September. Dr. Pevsner lunched at Brooks's. He gave me four alternative subjects about Robert Adam to write for the *Architectural Review*. This man, whom hitherto I have pictured as dry, pedantic and rather carping, proved to be friendly, eager to assist, and encouraging.

Wednesday, 20th August

Went to Hampstead in the afternoon to call on Mrs. Angeli, the daughter of William, niece of Dante Gabriel and Christina Rossetti and granddaughter of Ford Madox Brown. She suffers from heart, is about seventy, very frail and ill. She lives with a daughter, very Italian in looks. Mrs Angeli is surrounded with heaps of books, piles of furniture, china and framed drawings by Dante Gabriel, in confusion indescribable, her house having been destroyed by a bomb, and she and her daughter now lodging in a clergyman's house. She offers to lend us a quantity of pictures for Wightwick Manor. She told me she owned Shelley's sofa, bought by him in Pisa and slept on by him the night before he died (why and how?). After his death Mary gave it to Leigh Hunt, who gave it to Trelawny, who gave it to William Rossetti.

Went this evening to Westminster Abbey to see Henry VII's tomb. The burnished bronze pilasters at the four corners, the angels, the bronze – or are they black marble? – wreaths. How strange too are the Darnley and Buckingham tombs on either side, both so proud, extravagant and meant to endure. And so they have by a miracle survived the war. Yet 'not marble, nor the gilded monuments of princes shall outlive this powerful rhyme'. And Shakespeare will be read when they are reduced to molten sludge and slime. I looked too at Hugh Easton's RAF window. It is true the colours glow and give promise of eternal life, but the design is somewhat banal, confused and laboured in a neo-Pre-Raphaelitish sort of way. I like the silver altar rails and two candelabra. These are the dear Professor's [Richardson] work.

Thursday, 21st August

Today is my Uncle Robert's birthday; and he died thirty years ago, cannon-fodder he was, and his name is known to a very few. Yet I shall remember him.

Friday, 22nd August

Motored home this afternoon. It was fine, warm and sunny. My parents were sitting under the apple tree drinking gin and orange. Then Deenie came and we dined at the long teak table on the west side of the cottage watching the sunset. My father declared he had never been happier in his life.

Saturday, 23rd August

Went to Overbury Court. I was late and Ruby Holland-Martin had gone out riding. His mother showed me the collection, formed by the father, of old brass which might do for East Riddlesden Hall. Some of the ink pots are almost elegant. Old Mrs. Holland-Martin deplored the moral decadence of the English people. How could I respond but by sighing sympathetically? Called at Harvington Hall, Little Moreton Hall and slept at The Macclesfield Arms Hotel, where I was given four courses of which lobster was one.

Sunday, 24th August

At Lyme [Park] was conducted round the house by the Town Clerk of Stockport, by name Morgan. Considering the vast hordes of visitors who come here – 45,000 into the house alone since mid-June – it looks fairly well, and there is not much that jars. I lunched with the Morgans in their house, Belmount, a large substantial villa, the rooms painted diarrhoea, stippled walls, lincrusta ceilings; furniture wicker and leatherette. 'Tasty' and comfortable. Huge luncheon, badly cooked. An important alderman and wife to meet me. All very polite, kind and dull, *dull*. Weak coffee in the 'lounge' and dreary platitudes about cricket and sport. Yet I liked Mrs. Morgan, a sweet, bright, pretty woman and keen housewife, aged fifty, with grey hair, permed. The alderman and wife have just been to Switzerland for a holiday and were full of complaints that they were not allowed to spend more than £75. Ten years ago they had never heard of Switzerland or £75.

At last, party over, they drove me back to Lyme, and I was entreated to witness the scene at the height of its numbers on a beautiful summer day. It was a nightmare of crawling, shirt-sleeved, smelly, happy people. All behaving extremely well. There was one moment only when I hated them, seeing and hearing them stamping up the grand staircase like a herd of untameable buffaloes. The furniture looks drear enough behind the ropes, but what can we do when there are such crowds? I left at four and stopped at Wythenshawe Hall. This small park likewise crawling with and trampled thin by people. A melancholy, over-restored, black-and-white house, with a red brick Georgian far side. But shut up and empty. Then drove to Hale Manor, near Widnes, to stay with Peter and Monica Fleetwood-Hesketh in a very pretty 1700 red brick house. We walked to the ruins of Hale Hall, the 1806 facade by Nash standing alone, gaunt above a flat stretch of land to the Mersey, the starkness spoilt by a row of strident red-roofed villas on the skyline.

Monday, 25th August

This morning walked with Peter down to the Mersey, gazing across at the chimneys of Runcorn and the great iron bridge-conveyance, called a transporter, of Widnes. There are a pretty white lighthouse and cottage on the shore below Hale where the coast runs towards Liverpool. After luncheon I drove the Heskeths to Speke Hall where we were met by the Town Clerk, the City Engineer and a member of the Finance Committee, all smelling strongly of drink. I was not at all satisfied that this house was being looked after by the right committee, and gathered that the inside of the house comes exclusively within the control of the City Engineer. At present all the contents of Miss Watt's trustees are still in the house waiting to be sold. There is much that is really horrid, oak furniture black as pitch. But Peter rightly remarked, the point about these old

Lancashire houses is that the rooms should be filled with black oak and be 'rather terrifying'. I think it would be a mistake entirely to replant the wood between the house and sea. There is still a definite country house flavour about Speke, marooned though it be, for it is wonderfully sheltered from the aeroplane factories and housing estates around it. After tea we motored in Peter's Dodgem, made in 1929, to Ince Blundell Hall, the home of Mrs Weld Blundell. It is lived in by her husband and daughter, whose name is Montagu, and the brother-in-law, also Weld Blundell, born Weld, and his children, called Weld. It is a romantic Papist establishment. The Pantheon, built *circa* 1810, is marvellous, filled with Roman statuary collected by a Mr. Blundell of the day. It must be one of the finest statuary collections left in private hands. The acoustics in the Pantheon are so bad that you cannot hear a word distinctly. The picture-gallery and dining-room, added *circa* 1850, are in the eighteenth-century style. The main portion of the house is George I, and might be by Talman. Unfortunately the windows have plate glass. We were given cocktails before leaving.

Some of the new Liverpool houses being built are admirable, of decent materials, neat designs, especially those near Knowsley.

Tuesday, 26th August

The Heskeths are very late people They dine at nine, and there is lots to drink. Last night two bottles of champagne and bed after one. Even then I had to insist upon retiring, contrary to Peter's inclination, I think. His ideas about N. Trust properties are absolutely right, just as his taste is faultless. He is an escapist from realities, a civilized being. At 10.45 we left for Rufford Old Hall where we were met by the chairman of the local committee, the architect, the curator Ashcroft, and old Jarrett, who spoke to me about his book on Shakespeare which is still unpublished. Rufford looked well kept and tidy. The armour needed cleaning, and the varnish removing. We went on to the roof and examined the leads and stone tiles. Peter and I lunched with the chairman, Mr. Gosselin, and the architect at the Park Hotel, Preston.

After luncheon we motored to Ribchester, up the Ribble valley. Here the country at once improves and Lancashire ceases to be industrial, and becomes rural. The mountains are

205

in the background. The new curator, installed in the dismal Museum, grumbled about the conditions. Considering that she has one small room to keep tidy I was not very sympathetic. The state of the ruins is poor indeed, but work on them is to start in the autumn. From here we drove to Parrox Hall, across the Fylde of Lancashire, a district distinguished by the trimness of its coverts and its white-washed houses. Parrox Hall has great charm. It too is white-washed; stands in a miniature park with, alas, some nasty development close to. It is a typical small squire's homestead. Probably late Elizabethan, or Jacobean, with low, latticed windows, and a stone Gothic portico added to the front *circa* 1820. It is cheerful and homely. The hall has a flagged floor, dark panelling with lozenge pattern panels, a stairway leading directly off it, and much dark oak furniture. Among the furniture in this room are several late seventeenth-century chairs with original leather seats and backs inscribed with a crown, brass studs and finials, said to have come from Portugal. Several four-post beds, one very fine Jacobean bed in which Cromwell is said to have slept before Prestonpans. Each bedroom leads to the next, for there are no passageways. Much of the oak is made up and heavily varnished in the Lancashire fashion. Mrs. Elletson, mother of the owner, lives here with her unmarried sister, a Miss Philipps. The owner was abroad. There are two bachelor cousins, aged seventy-six and eighty-five, staying. They have stayed here every summer since they were boys. Mrs. Elletson is nervous about the Trust and asked sad little questions, like: 'Would her sister still be allowed to paint in the garden studio?' 'Would the servants be allowed to stay on?' Would they not? One feels that the mode of life at Parrox Hall has not changed since the house was built.

After tea we left at 6.30. I dropped Peter at Lancaster station and drove through the romantic Lune valley, past Hornby Castle, Melling, Thurland and Kirkby. Stayed the night at Barbon Manor, a large, baronial, 1870 house high above the village, remotely and beautifully situated. Roger Fulford lives here with his wife and step-son, Lord Shuttleworth. The house teems with sons and daughters. After dinner we talked politics. Roger told his experiences as a Liberal candidate at the last election and in 1931, both times unsuccessful. When I gave vent to my right-wing views they were horrified, but amused. Mrs F. said she admired my honesty. Barbon is a Liberal stronghold.

I wrote letters this morning in Roger's eyrie at the top of the house overlooking the Lune valley, where he works. Then he took me in his car to Dent, a perfect, small mediaeval village, or townlet. Roger drives as slowly and carefully as he speaks. He recounted the Shuttleworth story: how the old Lord died during the war; his two sons were both killed in the 1914-18 war. The elder son's two sons were killed in the last war. The present Lord's younger half-brother, Mrs. Fulford's son, a Lyttleton, was also killed in the last war. The present Lord himself lost both his legs in battle. He lives here and at Gawthorpe, crippled by death duties.

We lunched at The Sun Inn, Dent, which is still governed by twenty-four 'Statesmen'. Its streets are cobbled, its cottages all of cob, painted white. It has a large church and a fountain. Open country runs up to it from all sides. It seems to be the end of the world. We approached it by a rough lane along Barbon Beck, over the mountains. On my return I packed and left. I enjoyed this visit immensely. Mrs. F. pressed me to come again – very kind considering the polarity of our political views. She is intelligent, vivacious, handsome and some years older than Roger.

I stay tonight with the Bruce Thompsons at Troutbeck.

Thursday, 28th August

I wrote many letters this morning. Bruce motored me on a tour of N.T. properties in the Lake District. Cartmel Gate House was first on the list. In the church is a 1620 rood screen with classical entablature and baroque pillars with vine leaves entwined. Then Hawkshead, where we lunched. Then Hill Top, Beatrix Potter's house, with all her personal belongings lying around loose, the prey to any thief. Yet it is the best showhouse of an eminent person I have seen, still of course fresh and new. But what will it be like when Beatrix Potter is no longer revered and the little cottage is worn out, and the carpets and rugs threadbare? And on we went to Borran's Field, Ambleside, Town End. Bruce, who is a master of show-manship, the most meticulous of guardians and the oldest member of the staff, took my criticisms, such as they were, with amused tolerance.

We dined at Windermere and called at Sir Samuel Scott's after dinner. He is a snobbish little man speaking with dis-approval of so common a man as Lord Woolton being elected to Brooks's club.

Terribly upset by the announcement that the basic petrol ration is to be cut off and all foreign travel to cease.

Friday, 29th August

Sent Mama a birthday telegram from Northumberland. Went over to Huntingstile, the Wordsworths' house on the west side of Grasmere. This is a Victorian stone-built house, ugly and large, which looks north-east and gets little sun in the summer and none in the winter. I left my car, and Gordon and Doreen Wordsworth drove me to Hotbanks Farm and Housesteads on the Roman Wall, and a wonderful drive it was, up to Thirl-mere past Saddleback, to Penrith, over the moors towards Hexham and the Allen Valley to Hotbanks. Here we lunched under a wall. Gordon had business at the Farm and Doreen and I walked upon the Roman Wall to Housesteads Camp. It was superb tracing the undulating line of the wall along the ridge of the wild rolling country, now a thick raised embankment with a flat path-like top, now a thin snake. The Fort is one of the most evocative Roman remains in England, for vast excavated foundations survive, gate-piers and two water tanks, their stone sides worn from the women washing and scrubbing linen, their lead joints, the runnels of the latrines. The Fort stands on a sloping hill and is impressive seen from the road. There are likewise remains of terraces on the opposite slope, seen from the Camp.

It was so hot we stopped for bottles of mineral lemonade, drinking in the car in shirt sleeves. We visited Allen Banks and walked through the wooded ravine. There were people pick-nicking on the rocks in the middle of the river, which is so dry. Drove back through Ullswater, looking at the new property at Glencoyne, and dining at Huntingstile. I went back to Trout-beck at ten. Received a letter from my bank that I was overdrawn £400 which depressed me very much indeed, for I thought I had been reducing, not increasing my overdraft.

Bruce Thompson and I motored in my car to Armathwaite Hall Hotel where he had a directors' meeting. I went on alone to Cockermouth to see Wordsworth's House. It is let as an antique shop of a superior sort, and so is well furnished. Apart from its association it is a good house built in 1745. Plain outside but untouched. Interior unaltered too. A particularly good drawing-room upstairs with pedimented doorcases. To think of the Wordsworth family living here in a room which to their simple taste must have been ornate and ostentatious. The garden with raised terrace is as the poet knew it. I bought for £3 a set of steel fireplace implements, date about 1800. Condition perfect. Felt impelled to spend because of the bank's letter. Bruce and I motored in the afternoon to Keswick and at Stable Point on Derwentwater took the Trust's boat from the wood-man and rowed to Kempsholme Island and Lord's Island, where we landed. Then to St. Nichol's landing-point. Here we picked up two spinster girl friends of Bruce's and rowed to another small island and ate sandwiches for tea. We left them there and I rowed from St. Nichol's back to Stable Point. I can think of nothing more sublime than this lake, surrounded by steep mountains, lawns sloping to the shore, Derwent Isle woods and St. Herbert's Isle Woods. We motored to the Druids Circle. This miniature Stonehenge is not only roman-tic but 'aweful' in the eighteenth-century meaning of the word. On a small, flat plateau it seems to be the centre of the universe, for it forms the hub of a vast circumference of mountain tops and is solemn and sanctified by the ancient folk who frequented it, not knowing anything of the world beyond their horizon, across the barrier that encircled them. I stay tonight and the following night with the Wordsworths at Huntingstile.

After dinner Gordon read, extremely well, Canon Rawns-ley's conversations with old peasants and Wordsworth's but-ler, all of whom had known the poet. He pronounced very skilfully their own words in dialect, which he can speak. They conveyed a convincing picture of the old poet, gruff, aloof, moody, and mumbling and bumbling to himself as he roamed the dales by lamplight. Gordon told me that, when as children he and his brother and sisters lived with their parents at Whitemoss, American visitors used to beg his father, who was a parson, to be allowed to shake hands with him as Words-worth's great-grandson, for a fee. The father hated these attentions and would dismiss the officious Americans with distaste. But the children, whenever they had the chance, used to indulge in these little transactions themselves, receiving small tips for the privilege of allowing a pat on the head.

Sunday, 31st August

Motored to Ambleside for Mass. The young priest gave us a whigging for not turning to God in our present extremities. How did he know that I don't? Gordon and I went to Allan Bank at 12.30 and Mrs. Rawnsley, widow of Canon R., one of the co-founders of the Trust, showed me the house. The Wordsworths lived here before moving to Rydal Mount. It is a plain house, modernised, ugly and spoilt. Mrs. R. has a collection of Wordsworth manuscripts, and portraits of him and Southey. She is about seventy-five, very intelligent, talkative and well informed. I liked her. She came to lunch at Hungtingstile and then took me to Grasmere churchyard. She told me the yews were planted by Wordsworth. Showed me the Greens' grave, but would not go up to the Wordsworths' because, I suppose, of the trippers. Took me inside the church with its curious arches and superimposed arcades which divide the two aisles. All but one old pew have gone. The poet's mural tablet is by Woolner. She then took me to Dove Cottage, quite a humble little place with a tiny garden. As she says, the vast numbers of visitors have dispelled much of the sanctity of the place. There is little inside, except the wainscot-ing and doors, that is original. The kitchen is minute and pitch dark. How they all, with children, squeezed in is difficult to imagine. Then she showed me the museum, but one must be alone to study the letters. Mrs. Rawnsley has a dark, swarthy face with suspicion of a moustache. She thinks highly of Gordon.

After tea we walked round the lake by Loughrigg Terrace. The shadows began to lengthen, the bells of Grasmere church to ring. It was very still and beautiful; but there were too many people on the hills and the road. Rydal Water has tall rushes at the shore's edge. Gordon loves this district passionately, but Doreen hates it, and this is very distressing for him. It does not predict domestic content.

I left Grasmere at 9.30 on as beautiful a morning as I could wish
for: the lake absolutely glassy, a faint mist obscuring the far
shore. I motored through Lancashire, diverging just a little to
have a look at Borwick Hall, near Carnforth, happily inhabited and cared for, and stopping at Lancaster, of which the
bridge is by Carr. Lunched at Wigan where I left my camera in
the hotel, only remembering it when I got to Wellington at tea
time. Before Wigan at the approach of the dreadful industrial
country, the sky darkened. I thought storm clouds portended
much-needed rain, but not a bit of it, only the filthy smoke
which gathers in the sky here every day of the year, fair or foul.
However before Wigan I diverged to Chorley to see Astley
Hall, a truly remarkable house, Jacobean but altered in 1666.
Very well kept up, both grounds and house. My only adverse
comment the turnstiles at the front door into the hall. The
astounding features are the ceiling and frieze of the high hall,
and the ceiling of the adjacent drawing-room. These ceilings
in Wren-style compartments have stucco foliage in the very
highest relief, and putti dangling from them in the round. The
putti are of large size bearing arrows, and slung, as it were,
invisibly from the soffits. The drawing-room ceiling is low
and these heavy ornamentations are quite oppressive,
although so beautifully fashioned. It is remarkable to find this
gem of a house in such lugubrious and polluted surroundings.
The country south of Lancashire is in colour burnt straw. I got
to Wickhamford at seven to find the garden, dry, parched and
sad. Mama was in the orchard watering the beds.

I left at eleven and after Chipping Norton drove straight to
North Crawley where Mr. Chester now lives in the Old
Rectory. He has let Chicheley to a school. He and his wife
showed me ten chairs of walnut, parcel gilt in a rich manner,
temp. 1730 with original gros-point backs and seats. The
needlework is in excellent condition and the colours are
unfaded. It must have been kept covered all these years when
not in use. I have never seen chairs so lovely. There is likewise
one gilt console table of Kent style, which is very fine.
Afterwards I motored to Chicheley and looking at the outside

met the headmaster. I said, 'I am afraid I am trespassing.' He was in his shirt-sleeves about to garden. Nevertheless he showed me all round, taking me into the house. There is an entrance hall with marble arcade, a ceiling canvas supposedly painted by Kent, and a wide staircase leading from the hall. Many of the Chester looking-glasses and pictures are left in the room. For a boys' preparatory school the house is exceptionally clean and well kept. I congratulated the master like anything.

Found at the office a parcel from darling Vita, containing present of a silver pencil with engraved inscription, 'J. from V. August 5-15 1947', a souvenir of our tour. Nothing could have given me more delight. Dined at Sibyl's. Not much fun. Jamesey walked into the flat while I was in the bath to say goodbye for he is off to France tomorrow morning for three weeks. He said with a wry look that Maurice had married on the 1st and now it had happened, in spite of his having engineered it, he rather regretted it.

At 11.30 I went to see Lady Astor in Hill Street at her request. Although over sixty she is a great beauty. White hair, healthy complexion and vital movements. She has dignity and deportment, in spite of her vulgarisms. She wanted to impress upon me the necessity of keeping Miss O'Sullivan at Blickling. As she advanced into the room she said, 'Why are you a convert to that awful Catholicism? Do you not bitterly regret it?' I replied, 'Not in the very least.' She said, 'My greatest fear and horror is Communism. Roman Catholicism breeds it.' I replied, 'Roman Catholicism is the only hope left in the world of combating Communism which I too abominate.' She said, 'It is only Catholic countries that go Communist because of the poverty and discontent fostered by the priests. No Protestant countries become dictatorships.' I protested vigorously, and she hissed, 'How dare you say so? You wicked child. Philip Lothian left them. He saw how evil they were.' All this was delivered with vehemence and good humour. She said we must meet again and have a proper battle. Then she said, 'You are in earnest and you feel passionately, and I like that.' As I said goodbye I replied, 'And you care passionately, and that is why I have always admired you.' It was a curious little encounter.

I bought six plates and dishes and went on a shopping spree in spite of my terrible financial straits. Perhaps because of them. Also returned to Mama the £100 she had generously lent me.

Monday, 8th September

Gerald du Gouray invited me to a cocktail party at Claridge's given by the Regent of Iraq in his sumptuous suite. The Regent and Queen Mother want to buy a house in the country, but near London, for the minority of the young King, now at school in England. The Regent with whom I spoke for some time – painfully – is rather short, well-built, fairly handsome, with pleasant brown eyes. He has a roundish face and is neatly dressed in a smart brown suit, very western. I could of course think of nowhere for him off the cuff, but promised that, if given full particulars of his needs, would look around. A stiff sort of function, like all royal occasions.

Tuesday, 9th September

Had planned to dine at home and work. But a young man, by the name of Peter Tunnard, rang up asking to see me. He wants a job with the N.T. I asked him for a drink and he came at 6.30. He is about twenty-six, dark, personable. He stayed till eight so I asked him to dine. He knows Rome and was able to give me information and advice. Result: work went by the board. After dinner I walked with him to Dickie Buckle's house where he is staying, and I did not get back till midnight. Enjoyable evening. Oh, the weakness of my resolutions.

Friday, 12th September

Feeling unaccountably – on the other hand perhaps account-ably – depressed; toothache at nights, fear of the aeroplane and fear, just a slight one, that if not careful I may never fall in love again. Mindy Bacon lunched. He is enormous in size, a head taller than me and doubly broad. We talked of Gainsborough

Old Hall. During the evening, dining alone I became very sad and unhappy, a rare thing to happen to me these days. All this weekend I have worked at a beastly article for the *Architectural Review*, which bores me stiff.

Sunday, 14th September

At tea time Peter Tunnard came and we drove to Polesden Lacey, then on to Midi's. She has just come out of a nursing home, and is very thin but pretty, and rather shaky on her feet, poor dear. Peter and I dined at home. I feel guilty that someone as young as he and with a splendid war record should be without a job. Although worried he is very cheerful about it.

Thursday, 18th September

Old Mrs. George Keppel has died. It was curious to see that little, bent old woman scuttling about the Ritz this year, with the white face of a grey mare, and to know that she was King Edward VII's magnificent, upstanding, beautiful, powerful mistress. A ghost from a past more remote from today than the day of Marie Antoinette from hers.

I motored Eardley to Stourhead where we spent the afternoon. Mrs. Hoare at home, looking extremely lost and harrassed, arranging dahlias in servants'-hall pots. She has no taste. At least E. and I decided upon a plan of campaign: we would get the experts, Professor Waterhouse, Leigh Ashton, Mrs. Esdaile, Margaret Jourdain, to go through all the contents. When we had their advice then we would do the arranging of the state-rooms ourselves, which will, I think, be great fun, provided Rennie Hoare leaves us alone.

We drove on to Taunton where I left my car to be repainted. I chose dark blue with black wings which sounds chic enough. Returned to London with E., had a delicious supper in his flat at eleven and walked home.

Saturday, 20th September

To the office and then lunched with Margaret and Ivy alone. Talking of Charlotte Bonham-Carter, with whom they had just stayed, they remarked: 'She never will say a single disagreeable thing about anyone. A most tiresome woman to be with.' Ivy has found an American publisher whose agent over here treats her just as if she were one of her own characters of fifty years ago. 'Of course there will be no drink if you come to my flat.' And, 'If you lunch at this restaurant you can be sure no one will speak to you.' But, Ivy says, the trouble is that she has no biographical material. 'There just is none.'

Sunday, 21st September

This weekend I have read a second book by Stratton on the Italian Renaissance. Spoke to Joan and Garrett Moore who are flying to Rome the same day as I leave, but by a different plane, they flying direct. It is very disappointing. A girl came to tea called K. Hopkins. She rang me up yesterday having seen a letter by me in *The Times* and remembering me from Grenoble days where, she says, we were great friends. She came, and still I could not remember her at all. This, she complained, was no compliment. I am suffering from toothache, and will have to lose two teeth, so Mr Boutwood informs me with glee in his eye.

Monday, 22nd September

Bridget dine with me at home. It is the first time I have seen her for weeks. When I do see her after an interval I realise how devoted I am to her, in spite of her incessant grumbles. She started off with complaints against Michael for preferring the Messel family to his own. 'Well, perhaps he does,' I said.

Tuesday, 23rd September

Sibyl lunched alone with me at the Ritz. She had thought she might be staying in Rome too but, rather to my relief, the project is off. She is difficult to hear. Her voice is indistinct and her poor head is bent downwards. She has given me an introduction to Berenson in Florence, and says I must go and see him. She told me that before the war the Ritz management called her in to redecorate the hotel, but she gave them a straight talk and made them promise they would never touch the interior which had more distinction than any other hotel in London. If they did, she would make life hideous for them by ventilating their philistinism in the press, the House of Lords and Commons and over the wireless. We owe her a great debt.

John Wilton dined with me at Brooks's. He was very charming but has grown stout. I gave him warning to take heed or his jaw would become as pronounced as Lord Fairhaven's. He thinks he will not rent Coleshill after all and wishes to buy Trafalgar.

Wednesday, 24th September

Lunched at the Ritz with the Pryce-Joneses. Sat between Poppy P.-J. and Karen Lancaster, and had nothing to say to either. Osbert L. was present and Princess Marthe Bibesco, dressed very oddly, her flat hat entwined in a green veil which issued therefrom and like a waterfall enveloped the rest of her person. Her thick legs were encased in black stockings over which she wore bottines. She has an intelligent, whimsical face and talks learnedly of French literature. I went to the dentist again. Mr. Boutwood is busy viciously killing two nerves in two teeth.

Charles Fry, with whom I had a date to dine last night but who was delayed by the Queen Elizabeth, made me go to his flat at seven for a drink. He is back from the States for three weeks, then returns for good. I thought it politic to see him. He was exactly the same as before, drunken and boastful. He says I must stay with him next year in New York – I would sooner die than do such a thing – and write a book on America. Why not on the world? I have spent little time in packing, hoping to supplement a scanty wardrobe in Rome.

Thursday, 25th September

At 4.40 Emily, good soul, called me to say my bath was ready. It was pitch dark but a hired Rolls came punctually. I picked up a dear old lady, but at Terminal House discovered that we were on different aeroplanes. Mine did not leave the airport till eight. A sunny morning. From the air one sees that London is sprinkled with reservoirs, as though the metropolis were in flood. The fields and hills of Kent are wreathed in mist like dirty snow, but I watch the sun literally scoop the mist away. Over Deal we run through a dark storm and there are splashes of rain against the glass windows. I think how lumbering and slow aeroplanes are, like old buses. I wonder they do not take longer than they do. Apart from the clicking of ears I am unaffected by change of altitude. In an hour and a quarter we circle over Brussels and land. And there is Geoff Lemprière, with whom I have barely time to exchange greetings and be handed by him two yellow pills to take over the Alps. There is no time for breakfast, and I have coffee and an apple at a bar. We immediately change into another Sabena, rather an old machine, and in no time are off. The journey is foolproof, yet there is much hanging about. I am writing this in the air over France, at a great altitude, rising every minute over dense forests. It is getting cold. In spite of the height we are not in the sun, and there is a leaden canopy overhead. I wish they would bring me something to eat.

We find ourselves over the Rhône because they say the weather is too bad to risk the Alps. Here it is clouding over and becoming misty. How long the Rhône is. We follow it for quite three-quarters of an hour, and as there are hills on either side it is not very agreeable. We seem to be on a level with the tops of them. Passing Marseilles and over the sea it becomes stormy. Angry purple clouds gather. It is becoming bumpy. Many passengers are sick, and it is considered a bad journey. Somehow I don't feel at all sick. After the bumps it is smooth again. There is not the horrid rhythmical roughness of the sea. Then we turn back and there is some difficulty landing at Marseilles at 2.45. We stay at the airport till 6.30. Every kind of inanity takes place. All our luggage from the aeroplane is taken to the *douane* and the French go through our bags, which are then returned to the plane. At last rooms are found for us at Cassis, fifty kilometres away. The bus driver loses the way, and we do not arrive till nine. We dine and are sent to a tiny lodgement to sleep. A terrible storm gets up in the night and at 6 a.m. we are woken up with a bowl of nasty acorn coffee and hard black pellets of bread.

Friday, 26th September

All the telephone wires are on the ground and the battery of the bus has been allowed to run down. We cannot therefore go to Marseilles to catch a train, and the weather is too bad to fly, so we may have to stay here another night. At seven I walk into the town. All the fishermen's boats in the quay are smashed by

217

the storm. It is a nice little old town, endurable no doubt in sunny weather, but with no buildings of any distinction. There is hopelessness, inefficiency and depravity in the faces and mien of the French here. Many of my fellow passengers say they will never again travel by air.

This unexpected visit to Cassis is like a story by Rose Macaulay. We are cooped up in a horrid hotel, cut off from the world. Inevitably the party separates into little groups of companionable malcontents. The nun, to whom our misfortunes are attributed, is left severely alone. So is the Roumanian suffering from asthma. My group, which is by far the best, consists of an American of Italian extraction who speaks indifferent English, is President of some international company, cashes cheques and drinks steadily; an English-born girl, Mrs Gregory, married to an American pilot, and a Russian lady, age about fifty, who lives in Milan. We become intimate friends and are quickly on Christian name terms. With one it looks as though I shall be on still more intimate terms before another twelve hours have elapsed.

In the afternoon we hire a taxi to Marseilles and at the Air France office discover that our aeroplane was damaged on the ground during the storm last night and we certainly cannot leave before tomorrow. We despatch cables and telegrams and drink dubonnet and eat good cakes at a café, watching the crowds of ugly, shoddy, sullen, hard-faced, hostile Frenchmen and women. When we communicate with them they are unsympathetic, un-cooperative and prone to cheat us. We dislike them. On our return to the hotel at Cassis there is a fearful row with the taxi-driver who, supported by the proprietor and his wife, certainly would cheat us, did we not prevail. The consequence is that the hotel staff is uniformly unpleasant for the rest of our stay. But we are the enforced guests of Sabena Air Line. During dinner my group becomes still more intimate: the Russian confesses that she has loved her husband consistently for thirty years; the American that he has loved his wife for six months and now has mistresses whenever they are available; Mrs Gregory that she has had two husbands, plans to have a third, and, looking me straight between the eyes, indicates that she intends to have me tonight as a sort of supplementary. I have nothing to confess, at least in this company.

To my horror, we were called this morning at 4.45, in fact just after I had got back to my own bedroom, like a thief in the night. Consequently I am dog tired all day. We are given a horrid breakfast at the big hotel. The black bread is barely eatable, the acorn coffee barely drinkable. There is no butter and no milk. Poor Mrs G., having as I alone know had no more sleep than I had, is in despair how to feed her baby of under two. I do not know how babies in this country are able to survive. We drive in the charabanc to Marseilles airport and leave at nine. We fly over huge, ugly Marseilles, and over that sink of iniquity Cassis, and Toulon where the sunk battleships in the harbour are clearly visible, just as I recollect having seen an aerial photograph taken of them after the sinking during the war. There are still clouds and lightning storms, and over Lombardy there are low, fleecy white clouds, pierced by shafts of sun like sharp lances. The fields are inundated by the torrential rain of the past days. We make for Bergamo but turn back because they tell us we may land at Milan after all. We are the first plane to do so for three days. Here we wait four hours. I decide not to stay in Milan after all since there is a spare seat on the plane to Rome. So at the risk of incurring further expense I, with the kind assistance of the officials and a friendly Italian traveller, book the seat, for which I am to pay at the other end. There are only coffee and biscuits to drink and eat here, but both taste delicious, and the Italians are politer, just as they are cleaner than the Frogs.

At 2.30 Mrs. G., her child and I, the 'incommunicada' nun and the kind, silly Italian traveller get into a Lai plane and fly for Rome. We are the only passengers from the lot who started from London. The weather over the plain of Lombardy is clear. The country looks incredibly neat, smiling and gracious. The Po is yellow as ochre. I suppose there are few sights more beautiful than the country between Milan and Rome on a fine day with intermittent clouds, seen from 9,000 feet. Stepping out in Rome one is struck as by the air of a conservatory. An American friend greets Mrs. G. and by some extraordinary act of generosity which I do not understand settles my extra fare, plus 700 lire for excess luggage, as though I had been a guardian angel and not a wicked seducer. Simply do not understand. Yet I cannot like this tall, middle-aged, slouching, oh-yahing and utterly philistine American friend. Nor do I care for the husband, when we meet him; nor the newly-furnished flat with its ferns, laced window curtains, spanking walnut dining-room suite, and plethora of silver mugs. They are all very kind to me however, and even send me in their car, after profuse goodbyes (Mrs. G.'s slightly guarded perhaps) to the Hôtel de Ville where I am staying. Here I wash and try to undeafen myself before calling on the Moores at the Hassler next door. Joan welcomes me with an embrace and Garrett orders himself a drink which he has in his dressing-gown on the terrace of their room overlooking the Spanish Steps. I dine alone in my hotel for 1170 lire, a fearful price.

Sunday, 28th September

Sleep soundly after my debauch and succession of early rises. It is terribly hot all day and I have brought the wrong clothes. Garret calls me and I go round to the Hassler where poor Joan is in bed with a bad stomach-ache and cannot get up. So Garrett and I walk to the Villa Medici, but cannot see inside it. Then we walk down the Via Sistina to the Baths of Diocletian. Here Garrett with great efficiency engages a guide who turns out to be educated and knowledgeable. For an hour and a half he conducts us round the sculpture gallery. I like the mosaics, particularly the Grecian one of a skeleton and the tag, 'Know Thyself'. I lunch with the Moores in their bedroom, then have a siesta till four, sleeping soundly. Garrett wakes me up rudely by walking into my room. We go off to Santa Maria Maggiore. The Sangallo ceiling in gold, the eighth-century mosaics, which almost make me sick with excitement. Then we walk to San Pietro in Vincoli to look at the Moses, as colossal in aggression as in conception. Here there is a tomb, no, it is in San Clemente, of Cardinal Roverella dated 1476, which is pure Renaissance. Such a thing I have never seen in my life before. In another church immediately beneath this one are the remains of a Roman plaster ceiling in square panels and one long panel of arabesques very similar to the tomb which unconsciously followed it hundreds of years later. These underground basilicas are immensely impressive and moving. I dined at a *trattoria* very well. With wine it cost me 800 lire. Then sat and talked to Joan.

It is a step to the Pincio gardens where I walked in the early morning – holm oaks, statuary, fountains and horse-drawn *carozze*. I looked at the Pantheon, the prototype of so much I love and endeavour to preserve. The most complete Roman building, I suppose in the world – the interior a cosmos in miniature like something pendant from the heavens, columns of giallo antico and pavonezzetta and porphyry floor. The emptiness, the solemnity of this extraordinary globe. Then I looked at the Cancelleria Palace, the church in it by Bramante, the *cortile* of the palace so chaste and beautiful. Lunched alone at another *trattoria* and after a siesta met Garrett and Sarah Churchill. We looked at Santa Maria della Pace, the cloisters there by Bramante, likewise austere, and within the church Raphael walls and a chapel with 'overladen reliefs' – according to my Murray – by Simone Mosca. We then drove to the Capital where Sarah left us. She, an intelligent girl, has lived in Rome six months and yet has never been to the Pantheon, or St. Peter's. Her skin is translucent like alabaster. Garrett and I looked at the outside of Michelangelo's piazza and palaces, Marcus Aurelius's equestrian statue (traces of gold paint still visible on the horse's head) and the Forum, and the Mamertine prison in which St. Peter was incarcerated. I never need go to the last place again.

So hot that I bitterly regret not having brought more suitable clothes, but this afternoon walked in my shirt and a pull-over without a jacket. Found Peter Tunnard's tailor, Ciro, who will make me a suit for the equivalent of £30, which I am to pay in England. Walked to St. Peter's. I think Mussolini was right to pull down the old buildings in the Borgo for now one can for the first time see the basilica, dome and all, from the Ponte Sant' Angelo. What a mistake the Latin cross was, and how angry Bramante and Michelangelo would have been. I was too tired to join Garrett and Joan this afternoon and, after a siesta, walked to San Pietro in Montorio. The best evening view of Rome is from the Janiculum; the best morning view from the Pincio, with the sun behind one. I walked along the Tiber, looking at six or seven palaces.

Walked to the Palazzo Doria, stopping at the Trevi Fountain, that rococo delight, on the way. At ten o'clock Prince Doria greeted me. He is so exceedingly polite and smiling that I deduce he shuns intimacies. He is rather bent from the waist like an old apple tree. He has had tuberculosis of the spine, poor man, and was tortured by Mussolini, I believe. His Princess, with broad Scotch accent, like a comfortable nanny, is an angel. To my surprise we were joined by Garrett and Barbara Rothschild, brought by the friendly Italian father of Yvonne Hamilton, whom they call Papageno. For two hours we were shown round the *piano nobile* of this gigantic and gloomy palace. Pictures v. important. Memling and Lippi and to crown all the Velasquez of Pope Innocent X. Beautiful rich Genoese velvet stuffs, curtains and chair covers. Some curtains of a Neapolitan yellow ground. Some terra cotta wall hangings, others crimson and brown. The grisaille ceilings in arabesques poor. In one room stands the Pope's velvet covered throne turned to the wall, a customary protest among the Roman nobility against the Pope's incarceration within the Vatican city in 1870. A few princes only have the right to invite the Pope to their palaces. Another princely privilege among the Black Nobility is the Baldacchino (the Doria one sheltering the portrait of Innocent X) on either side of which repose the velvet cushion and umbrella carried in the Prince's carriage in case he meets the Pope's equipage in the street. In which event he is obliged to descend and kneel, if needs be, in the rain and mud. Nearly all the gilded furniture in the Palace is swathed with thick leather case covers. Prince Doria says that only the Palazzo Colonna is still inhabited as a private dwelling by the family, in addition to his own.

At 12.15 we parted and I looked at the Palazzo Vidoni, Palazzo Linotte and Palazzo Lante. Then went to the flat the Moores have been lent for two days in the via Margutta. Sir D'Arcy Osborne and Barbara Rothschild were there. After luncheon we questioned Sir D'Arcy about the Vatican. He said he had the highest opinion of Vatican diplomacy although the Vatican was not as well informed on foreign affairs as might be expected. The Pope [Pius XII] was a saint, and had the charm of our Queen Elizabeth. He was now launching into unequivocal condemnation of Communism. He had hated the war and went to every endeavour to end it. But so rigidly did he maintain his neutrality that he pleased no one. Far from being Machiavellian the Cardinals were the kindest of men. Sir D'Arcy ought to know, having spent the whole war shut up in the Vatican, and being an unprejudiced Protestant to boot.

This evening I walked miles, past the Quirinale and the Colosseum to the Tiber, finding myself beside the temples of Fortuna Virile and Vesta, two of the best preserved in Rome. I walk everywhere, intending to know every street and square inch of the old city before I leave. Dining with the Moores Barbara Rothschild said that Garrett and I made the oddest spectacle walking the streets on Sunday, two of the tallest, slimmest and seemingly most disdainful men who could not be anything but English. The Moores and Barbara all leave tomorrow, and I shall miss them.

Thursday, 2nd October

A rather lonely day. Not one of the seven people to whom I have posted letters of introduction has so far replied. The only letter I get is one from Sibyl Colefax asking me to bring her back a pair of shoes. I spent the whole morning in S. Maria del Popolo. A treasure house for the student of the Renaissance. Then walked through Vignola's gate up the straight drive of the Villa Borghese to the Casino. I believe that the balustrade still in the forefront of the house is the original one and that Lord Astor took away the other balustrade on the garden side, without replacing it. At any rate the brick fillings at Cliveden should not be left in their nakedness but be plastered and washed over.

In the evening I walked miles again to the Baths of Caracalla where Shelley wrote *Prometheus Unbound*. Was disgusted by its condition. It has become a dump for old war material and barbed wire. There is no romance about it, no vegetation, no clinging vine or trailing ivy. Inelegant, naked brick ruins bore me. I continued to the Porta Latina, looking at the tiny chapel, reputedly by Bramante, of S. Giovanni in Oleo, octagonal, brick-filled, dated 1509, with a wide terra cotta frieze of large honeysuckles and a stone finial capping the whole. There were motor-bicycle trials in progress, and discords rent the air.

At Rampoldi's this evening for a drink I was introduced to Prince Wolkonsky, a middle-aged silly, who said he would cash my travellers' cheques at the black market rate which is far more favourable than the bank rate.

All night it poured with rain. This morning the rain fell in hard, straight prongs. I got up late, for where could I go? Also I am suffering from slight diarrhoea, a common complaint here. Barbara R and Joan M have both been victims. So I took a taxi to the Vatican Museum. On my return found an invitation to the Legation for luncheon tomorrow and another from Roger Hinks. At 9.30 Guy Ferrari came, but an interruption at the door frightened him. It turned out to be merely a telegram, not a policeman which G for some extraordinary reason feared. He said he had momentarily forgotten that the Occupation was a thing of the past.

I was conducted by a guide with an inadequate electric torch down to the enormous Golden House of Nero below the Baths of Titus. It is dark, gloomy, muddy, full of rubbish, and sinister. But I was fascinated by the remains of Roman paintings, the arabesques which Raphael copied in the Loggie and which Adam studied when in Rome. He must have been let down through a hole on the end of a rope, with a candle in a lantern. My guide, an old ruffian, smelling of drink, was very informative in bad French. These arabesque fragments date from the first century A.D. They represent birds, flowers, foliage. The Throne Room is barrel-vaulted and divided into squares, painted. There is no stucco.

At luncheon time I went to the Chancellery where I met Victor Perowne, the Minister to the Vatican, who motored me and Roger Hinks to luncheon in his house near the Baths of Caracalla. He is tall, languid, cultivated, slightly cynical, a typical British diplomat. His wife is a sad little thing, with a peaky face. After luncheon Perowne motored me to the Villa Madama, which is not open to the public but is being prepared for the head of the State. Saw the famous loggie begun by Raphael and Giulio Romano for Cardinal Giulio de Medici. The loggie are now glazed. They remind me of Adam's or rather Rose's stucco in the rotunda at Kedleston. They are unpainted and white. There is one deeply coved room painted in arabesques and two wooden panelled ceilings with Medici arms. Victor Perowne confirmed that the Pope's charm was overwhelming. His manner was affectionate. Unfortunately he seldom saw him. Dined with Sarah Churchill and the Duchess of Marlborough, a typical English lady, conventional, limited and hard, with large feet.

Sunday, 5th October

Sarah dined with me in a *trattoria*. Her beauty is of a very frail sort, her hair Botticelli gold. She is of a romantic disposition. There is something guileless about her, like Johnnie, and she will be the victim of disillusions. She says that Randolph, to whom she is devoted, is most unhappy. But then it is his own fault for being so objectionable to everyone he meets.

Monday, 6th October

A most glorious, translucent day, and hot again. I met Ruth Lowinsky at the Chancellery and we drove to S. Maria del Popolo. I have never seen a woman sweat so much, but she was wearing a thick tweed coat and skirt. Guy Ferrari came to see me in the evening and very nearly cried when I told him I was leaving on Friday. He said he wanted to become an 'English' architect, did not like Italians. But since he is one, was born and has always lived here and must go on living with his compatriots, I told him he could not be silly and must try to like them.

Tuesday, 7th October

Early this morning I walked very slowly through the Pincio and the Porta del Popolo to the Villa Papa Giulio. What a glorious surprise it was. It is a museum of Tuscan figurines, rather dreary and even ugly artefacts, but some fine Greek and Etruscan vases, amphora, kraters. The garden is laid out with stone screens. Arabesque stucco panels, steps leading down to a sunk water basin – alas, the fountains are dry – and caryatides upholding arches, too heavy for them. Stage scenery of rococo delights. Few people there at this early hour. On the garden side of the casino is a hemicycle colonnade, decorated with

225

painted *treillage* work of vines, cupids, peacocks, storks – what James Adam, I believe, condescendingly described in his diary as 'vastly well for the country'. It is one of the prettiest scenes of fantasy I have seen in Rome.

Alice Gainsborough and her son, Gerry, turned up this morning and I got rooms for them in my hotel. We walked to the Pincio for tea. I dined with Roger Hinks at an extremely good restaurant where we were given lots of butter. Apropos of contemporary art books he complained that it was considered fashionable and gentlemanlike to be inaccurate, and this drives him mad. He was full of complaints and, like Guy, dislikes the Italians.

Wednesday, 8th October

Tried again to leave my note on Sarah, but at 9.30 got no answer when I rang at her door high up on the topmost floor of the Palazzo Buonaparte – I had tried with Roger Hinks last night with no success. So I proceeded rather unhappily to the Capitoline and entered the museums. Looked idly at the sculpture, but not seriously. It is foolish to go to galleries on the mere chance of finding something that may interest one. One should go with a definite quarry in view, and then allow one's interests to be distracted, provided one returns to pursuit of said quarry afterwards. Then I ate three delicious iced cakes and drank orange juice, and visited my tailor. Lady Gainsborough and Gerry lunched at a *trattoria*. They have no interest in profane Rome whatsoever, only in sacred Rome. They have fixed up an audience with the Pope for themselves and for me on Saturday, but I cannot stay till then.

After a happy siesta, induced by copious white wine, I walked to the Protestant Cemetery. I have a sore throat today and am starting a cold. Damn! The lovely sad spot has horrid blocks of flats built up to its walls. From within one can hear the squeal of trams like the shrieks of the damned from inside the gates of paradise. For the Cemetery is enclosed within a barren, soulless, squalid suburb. Nevertheless it retains its special peace, serenity and poignancy. I picked a shred of box from Keats's grave and of lonicera (inappropriate shrub) from Shelley's. This was the only way I could pay my respects. I had nothing to give them. So I took from them, as I have taken all my life. There is something presumptuous in Trelawny's

226

officious proximity to Shelley's remains; but Severn's to Keats's is touching, and well earned.

Then I rang up Sarah, and hurray! she said she would dine. After a cocktail at the hotel we dined at Nino's. How good it all was. She has a way with her which melts the susceptible hearts of Italians. We ordered prosciutto and salami, and her favourite dish of grilled turkey, wrapped in bacon, with cheese over it. We drank much red wine. It was a successful evening. She is bright, independent, bohemian, yet elegant, which is a welcome contradiction. She has a sense of humour and poise, awful word, but what other is there? She is quite uneducated, which is strange considering who she is. She is dedicated to her own art however. She explained to me why she loved Rome. She does no sight-seeing and has no understanding of architecture. She says it is the movements of the city which she relishes: movements of the statues, the fountains, the bridges, the curves of facades of churches, the actions of the Romans in the streets, and even the mudguards of the *carozze*. I really am intrigued by her. I walked her home and was amused by the impression this blond beauty, apparently unnoticing, makes upon the staring, lascivious Italians.

Thursday, 9th October

My cold is worse. I had a night of fever and sweated like Mrs. Lowinsky. It thundered and today is raining intermittently. I have done little, feeling ill. I called on Sarah in her garret at the Palazzo Buonaparte, just to see how she lives. It is charming, right under the eaves: only two little rooms. Then she dropped me at the Palazzo Rospigliosi where I lunched with Sir D'Arcy Osborne. There were Monsignor Hemmick and Count Eddie Bismarck. The first is a worldly prelate, cackling and gossiping like an old woman, yet just avoiding scandalous talk; the other a middle-aged sissy, the younger brother of Prince Otto who figures so prominently in Ciano's *Diary*. Sir D.'s apartments are spacious, dark and cool, his *salone* dating from the seventeenth-century. Amused I listened with flapping ears, but closed mouth to the gush of gossip about people of whom I knew nothing. Harold Acton has arrived in Rome today by air from Ireland. He left Birr yesterday evening. He and I and Roger Hinks dined in the restaurant in the Palazzo Colonna.

All day it poured with rain and my cold was at its height. Harold walked up to the hotel at 10.30 and we went to the American Express. He then lunched with me at the hotel. What exquisite manners he has, never intruding, deferring to women with charm and attention. And what is going on in his mind all the while? He lives for literature, the arts and things of the mind. At 1.30 I left for Florence. Sarah telephoned before my departure.

At the Grand Hotel I have a luxurious room with bath, overlooking the Arno and Bellosguardo. Geoff Lemprière and his Italian business agent, boring man, met me. We dined and walked round the Duomo and down the Arno in the lamp-light. I was horrified by the amount of bomb damage around the Ponte Vecchio, of which the houses in the middle have been destroyed. Geoffrey, who is a good fellow but by no means a highbrow, has the irritating qualities of the perpetual schoolboy. He will be facetious without ever being witty.

Saturday, 11th October

In the morning visited the Duomo and San Lorenzo. The first cold and brown, almost ugly inside. Donatello figure on south wall of Joshua redeems all. Dome pineapple shape. The second so full of treasures that a cursory visit leaves the mind in turmoil, not to be expressed.

The last time I was in Florence was 1937. The first time 1927. I was with Hoel Llewellyn, fresh from Eton. We drove from the station to a remote and squalid door which was opened by a sinister gentleman in dirty pyjamas. We instantly decided the address we had been given was a house of ill fame and terrified, silly little fools, turned on our heels dragging our luggage, having dismissed the taxi.

Most of this afternoon I slept, feeling rotten. In the evening met Hamish [St. Clair-Erskine] in the Grand Hotel and had drinks with him. As he was going to stay at Berenson's I gave him my letter of introduction. He returns on Tuesday to Venice where he too is staying with the Chavchavadzes, so I was able to give him a letter to George likewise.

A lovely, clear, keen autumnal day, in so far as there is any sense of the seasons here. I am feeling better. Drove to San Miniato, listened to a Mass and sat for an hour ensconced in one of the deep walnut choir-stalls. Seldom have I seen a more exquisite church, eleventh-century; Byzantine mosaics in the apse; tabernacle by Michelozzo, soffit of glazed terra-cotta, sea-blue ground with white rosettes by Della Robbia. Marble pulpit Romanesque. Then drove with Geoff to Fiesole duomo; afternoon the Bardia, Fiesole.

Geoffrey and the business man left early, to my intense relief. Once more I am on my own. At 12.40 the Berenson car called to take me to I Tatti to lunch with this grand old man, of whom I am mortally frightened. I found Raymond Mortimer there, very friendly. He told Berenson that we had known each other for twenty years and he hoped I valued his friendship. Signorina Mariano lives here as hostess. Sweet woman who relieves tension and makes one happy. She said she had received six letters from Sibyl about me. I apologised. Then in came the great man. The great man is a tiny man, white-bearded and eighty. Looks frail and tired, and is neat. When he speaks he speaks to the point. No irrelevancies, no pleasantries. I felt very shy and was tongue-tied. He saw at once that I had nothing to communicate to him. But I was fascinated by listening to his talk to others. My fellow guest was Mrs. Bliss, a grand Henry Jamesian lady, old, and described as a wise goose. Berenson is tiresome in that he is very conscious of being the famous art-dictator and sage, surrounded by applauding disciples. This expectancy of deference does not make for ease. And no small talk is allowed. After all a modicum of small talk does oil the wheels. In stony silence he dismisses a conventional advance as a triviality, which it doubtless is. When he talks he demands attention, and is not the least averse to obsequious confirmation of his utterances. He speaks scoffingly of religion and observers of the Christian principles, like T.S. Eliot. In the late afternoon while the others were having siestas I wandered into the library. I have never seen a larger private library. Every art book published must be here. And portfolios of every known work of art recorded. I took out a book about the Villa Madama, Rome, and read it on the terrace. Probably this was against the rules. Before tea Raymond and I strolled up the hill, he expatiating upon the beauty of the grey-green landscape. I thought the little brown farmhouses, villas and villinos dotted upon the hills were what constituted the Italian landscape, which is essentially suburban, the very quality which in England we consider an affront to our landscape.

During tea in the loggia Berenson sat in the full sun, talking of London. I asked him if he had not thought London beautiful before 1914. He said No, the mews were filthy slums, the fogs were stifling, and the number of drunk women and their smell overpowering. Talked about the Italian temperament. When Italians complained to him that the Americans were pluto-crats, he told them they were heliocrats. He is a little deaf. He conveyed to me the impression of a great man striving to be something which he isn't. Perhaps he wishes he were an aristocratic connoisseur, and not a self-made professional expert.

Tuesday, 14th October

This morning Santa Croce. Ugly 1860 marble front. Wonder-ful things within an unsympathetic building – Giotto frescoes, door by Michelozzo into the corridor, and the Pazzi Chapel surpassing words. To the Bargello. By noon everything shut, virtually for the rest of the daylight.

At 4.30 Peter Rodd and Adelaide Lubbock, who are staying at the Grand because their car has broken its axle, shared a taxi with me to the Villa Pietra. For the first time I met old Mr. and Mrs. Acton, he very English, she very American, with white hair, pretty, pencilled eyebrows, and bearing no resemblance to Harold either in looks or speech. They nag at Harold and ask him to fetch the ash-trays, to ring the bell, to turn on and off lights and generally fag. All this he does with good humour as a matter of course. The garden, entirely made by Mr. Acton out of nothing, is ideal, straight walks between evergreen trees, with copious statuary, some very good, and stone gateways. In many respects the loveliest garden I have ever seen. The villa is sixteenth-century, compact, large, stuccoed and washed a pale lemon. It is so full of works of art and primitives that it gives you a headache. It is splendid, but not cosy. Dined tonight with Peter and Adelaide Lubbock. They were gay and entertaining. I had thought I disliked Peter, but I now discern a latent charm. His knowledge of Roman and mediaeval history is stupendous, but his delivery is relentless and boring. He has inspired me to devote myself to a course of Gibbon and Gregorovius.

Cold over except for catarrh which vitiates taste and makes smells of tobacco and petrol like hell's sulphur. Walked this morning to Santo Spirito, the purest Renaissance church in Florence after San Miniato. The continuous arcade of Corinthian columns at the crossing really is like a forest of smooth tree trunks. Met Peter and Mrs. L. at a small *trattoria*. She said she was suffering from Primitive indigestion. Ate succulent chicken breasts.

Every Englishman seems to come to this hotel at some time or another. This afternoon I met David Horner with Osbert Sitwell. The latter walks with a stick like Malcolm Bullock. His voice resembles Sachie's, low and modulated. He is of heavy build, with a strong Hanoverian face, straight grey hair running back from the forehead. He shakes hands with a large, soft, yet firm grip. I dined with the Moores at their little house in Costa di San Giorgio, rented from Mrs. Leith. Besides Barbara Rothschild (impossible not to love) there were Una Lady Trowbridge and Julian Amery, who sat next to each other. I, being shortsighted, was surprised when approaching Lady T. to shake hands, to discover she was not a man. She wears close-cropped, straight white hair; small ear-rings it is true, but a man's dinner-jacket and black bow tie. She lives entirely in the past and talks of Miss Radclyffe Hall as 'John'. 'John' and I did this and that. She told Garrett all about the prosecution case over *The Well of Loneliness* and the way the two of them had been persecuted. She spoke intelligently of D'Annunzio. She is a devout Papist and believes in miracles. Said she was now always lonely and unhappy, yet preferred a good climate without friends to a bad one, like England, with them. To my embarrassment I saw her turn to Amery and heard her ask, 'Are you the brother of the boy they hanged?' Then she expressed to him her feelings on that subject. I walked her back to her very small *albergo* on the Lung 'Arno.

The Pitti Palace is full of middle-aged spinsters making miniature copies of the Raphael Madonnas and, if one so much as
looks over their shoulders, trying to sell them to one. Like
Hampton Court there are too many state rooms in a line,
broken by no passages. Found Prodd and Mrs. L. still in the
hotel awaiting a new axle; we lunched again at our cheap and
good *trattoria* where the charming waiter looks like Oliver
Messel and runs up to our table with a skip and a jump,
showing very white teeth. I saw them off in their car and went
and read *The Moonstone* in the Cascine, very uncomfortably,
for in Italy there seem to be no benches with backs to them,
only cold marble slabs at the best.

Harold gave me dinner tonight. He walked all the way from
his parents' villa, carrying a large stick with a knob in case of
trouble late at night. An excellent dinner; felt rather sick
through over-eating. We walked down the Via Tornabuoni,
along the Arno, through the Palazzo Uffizi arcade and past the
Palazzo Vecchio. Harold taught me to appreciate the endur-
ing monumentality of this building. We walked down the Via
San Gallo and after admiring the Palazzo Pandolfini, parted
there.

Observations on Florence. (1) Walks at night, when the
main streets are empty and quiet. Narrow, tortuous streets are
mysterious and forbidding by lamp- and particularly by
moon-light. Then you can appreciate the vast, rugged, abstract beauty of the palaces in the sharp shadows of semi-
darkness. Things not noticeable by day loom into sight. Here a
window pediment, there an armorial escutcheon suspended
over a doorway. (2) Although mercifully the chief monuments have escaped the fighting the spirit of Florence has been
very seriously impaired by the destruction of the bridges and
houses along the Arno. (3) The Florentines are not quite so
beautiful, nor so lively, as the Romans. (4) A Vespa (motor
scooter) would be an ideal vehicle in London, nipping in and
out of the lumbering traffic and the queues.

On my return on foot along the Arno I met the handsome
young Italian who had been in the hotel with a party of
tiresome English people last night. He was sitting on the
embankment wall tapping the stone with his heels. Very sweet
he was. He took me in a taxi to the Porta Latina where we got

out and walked arm-in-arm towards the pitch darkness of the Boboli Gardens, which were shut now. 'But I know a way in,' he said, 'and we shall have it entirely to ourselves.' We did. When we parted I walked home under the stars. I salute his evanescent youth and beauty.

Observation (5) Berenson is a vain, blasphemous, tricky Jew. (6) Made before: the Italians don't like sitting down, nor do they mind about comfort.

Friday, 17th October

I write this on my bed at the Hotel Touring, Milan, waiting for Geoff to turn up. I hope he does soon for I hate this soulless commercial hotel and this vast, evil and ugly city. Instead of stopping at Bologna on my way I took the eleven o'clock *rapido* straight here, an easy journey, having paid a last visit to San Lorenzo and that lovely sacristy with the 'intarsia' wooden pews, and the very dull Duomo interior and the supercilious Joshua by Donatello. For five shillings I bought en route a carton of spaghetti, not very good, roast chicken still warm, chip potatoes, half a bottle of Chianti and an apple, and was happy. Why the hell can one not do this on an English train journey?

I walked to the Milan Duomo: the vertical perspective seen from the north-west striking; the west facade unsuccessful. Entering is like plunging into a very dense forest. Always dark, now that so much of the stained glass has gone it is darker still because the missing windows are boarded up. People move about mysteriously, but one can study nothing in detail. I strained my eyes at the St. Bartholomew flayed, carrying his own skin over one arm and looking perfectly nonchalant and composed, like Anthony Eden.

(7) The Italians are working like blacks rebuilding their bridges and small towns, badly destroyed between Florence and here. They are a nation of stonemasons. The new houses are mostly traditional and decent, if plain.

Geoffrey arrived at eight having been delayed by fog. I was as glad to see him today as I was glad to see him depart from Florence. We went straight to the Galleria, dined and listened to the band who were all enjoying themselves, singing and playing and singing in turns. We looked at the spot in the Duomo square where Mussolini and La Petacci's bodies were ignominiously exposed. But no sign of the petrol-filling station.

This morning we went to Santa Maria delle Grazie which has been fearfully bombed, but is in process of restoration. So well done that you can barely tell which parts are new. Interesting to compare the terra cotta work on the apse by Bramante with our similar and almost coeval stuff in England, such as the tombs and screen in Oxburgh church, which derives from it. The Cenacola, badly damaged, was not visible. Then to Sant'Ambrogio to see the atrium, an interesting survival of the old basilica. Detail here very Byzantine. I insisted upon visiting Sant 'Eustorgio to see the Portinari chapel by Michelozzo. It is as gracious and sweet as all his tabernacles and chapels, but has been altered to some extent since built. The plaster decorations down the piers and the reliefs upon the frieze of angels with bells, all coloured. The sacristan showed us with relish the grizzled black head of St. Peter the Martyr, much decomposed, the flesh like old, hard, untreated leather. It occurred to me that Guy's comely black head might resemble the Martyr's in 400 years' time. Geoff left for Rome at 1 o'clock and I for Venice at 2.45. Had a horrid journey standing much of the time, or diving into the restaurant car for drinks, chiefly to get a temporary rest on a seat.

Reached Venice at 8.10. Already dark. To my great relief was met by the Chavchavadze's gondolier at the station, who said, 'La Principessa ha detto che Lei era grand' uomo.' This made me happy, not because I was a tall man, but because I was recognised. What a lovely gondola! Jet black and sumptuously upholstered with brass figureheads at either side, brightly polished, crests and a coronet and black silk ropes and tassels. There is etiquette about gondolas too. The gondolier sees that you sit in the proper seat. When you accompany the Princess, her seat is on the right, yours on the left; and you, the man, must get out first. The first gondolier, wearing livery with wide sailor's collar, brass buttons, striped waistcoat, knee breeches, a beretta with big, black pom, takes the prow. Behind him stands Mario, the second gondolier. There can be few things more romantic, more transporting from this dismal modern age, than to find yourself at dead of night, under the stars and dim spangled lamps, skimming down the small canals, the gondoliers shouting, 'Hoih! hoih!' as you approach a corner. Rhythmically, swiftly you glide, your wake gently lapping the palaces, faster seemingly down the narrow canals, slower into the Grand Canal, where indeed the romance is not lessened, if anything intensified at this hour by the noisy *vaporetti*, whose rough wake rocks the gondola and rudely smacks against the prow. Never once do the *gondolieri* pause. We reached the Palazzo Polignac, very sombre in the darkness, its great striped *pali* rising from the water at the steps. This is a fine Lombardi palace and the Chavchavadzes rent the second and top floors, which are splendid and high. There are many servants, all male, silent and respectful.

We dined at 9 o'c, the Cs' usual hour. George delighted to see me and as charming as ever. Elizabeth, bigger than before. Hamish and a young 'cellist staying. A brigadier and wife, a daughter of Bourne & Hollingsworth, dreary folk, came to dinner. When they left we talked till two.

Sunday, 19th October

I woke at 9.30 and rang for coffee and fruit. My room is large, with a floor of scagliola, a large bed with white and gold posts, raised on a dais, the windows looking up the Grand Canal through the high-arched Accademia bridge to the Palazzo Fornari, and down the Canal towards the Salute. Elizabeth says Venice is so fragile that each time she returns, it is with relief that she finds it still there, and not dissolved. How long can it survive, its huge palaces supported on wooden piles? She and I went to the steps of the Piazzetta in the gondola, and walked to High Mass in St. Mark's, standing tightly wedged, for Mass was said by the Patriarch himself on account of the visit of St. Somebody from Hungary, his 700th anniversary. He was behind us in a glass case, embalmed and wearing red gloves and slippers. I did not feel in the least devout. There is a cold wind blowing through the *calle*. But we were sheltered and warm, drinking coffee in the Piazza.

Monday, 20th October

It is distinctly cold. In the Palazzo large wood fires are lit, and the stoves are being cleaned out. Walking in Venice today I caught, mingling with the smell of fruit and the moist, excretal smell of the lesser canals which I love, a scent of firewood that is faintly English and preposterous. I am not taking my sight-seeing very seriously here. I did too much of it in Rome and Florence. Furthermore, I am luxuriating in the comfort and superb meals of the palazzo, the flow of wine and the late hours. The first night at dinner there were, after martinis with fresh lemon peel in them, white and red wine and two sorts of champagne. After soup there is invariably a fish or some such course before the meat. After tea I sit upstairs in George's attic while he practices the piano. Then at eight have a bath. This afternoon Hamish with the 'cellist, Dimitri Marcovitch, who is twenty-five and of some renown, went by gondola to look for Tiepolos in the Madonna del Orto and San Giovanni in Bragora. Hamish says that Mario, who stands at the helm of the gondola, looks as proud and beautiful as Michelangelo's Adam.

Wednesday, 22nd October

Today George motored Hamish and me to the Villa Maser. George's car would not start and a typical Russian scene ensued for an hour, of George shouting, his Mexican valet, the two gondoliers, five garage men and ten small boys pushing and offering advice. The battery was flat. Finally we got off. The car is an enormous American Cadillac. On arrival we were told that our hostess was away with her father, Count Volpi, who is dying. Her daughter, Esmeralda, acted hostess. She is a lovely girl of twenty, with black hair piled on the top of her head, olive complexion, the reddest lips, and prune dark eyes with velvety lashes. We arrived at 2.15 for luncheon. I had heard so much about the Villa Maser that I was disappointed. I know it to be one of the great dwellings of the world, the work of three outstanding artists, Palladio, Veronese, Vittoria. But it presents a cardboardy appearance and is over-restored. The Veronese rooms are approached upstairs, on the *piano nobile*, which at the rear leads straight to a little enclosed court, with central pool, semi-circular arcade with statues in niches, grotto and a maiden spouting water into the pool through her breasts. The villa is built on a steep slope. Vittoria's stucco-work inside has lost its crisp mouldings because too often repainted or lime-washed. The Veronese rooms are of course

236

superb in conception, but the execution is not entirely satisfactory. Nevertheless they are extremely pretty. The colours vary in a dozen shades of green and yellow. The whole is light and cheerful.

The landscape in front of the villa is rather dull, but the little church is delightful. A rotunda, with two projecting square towers, a round, stepped dome with cupola, and a Corinthian portico of marble columns, the capitals connected by stone swags of carved foliage. The interior is circular with balustraded gallery running just under the dome. The quality of Vittoria's stucco here is far better than in the villa. George was a trifle upset that I was not more enthusiastic about Maser.

Friday, 24th October

The sun has gone. It is grey and cold. Paid a visit to the Biblioteca Marciana. Palladio called it Sansovino's masterpiece. Vittoria's stuccowork is by no means as refined as that of the Adam brothers. No wonder they despised Palladio's interiors. Visited the inside of San Francesco della Vigna. One chapel decorated by Vittoria shows that he could be less of an artist than Oliver Messel. In the afternoon the gondola took me and the Mexican to see the two Palladio churches across the water. In the niches of Il Redentore are painted wooden silhouettes of saints, rather like the Jacobean figure doorstops at Knole, a form of statuary I have not seen elsewhere in Italy.

Many, too many people came to the Palazzo this evening. I remained silent. I do not find Elizabeth Chavchavadze very sympathetic, and polite and kind though she is to me, I think I bore her.

Saturday, 25th October

I left for England today. It was raining hard in Venice, and was cold. Hamish, Dimitri and Elizabeth accompanied me to the station in the gondola under the *felze*, which was put up. It was like riding in a sedan chair. They left for their tour to Bologna.

An American girl in the train between Dover and Victoria, her first sight of England, said to me, 'My, what a number of chimneys! In our country we may have one chimney to each house; here it must be one chimney to each room.' That is one manifestation of England's cosiness before the war when every chimney would be smoking. Now the grates are empty, or nearly so. Tonight I went to the Albert Hall in the Rosses' box to hear Bruno Walter conduct the London Philharmonic – three glorious symphonies of Beethoven. The Eshers entered, and he said to me, 'You are to go to Harewood at once. The Princess Royal has been on tenterhooks, awaiting your return from Italy.' Then, 'You will have to treat her with less of your usual easy-go-lucky manner, my lad.'

In the train to Evesham I talked to an old English woman just returned from Germany where she had been staying with her sister, married to a German landowner outside Cologne. She was still in a state of shock from what she had seen and enraged against the Allies for keeping the Germans starved. Where, she kept saying, does the food go to? Her sister's family eat day after day boiled carrots and potatoes at every meal, served on silver plates by footmen in white gloves. They have no tea, coffee, butter, bread or meat. The Germans are utterly done for, and in despair. Her sister's son, born and bred in England, was killed on the Russian front. The tragedy of Germany, she says, haunts her.

James lunched with me on Friday. He looked thin and ill. I was almost worried about him, and at once was made to understand that something dramatic had happened to him. He told me over coffee that E.P. was engaged, and that was the cause of his distress. He is so upset that he begs me to make no reference to it again. It is a little difficult to sympathise because, when she was disengaged, Jamesey made no endeavours to marry her. He refuses to go out in the evenings and has to complete the first volume of Lord Houghton by the end of the year.

Everyone I meet complains of distended stomach and attributes it to the starchy food. The food in England is worse than during the war, dry and tasteless, even at Brooks's.

Monday, 3rd November

Motored to Brockhampton. In the afternoon members of the Barneby family arrived and by a sort of muddled arrangement we distributed to them certain things they severally wanted, for which they paid probate figures. The Admiral, who was present, behaved very well, and saw the point of the Trust behaving like gents and not bureaucrats. Now the Ministry of Works would never have allowed these poor people to have a few family trinkets, which have little monetary value and mean all the world to them.

Wednesday, 5th November

John Rothenstein showed Sir Geoffrey and Lady Mander and me all the Pre-Raphaelite things of Mrs. Angeli's which he is storing and agreed to exhibit them first of all at the Tate. This will give us good publicity and furthermore the Tate will clean up and catalogue them for us, for nothing.

I dined with Barbara Moray who arrived very late having been at a cocktail party at which the King and Queen were guests. The K. and Q. did not leave till nearly 8 o'c, so no one else could go before them. Barbara said the King remarked to her naively, 'We keep wondering whether Philip realises what he is in for.' The Queen loves informal parties where she meets people who are doing interesting things in the world, and she hates leaving. At dinner tonight were Mr. Clare and Lady Doris Vyner. They spoke of Fountains Abbey and said the deal with the Roman Catholics was off, much to their disappointment. Tonight Barbara was very sparkling and witty. She is sharp and intelligent. But is there softness underneath? She has taken up weaving.

Thursday, 6th November

Another conference in the City over Osterley. I made them deal with points in which the Trust was interested, and then left for tea at Old Battersea House. This time poor old Mrs Stirling was less irritating and spoke sensibly of her wishes concerning the future of this house. She also showed me the twenty-four pieces of de Morgan pottery which Miss Stopford-Brook has bequeathed to the Trust. This house is a muddle. Again I was impressed by the Botticelli-like portrait painted by Mrs. de Morgan. The technique and the lavish gold are deliberately Botticellian. Very beautiful one must admit, and little the worse for being derivative.

Walked home in the fog, and then to the Albert Hall for the Bruno Walter concert in Bridget's box. The Mahler First Symphony nostalgic, moving, dreamy, but too long drawn out. Could not make up its mind to come to an end. The Albert Hall beautiful in the fog. You could not see the roof. Only the outline of the arcades, the capitals faintly lit, were visible on the opposite side of the hall. We walked to Adelaide Lubbock's afterwards, cars crawling, their drivers leaning out of open windows, buses guided by conductors holding flares. Very *gemütlich*, and general anxiety making people friendly, not irritable. I am the only person who loves the cosy, muffled mystery of London fogs. Poor Oggy Lynn had to walk miles guided by Christopher Sykes. A. Lubbock a very sympathetic woman. Whimsical too.

Friday, 7th November

At noon went to Lord Lytton's Memorial Service in Westminster Abbey. The largest attendance I have ever seen at a memorial. It was very beautiful indeed. I represented the National Trust and went in at 11.50 to find the Abbey already full. I sat in the north aisle close to Asquith's memorial, which his daughter, Lady Violet Bonham-Carter went up to after the service and scanned minutely. Mrs. Churchill facing me, sitting in the end canopied stall, marked Lector. The sun streamed in strong gushes through those windows which are still filled with glass. It is so difficult to disassociate the monuments from the architecture that one can overlook the arresting beauty of the vertical, aspirant piers, arches and vaults. It is one of the most noble buildings in the world. A long procession of deans and acolytes. A hymn to the airmen, composed by Lord Lytton, in honour of 'Anthony' I suppose, and set to music by Vaughan-Williams, was sung. I had grown to like it by the time the third verse was reached. I looked at these hundreds of eminent and intelligent people, the élite of

English brain and breeding, all of whom were for this h
hour concentrating their thoughts on one thing, their ov
impending deaths, their near conviction of annihilation ai
desperate hope of an unlikely survival.

Walked in the sun across St. James's Park to the Allies Club
where Barbara Moray and her youngest daughter, Arabella
Stuart, who was on half-term leave from school, lunched with
me. Mark [Ogilvie-Grant] came too. We had a tolerable meal.
Barbara touchingly kind, Arabella frail and pretty. May become a beauty.

At 6.30 I went to 55 Park Lane to see Sarah Churchill, a
meeting I have been much looking forward to. She distressed
me by explaining that she was not at all well, not having slept
for three nights owing to some worry, which she would not
divulge. She looked extremely thin. Was wearing a long
flying-fox fur wrap. She walks with a brave, galleon-like,
thrusting movement that is not inelegant, but attractive and
characteristic, as though always in a hurry and breasting the
storms of life. We went to the Italian film at the Curzon
Cinema, *To Live in Peace*. Returned to Thurloe Square to
dinner, and the fire. S warned me that she might fall asleep at
any moment, she felt so unwell. Consequently, although she
chatted away, she did not make the evening exhilarating.

She told me that her father was very elated by the municipal
election results, and was now confident that his party had a
following in the country. Already people in the streets were
more respectful to him.

Saturday, 8th November

Wrote another contribution to my N.T. *Guide*. I sold 120
books for £6 to a shop in the Fulham Road, which I happened
to pass by; and finished reading Coryat's *Crudities*. Also went
to the National Gallery to see the pictures which have been
recently cleaned. The exhibition is the ultimate vindication of
cleaning. I do not think any reasonable man could still object
to it being done by an expert with the scientific care that the
Gallery undoubtedly takes. I am inclined to think that the
photographs taken after cleaning make the originals look more
scraped and chalky than in fact they do look. I reached this
conclusion after comparing the detailed photograph of a

241

satyr's face in Rubens's Silenus with the painted face on the canvas.

On the whole a satisfactory weekend. I wrote a section on Attingham for the *Guide*. Dined with the Chaplins at the Allies Club. Ti Cholmondley joined us. She now wears her white hair scraped back and a crimson wreath stuck on the back of it. Instead of looking younger she looks 102. She told us in a disingenuous way how spiritual she had become and divorced from the physical. What an absurd woman. Anthony always amuses me. We talk arrant nonsense together, having got on to that beam. How does one get off it?

To Knole for the day. Had quite a profitable time with Robin and Mason settling opening hours for next season. In the afternoon I talked with Lord Sackville who seems happy, apart from a complaint that the Trust do not pay their bills and have owed him money for nine months. I said to Robin as we left: 'It is odd but I have little affection for Knole, although I know it so well.' He replied that the only quality it has which appeals to him is atmosphere. But I am normally very responsive to atmosphere. Here I don't seem even to catch that.

Lady Crewe has invited me to serve on the Keats-Shelley Memorial Committee, and the Princess Royal has asked me to stay at Harewood on the 26th. I dined with Dame Una Pope-Hennessy and James. Carmen Gandarillas was there. She said her father, Tony, rushed into the house today with a rumour that the Queen was about to have a baby, and if it were a boy, what would become of Princess Elizabeth? On the way home Carmen said that Dame Una's erudition and aggressive lack of small talk alarmed and upset her. How could one be at ease with a bluestocking like that? When I am sitting next to her now I just give up and make no attempt at conversation. This evening she spoke of Queen Victoria's wickedness in shaping the twentieth-century European disasters by her Bismarckian alliances and dynastic ambitions; then about Lamartine, on whom she is very set, Madame de Staël, Kingsley and her son, John's superior knowledge of Nicholas Hilliard to any living person's on God's earth.

Wednesday, 12th November

Historic Buildings Committee this morning. Eardley, who attended, said at luncheon afterwards that the meeting was the most entertaining two hours he had ever spent. It consisted of a public flirtation between Esher and me and the two of us Gerry-baiting. Esher said, 'I know no man, but the Duke of Wellington, who says "No" more often than Mr. Molotov.' He made Eardley purr by telling him that he always liked his ideas, E. having submitted a scheme that the Trust should put its country house libraries to public use.

Thursday, 13th November

Clifford Smith lunched at Brooks's. I wish this man were not so kind and fundamentally good-hearted, for then I really could dislike him. He pressed me to see that Margaret Jourdain was paid for any little jobs she undertook for the Trust, since she was so hard up.

Again I went to the Albert Hall in Michael's box to see – or is it to hear? – Bruno Walter conduct the London Symphony Orchestra. Superb – Brückner's Te Deum and Beethoven's Ninth Symphony. Charlie Brocklehurst said to me, 'This would tame even a Bolshevik.' X., and I suppose his wife, were in the box. His proximity made me feel self-conscious. I must have been no more than fifteen – if that – when I met my 'undoing' from his hands twenty-three years ago. I rather enjoyed it, although of course pretending not to. I still remember the smell of the soap he used. Cyril Connolly was in the box, looking like Rubens's Silenus.

Friday, 14th November

Immensely surprised to read in the paper at breakfast that Dr. Dalton had resigned on account of having given away to the press the headings of his Budget speech before delivery. There was much speculation in my office this morning whether Mrs.

Dalton would come to the Executive Committee. She did come, not punctually as she normally does to discuss with the staff before the meeting points of interest to her but, wisely, just after the meeting had begun so as to avoid general conversation. She was rather more truculent and talkative than usual, doubtless trying to maintain her *sang-froid*, yet I have seldom seen any woman so betray her true feelings by her looks. Her face when in repose was drawn, mauve and sagging. She was far from tearful, or abashed, just downright broken. I felt sorry for her. It shows how ambitious she is, how much she relished her horrible husband's position. It is interesting that humans, when deeply moved, cannot disguise their expressions, however successful they may be in disguising their manner of speaking and their gestures.

Harold Nicolson told me that John Sparrow has given him for his birthday present a letter to Byron from Lord Clare, written at Harrow, telling B. how unhappy B. had made him and admitting his love for him. On the letter in B.'s handwriting was jotted in later years, 'Just a foolish schoolboy's quarrel'.

After the Executive Committee I took the 6.30 to Taunton. There was a hideous scramble for seats in the restaurant car. I failed to get one, and dinner. The discomfort of travel by train in England is unsurpassed. The Castle Hotel, Taunton, were kind. As a concession they gave me, tired and ravenous, a whisky and soda and three ginger biscuits.

Saturday, 15th November

Fetched my car from the Taunton garage. It looks very smart, painted dark blue with black wings. The roof has been mended to prevent leaks. Other small improvements. My bill will probably amount to £60.

I lunched at Montacute with the Yateses. The house looking very spruce and the garden far tidier, now that we have our own regular gardeners. Drove back to London and dined late at Brooks's. Sat with John Walter who tells me he is a Liberal. He claims that the Liberals, if they were less ambitious and abandoned their silly pretence of winning elections, could in fact become a power in Parliament, for they would hold the balance in every debate and turn out whichever Government became unpopular. As a director of *The Times* he receives £250 p.a. but as a Walter wields little authority today. He says Colonel Astor's views are very limited now, but he is very powerful. Barrington-Ward is a rebel by nature and will always support the underdog; and Carr, the Foreign Correspondent, has to Walter's great relief, retired. It was he who made *The Times's* foreign policy so pro-Russian and foolish.

Rick S.-J. told me on the telephone that he met Ruth Draper yesterday. She said that during her English tour she has earned £38,000. What with American and British taxes she is £1,000 to the bad, after payment of her expenses. What a commentary!

Monday, 17th November

Joshua, in whose parents' house, Holbecks near Hadleigh I am staying, drove me to Colchester where we picked up Major Parker, who lives in a villa in this town. We went on to Faulkbourne Hall, which he owns. His mother, aged ninety, lives there. I had heard much of this house, but it is disappointing and even ugly. The park and landscape featureless. Witham town is creeping perilously close. It, the house, centres on a square red brick tower, fifteenth-century I suppose, or early sixteenth-, like Hadleigh Deanery and Layer Marney. It is built of small Tudor bricks. It has crenellations and delicate, degenerate – from the military standpoint, which was its purpose – machicolations. But the house has been extended from time to time, culminating in nineteenth-century makeshift corridors over back courts, most haphazard and untidy. Apart from an oak seventeenth-century staircase, somewhat altered, and a few William and Mary pine-panelled rooms, stripped, the interior is equally unsatisfactory. The surroundings make the outside even duller than it need be. I thought Major Parker a stupid man for offering the house and no land, apart from three or four fields, and no other endowment. I mean, he could not expect us to accept such a proposition. He says his son, just married, wishes to live here but will probably abandon it after a few years' attempt. Then what? A school, I suppose.

We dropped Major Parker at Colchester and went to Fingringhoe Hall to lunch with the Furneaux, he a brother of Lady Birkenhead. A nice couple with good taste. She is tall, handsome, outspoken, the type I like. This James I brick house is far nicer than Faulkbourne. She offers to lend the Trust two portraits of ancestors by Hoppner. The one of the wife in old age appears in the Hoppner book.

Joshua left early for Packwood. I had to take out all the plugs of my car, blow on and wipe the bloody things before the engine would start, which it finally did with the utmost reluctance. I visited the Deanery, Hadleigh. The gatehouse of rich brick-work overlooks the churchyard, and is similar in type to Faulkbourne. Reached Blickling at 1.30 and lunched at the Buckinghamshire Arms with the de Chairs who motored down from London. Went round the house with them and Carew Wallace, they deciding what colours they want for decorating. As C.W. says, we shall never get a licence to repaint all the rooms, and the de Chairs seem intent upon living in every room of this vast palace. After tea went to the Dell to stay with Maud Mosley. She in bed with a bad attack of bronchitis. Her grandson, Simon Mosley, Johnnie's boy, came to dinner. He is in the Coldstream and says he wants to be an opera singer – tenor. He is taking lessons in London. Says that fifty per cent of the guardsmen in his company refused to contribute towards a present for Princess Elizabeth. The dissentients came to him in a body and, quite pleasantly, gave him their reasons. *One*, they said the Royal Family did nothing for anybody, and *two*, the Royal Family would not contribute towards a present for their weddings. When Simon Mosley said that without the Royal Family the Brigade of Guards, with its privileges and traditions would cease to exist, they replied, 'Good! Let them both cease to exist.'

Wednesday, 19th November

Aunt Maud is much better today. She is distressed that the Sunday papers announced that she was sitting in the front row of Tom Mosley's political meeting last Saturday, when all the time she was ill in bed here in Aylsham. Already local Aylsham people have criticized her for being a fascist whereas she

246

has in fact joined the Conservative Party in Norfolk. They conclude that she is a fascist in disguise.

Friday, 21st November

My three days at Blickling have been profitable. Have shifted a great deal of furniture about. Drove to Wymondham church to see the terracotta tomb of the last Abbot of the Minster, a sort of canopied sedilia at the right of the great reredos by Comper. Arrived at Wingfield Castle to stay the night with Baron Ash. A lovely place it is. From 1 p.m. until 12.30 after midnight I was with Baron who did not once stop talking, fishing for compliments for his generous gift of Packwood to the Trust and praising himself. But his food was good.

The Castle dates from the 1380s. Retains its wide moat all round. You enter by the gate-tower of knapped flint work and dressed stone. You pass over the bridge – Baron longs to substitute a real drawbridge – into the inner court which, apart from the south-west wing where he lives, is now a shell. There are hefty chimney breasts and brick stacks. The wing drops sheer into the moat. We walked in the dusk to Wingfield church to see the de la Pole tomb made of wood. Baron is allowed no petrol for his car and is very isolated. But he does not mind. He sees himself as a mediaeval baron marooned and defensive within his castle, a happy isolationist.

Saturday, 22nd November

After climbing to the gate-tower roof, from which there is a wide all-round view of this singularly flat, yet not hideous country, and listening to the eerie screams of the wind whistling through the lead pipe in the gargoyle's mouth, I left at ten. The East Anglian wind kept me awake last night. It delighted Baron in making him feel more than ever marooned as though on board ship, himself the captain, nice Miss Eden his faithful crew and very efficient and solicitous cook-housekeeper. I drove to Framlingham and looked at the four well-known monuments in the church, dating from Henry VIII's reign. They are among the best examples in England of Italian Renaissance copyists' work. Tentative work, and unfortunately in bad condition. They are made of a coarse white stone which has cracked and is crumbling.

Rick dined with me at home, arriving late as usual, at nine. My relations with him are of the strangest. Charmed and irritated by turns.

Collected and catalogued my photographs bought in Italy. Gave an enjoyable luncheon party of Doreen Colston-Baynes, Roger Fulford and Ivy Compton-Burnett. Doreen wanted to talk to Roger about Queen Victoria whose young life she is writing. Roger is now publishing a life of the Prince Consort. I could see how happy Doreen was. They all stayed till twenty to four. Roger said to me afterwards, for we walked together to St. James's, that he feared from what Doreen had told him, the Royal Family were not opening their records to her, and questioned whether it was not because of the trouble he has got into from Queen Mary who gravely resented Roger's imputations that Prince Albert interfered in British politics. Ivy was very characteristic, speaking volubly in her breathless, sharp manner, and often being very amusing. She began by saying she never read the sort of books Roger and Doreen wrote and knew nothing of the subjects, implying that she cared less. Then she repeatedly interjected observations, which were very much to the point, while they were confabulating, which they did at length over coffee. The four of us then discussed how we wrote: Doreen never at a writing-table, which gives her claustrophobia, but preferably in bed, or sitting on a stool at the fire, or in a field on the grass, a pad and paper on her knee: Ivy always at her table at the window, with an electric fire the other side of her; Roger always at his writing-table, with piles of notes, carefully docketed around him, and several bottles of differently coloured inks; I at my little Empire bureau, if the weather is warm, or in my armchair as close to the fire as possible, if the weather is cold, papers balancing on the arms of my chair, a small table, a bookstand and the floor.

Roger was in the Abbey during the Wedding, out of sight in the triforium, watching the scene through field-glasses. He said the Princess looked pretty, as well as enchanting. He favours Prince Philip, as I do. Doreen does not. Doreen says she has been steeped so long in Queen Victoria that she knows her far better than her best friend. And who is that? She would not say.

Monday, 24th November

Mr. Elletson called this morning to say he had quite decided to hand over Parrox Hall and could provide an endowment producing £500 p.a. and a further £250 p.a. after his or his mother's death, whichever might die last. I lunched at the Écu de France with Mr. Sedgewick who had invited Jock Murray to meet me. Jock remains a boy, gay and simple, giggling and popping lumps of sugar out of his coffee cup into mine and back again. Correct Mr. Sedgewick was rather shocked by this odd behaviour until we explained that we had been at Eton together. 'Oh, Eton! That explains it,' he said ambivalently.

Tuesday, 25th November

A meeting in the office summoned by Lord Aberconway, at which he, Dr. Taylor and Major Bowes-Lyon, the Queen's brother, a genial man, represented the Royal Horticultural Society. They raised a matter long overdue that a Gardens Committee of the National Trust and the R.H.S. should be formed in order to raise money and to administer a select few of the very best gardens of England that could be given or left to the Trust. There are thousands of English people who love gardens even more than buildings, and would willingly subscribe to such a fund. I tried, and think succeeded, in guiding the discussion along the right lines. At least I knew the constitution of the Trust better than the others.

Wednesday, 26th November

Today went to Harewood. Took the train to Leeds and arrived at one o'clock. Was met by a nice, old-fashioned chauffeur, not in livery, and a bran new small Daimler limousine with a large silver owl on the bonnet, and driven to Harewood village. Immediately on leaving Leeds one enters the Harewood estate, on either side of the road. God, what England owes to the landed gentry for the trim appearance of their estates. Harewood village is a fine specimen of a planned eighteenth-century community. The little houses are uni-

249

form, for they were all built of a piece by John Carr. I lunched with Mr. FitzRoy, the Agent. He is a hunchback, with protuberant, pointed chest; his wife young and pretty. It is very cold up here, frosty, clear and beautiful. After luncheon I talked in Mr. FitzRoy's office. He told me the estate was faced with 75 per cent death duties, but the family were resolved to remain at Harewood notwithstanding. During conversation I suggested that the family might approach the Treasury and ask for the house, some 4,000 acres of land around it, and also the chief objects of art to be taken in lieu of duties and handed over to the Trust. Mr. F. was interested. Then he took me in his car down the Leeds road, and through the lodge gates to look at the house across the valley towards the Wharfdale and high ridge of hills beyond it. At once saw how important it was that a large area should pass with the house which is visible from such long distances.

We drove back through the main entrance, past the stable block by Chambers, to the house. Were shown into the old library to the left of the hall, and stood before a fire. While I was debating with myself how I ought to make my first obeisance, suddenly H.R.H. ran swiftly into the room and shook me by the hand without saying a word. When I realised who she was I just had time to incline my head. My first impression was how good looking she is, far more so than photographs suggest. She has a beautiful complexion, neat greyish hair, cropped but wavy at the back. She wore a grey tweed skirt, thick mesh wool stockings, dark leather indoor shoes, a grey jumper and one string of pearls. The effect not dowdy, but simple country dress. She is extremely shy, but dignified; sensible and natural in manner. Rather abrupt and has little small talk. When interested in a subject she becomes vivacious and communicative. It was now 3.30 and already getting dark. She took us round the state rooms until 5 o'clock. The hospital which occupied the state rooms has recently gone, and the rooms are being cleaned and put back. There were men working on the floor boards with a machine like a tennis court marker, sandpapering them. The Princess picked her way through, opening shutters, removing dust-sheets and talking affably to the workmen. In the centre library one workman was re-laying boards by the glass door, wearing his hat and smoking. When he spoke to the Princess he neither removed his hat nor his cigarette. When we left him H.R.H.

was very worried lest he might set fire to the house. I thought his behaviour abominable.

Tea was in the breakfast-room, as were all meals. I always sat on the Princess's right. She kept jumping up to fill the teapot from an electric kettle. She has a smooth-haired dachshund called Bruna, to which she is devoted and with whom she keeps up a flow of banter. It sleeps in a basket in her bedroom. The other day she upset milk on the silver tray and let the dog lick it up, then, for fear of what the butler might think, washed the tray herself. Miss Lloyd and Mrs. Balfour, ladies-in-waiting, were in attendance. The younger son, Gerald, came in from shooting. He is stocky, with large chin, slightly oafish, a mixture of David Lloyd and Auberon Herbert in appearance only. Has drooping, sensual mouth. He is very jolly with his mother, whom he teases.

The Princess has a remarkably beautiful, deep voice, and rolls her 'r's slightly. She has fine white teeth and a curious mark on the upper lip, as of a scald.

After tea she took FitzRoy and me to her private sitting-room where some of the best Chippendale satinwood tables and commodes are; also a pair of Sèvres inlaid cabinets. I then explained my ideas about the Treasury scheme and she asked many questions quietly and intelligently about domestic arrangements under the National Trust. Asked if she might have a small strip of the terrace to herself and dog on opening days, and proposed providing teas for the public in the stable block. 'One can get used to anything,' she observed rather pathetically. We talked until 7.40 when the Agent left us together.

My bedroom was in the semi-basement. It had a coal fire. There was no time for a bath. In fear of being late I changed quickly and dashed up to the old library just as it struck eight. At dinner there was no waiting, the Princess going first to the sideboard, helping herself, the rest following. There was plenty of banter during dinner. The P having rung the bell for coffee said, 'Now what is the betting that they won't answer it,' and two minutes later, 'I thought so.' The son then said, 'I will try, Mummie,' and his peals brought a response. The P. had changed with inordinate speed into a black dress, very plain, with black shiny belt and velveteen coatee, for she is still in mourning. After dinner, sitting till nearly twelve in the old library, stifling yawns, was a bit of a trial. Talk was about the crowds in the buses and tubes during rush hour, the smell of human beings on a muggy, rainy day (things which she can never have experienced), and then politics, and keen, anxious speculation over the Gravesend election. She says a little naively that, whatever happens, we mustn't emigrate or desert this country, however much we are tempted. I thought to myself, royalty never emigrates. It either stays put or is pushed out.

Thursday, 27th November

Breakfast at nine. I was up at 8.50 in case the Princess should arrive first. The ladies assembled in the breakfast-room. H.R.H. then came in. The two ladies curtseyed and I bowed. This was all the ceremony. Every sentence has a Mam in it, a slightly de-naturalising suffix. And reference to her presence or absence is to Her Royal Highness. I like this. After breakfast I was allowed to walk outside on the terrace and round the house by myself. Was specially commanded to examine the small group of playing children in a painting by Baurscheit, dated 1725. I could not admire these insipidly mischievous children as much as the urns the Princess has bought at the Clumber sale and put in the Barry parterre garden. At 10.30 the Princess reappeared and until 12.20 conducted me round the house again. She takes great pride in and has considerable knowledge of the contents. Her taste too struck me as very good. Indeed the rooms are superb and the long gallery one of the noblest apartments I have seen in an English house. It is amazing how convincing the wooden curtain boxes are, carved to resemble drapery. The quality of the French-style Chippendale furniture the finest possible. Together we pulled off covers, compared the suites of furniture, examined ceilings, pier-glasses, door-locks and handles, chimneypieces, carpets and pictures, about which she knows a great deal. We went into every bedroom and bathroom, deploring the effects of last winter's damp on many ceilings. Went into H.R.H.'s bedroom, with large, brown, modern mahogany double-bed, dog's basket and dozens of photographs of Queen Mary, the late King, present monarch and family. Rather wistfully she kept saying, 'I do hope I shall not have to sell this, or that.' We even descended to the cellar to examine the china. At the end I was asked if I was tired. Valiantly I denied it, although nearly dropping, and expressed the same anxiety about her. She said she never was tired showing the house to people who appreciated it.

I was motored back to Leeds to catch the 12.45 to London, and went to a party at Kew given by Mark Ogilvie-Grant, at which a Greek pianist played while the guests sipped flat champagne in a large chilly chamber. Papa is staying with me.

Saturday, 29th November

Unsatisfactory day. Worked at interrupted intervals. Lunched with Patrick Kinross at the St. James's Club. He is finally back from Egypt after seven years and is to retire to Devon where he intends writing a novel about his past and all his friends. God help us all. This will be no contribution to literature. I was delighted to see dear old Patrick who has grown enormous in length and breadth. He sprawls over chairs and tables and puffs a great deal. He is not notably chic or clean, but otherwise unchanged. The same, good-humoured, quizzical gently cynical, kind individual. We went to the Wallace Collection to look at the upstairs furniture which I wanted to compare with the Frenchified Chippendale at Harewood while it was still fresh in my mind. But you can't compare the French and English for the quality of each is so distinctive, and the English better finished in fact. I had tea with Ralph Edwards and his family at Chiswick Mall. Ralph was deploring present day amorality and said that only a religious revival could restore western civilization, the eastern having already gone.

Sunday, 30th November

I love having a Sunday to myself. A rare thing. Worked all day, finishing M. Jourdain's *English Decoration and Furniture* and began Hall's *Life of Henry VIII*. Then dined cosily alone with Colin Agnew who deplored the cleaning of the National Gallery pictures. Philip Hendy is a great friend of his. Nevertheless he thinks he has acted very unwisely and is entirely in the hands of a crook German scientist scraper of paintings. He says picture restoration has to be in the blood of families like the Drowns, whose fathers have for generations cleaned with turpentine and no chemicals and who understand the feel of varnish and dirt and can tell which layer of paint beneath is the true one.

Michael [Rosse] and I motored to Polesden Lacey. He was delighted with the arrangement of the house, which is Robin's doing and is a credit to him. We both liked too the railings designed by Professor Richardson to separate Mrs Greville's grave from the garden.

I dined with Ivy and Margaret. Charlotte Bonham-Carter and Soame Jenyns the other guests. It was the greatest fun, although there was only cider to drink, and it was perishing cold. Ivy and Margaret were at their best, playing up to each other and making strikingly pertinent and lively observations. I brought some lace from Brockhampton for Margaret's expert opinion. She found a number of pieces that are quite good and valuable, particularly two large pieces of Charles II date in excellent condition.

Took Sarah Churchill to the Charlie Chaplin film, *Monsieur Verdoux*, not up to standard, but there were flashes of the old humour and genius. The last dock scene makes an appeal to the world not to use the atom bomb, which is far crueller than Bluebeard's murder of his seven wives – no overstatement. Afterwards I dined in Sarah's flat, she having cooked the dinner. I did not leave till long after midnight. She is going on Wednesday to Morocco with her father. The King sent Prince Philip to lunch with her father in order to learn about the Constitution. Churchill liked him, finding him very intelligent.

Had tea with the Eshers in their small Chelsea house. There was an iced cake made for one of the grandchildren which he insisted on eating, to Antoinette's concern. He nearly devoured the whole of it. We discussed Harewood and he agreed that we should ask the Treasury if they would in fact take it in part payment of death duties and let the Princess Royal continue to live there.

Tuesday, 9th December

Eardley and I trained to Reading, picked up his car and motored to Stourhead where from 12 till dark, now 4.30, we worked in the house. This we continued the following day, and Thursday, I staying at Long Crichel for two nights. Stourhead in turmoil. We had to start from scratch, sorting, rejecting, with the minimum of help, carrying heavy furniture and busts together, back-breaking, yet giggling work. We sold a collection of sheer junk for £75 to the local antique dealer in Mere, who took it all away on Thursday, for which I hope the Trust will be pleased. We tried to trace all the younger Chippendale's pieces of furniture scattered about the house to put them in those show rooms to which they rightly belong. But we did no sort of arranging. It was the greatest fun, and oh how I enjoy Eardley's companionship. We think we make a splendid team, because we never spare criticism, neither taking offence; on the contrary each relishing outright condemnation of the other's efforts. I know we shall eventually succeed in making this house look splendid, we having picked the brains of all the experts, sifted, endorsed or rejected their several pieces of advice. The late Alda, Lady Hoare, has become a great mythical figure at Long Crichel. Eddy deplores our eradication of her appalling bad taste, and is going to write a novel about her. Desmond calls us the despoilers.

Friday, 12th December

At the Finance Committee I was appointed the Trust's representative on the Osterley Park Committee. Lord Esher said there was no one who knew more about Osterley than I, which is, I suppose true, after the years I have spent conferring with Jersey. Harold Nicolson said to me, 'Oh dear, I cannot get down to writing books for the constant interruptions. But I do not intend to abandon my other interests for a purely literary existence until I am seventy.' Eddie Marsh at luncheon at Brooks's told me three little stories in his clipped, Edwardian manner. Someone congratulated Lady Tree on the colour of her hair which he supposed she had recently dyed. 'How

255

sweet of you,' she replied, 'to say, *my* hair.' Winston Churchill when told that Mr. Attlee had decided not to visit Australia, remarked, 'he feared that when the mouse was away the cats would play,' and described Socialism as 'Government of the duds, by the duds, for the duds.'

Monday, 15th December

In talking to Doreen this evening I was overcome by an urgent desire to leave and get home to my work, and be alone. Doreen very shaken because last evening a burglar broke into her house, stole nothing, but left large footprints everywhere. Or so Doreen maintained, for sometimes I think she invents these dramas just to bring incident into her placid life.

Tuesday, 16th December

Sam Carr lunched and brought me the proposed jacket of the National Trust *Guide*, showing a pretty, fanciful coloured view of the Knole gatehouse. He said he thought the book would bring me in a steady income. I much doubt it, for it will soon be out of date. Lady Crewe had a party for Miss Ruth Draper to which I went out of politeness, but a horrid, heavy affair it was. I stayed twenty minutes and left with James who said, 'I only go to these parties for Peggy's sake.' I said, 'You mean you only go to Peggy's parties for Peggy's sake.' He said she loathed her own as much as she loathed other people's parties.

Wednesday, 17th December

Worked the whole day at the Stourhead guidebook. Malcolm Bullock dined at Brooks's and came back here afterwards. He would not go home but sat like Juggernaut telling funny stories about the Baldwins. Someone called at Downing Street. Mrs. Baldwin opened the door dressed as Madam Butterfly. She said, 'This is a surprise for Stan when he returns. I often do this. Last week I was a Turkish soldier.'

Thursday, 18th December

A harrowing visit this afternoon to see an old woman, Mrs.
256

Walter Tibbitts, in a private residential hotel in Inverness Terrace, Bayswater. She had offered her 'collections' to the Trust. From her description of the Benares ware, Poona brass, marquetry furniture and from the photograph she produced of a Hindu carved screen, it sounded appalling and unsuitable. Yet she had not a flicker of doubt that it was important and insisted that the collection be kept together. She is seventy-eight and must find a home for it before she dies. I left her feeling more depressed than words can describe. When the old have to live in soulless drabness, which this hotel is, alone, ridiculous and unwanted, they are pitiable. When they are slightly truculent, to keep their end up, it moves me beyond compassion to a sadness which haunts me for days. The agony of it.

Tea at Sibyl Colefax's. Harold Nicolson said that Eddie Marsh's new book was of schoolgirl badness. He and I left together. In the tube, in which we had to stand, Harold said to me: 'I find myself constantly touching my hat and offering my seat to tough middle-aged men until I realise that they are twenty years younger than I am.'

Friday, 19th December

This afternoon, after the dentist, I called at Batsford's and collected five advance copies of *The Age of Adam,* of which the jacket is the prettiest I have ever seen. Met Mr. Harry in the shop. He made me talk with him upstairs, and promise, rather against my will, that I would help in the editing of some guidebooks. I could not quite understand because of the coughing and spluttering whether it was the same old Methuen guidebooks on which he is so keen, or not. 'Now then, Jim darling,' he went on and subsided into catarrhal chuckles. The house telephone rang: 'God damn the bloody swine,' he shouted. 'Is that you, Sam darling?' without a break between the two ejaculations.

Saturday, 20th December

Bridget took me to Covent Garden. Three ballets, *Les Patineurs, The Three-Cornered Hat* and the new Lecoque one, very gay with Derain scenery. On the way to the Ivy – the best food I have had since my return from Italy – a man accosted me

257

and I, so Bridget said, was very snubbing. Indeed I did not recognize him until we had passed on. Then I suddenly remembered the sad, second-rate, hopelessly unpractical member of the A.R.P. who was in my platoon at the beginning of the war. The last person in the world I would wish to be unkind to. I left B. – angrily stumping the pavement – and tore after him. Alas, he had gone. Now for ever he will remember me as a cad, a man too proud while with a beautiful woman, to acknowledge him. He looked so thin, yellow, crinkled and *dégringolé*, which makes my behaviour worse. Perhaps he is starving and would have welcomed 5s. Instead B. and I continued to her flat in Mount Street where we drank whisky, were warm and happy.

Sunday, 21st December

Ugly hangover this morning. Worked all day. In the evening James dined here. After dinner we giggled so much over my book that we nearly choked. Then went to see Paul Wallraf who had Heinz Dietmar dining. Heinz said it was terribly depressing coming over to England from Germany. This annoyed James who observed tartly: 'Then I wonder you bother to come here at all,' Heinz having been a refugee from Germany all the war. Paul was cross with J. for his rudeness. I thought Dietmar a bore. Then France was discussed. James was angry with me for criticising the French before two Germans (who were after all his friends) and so the party broke up.

Wednesday, 24th December

I motored this morning early to Bibury. When not beset by angst I am happy motoring, for I can relax and assess my actions and tell my beads. I have given thirty-seven Christmas presents and, so far, received one, a wireless set from my parents. Financially, I am utterly broke. Most of my presents go to servants and friends like old Mrs. Strong, the caretaker of Carlyle's House. I suppose it is always the way.

Had a look at the Mill House at Bibury, which Eardley does not recommend, but which I favour on the whole. I like its great, stalwart buttresses. Then to Fossebridge to lunch with the dear Fairfax-Lucys, who are sweet friends and always give me a welcome – and a delicious luncheon. Called for Deenie at Stowe and motored her home for Christmas, just the four of us staying.

Thursday, Christmas Day

Immediately after luncheon I drove to Brockhampton to fetch eight velvet cushions, then back to Worcester and had tea with the Matley Moores in The Tything. The first thing I saw was a beautiful leather screen, which I admired. He said, 'Yes, we have just bought that at the Brockhampton sale.' Then I realised it was the screen I had bid for and did not even know whether or not I had been successful. Miss Matley Moore is already repairing it. It is leather, painted with birds and rabbits, date about 1695 they think; a lovely thing. She is one of the leading restorers of mural paintings in England. She has ascertained that those at Harvington Hall were done by four different men, one of whom was left-handed. M.M., gruff but kind and very well informed antiquarian, is the Ministry of Works representative of Worcestershire and Diocesan Adviser. By profession a dentist. They let me join their Christmas tea with their old mother of eighty and another old woman. Earnest and genuine people. I like them. She has a tame magpie which eats off her shoulder.

Friday, 26th December

The family went to Wolverhampton Races in the extreme cold wind. Papa's horse was third and Mama says it is a dud. All morning I read Virginia Woolf's latest essays. I really believe she is the best prose writer of this century. In the afternoon walked to see Maggie [my old nursery maid]. Her little boy, aged five, has fair hair and the most beautiful and patrician face, yet he hardly speaks. His eyes are melancholy, and beseeching. Maggie says she is forty-nine but looks as pretty and young as when I first knew her. They have thirty acres of fruit trees.

Saturday, 27th December

This morning took Deenie back to Stow, then on to Charlecote where I spent the day with Hollyoak, the agent, fussing

259

around with a view to improvements. Have an idea of making the morning room into a kind of state bedroom. Shall also get Kaynes-Smith to vet the pictures for me. Then to tea with Lady Throckmorton, that immortal woman whom I so deeply respect and admire. She asked if she might call me by my Christian name, which coming from someone of her age and generation is a compliment. She is very unhappy about the situation at Coughton [Court]. Her son has to renounce his lease and we discussed how she could continue to live there. It is imperative that we help her to do so. Upon that I am resolutely determined. She said a little poignantly, 'You and I alone must work upon it.'

Sunday, 28th December

Motored to Stoneleigh [Abbey] this morning at 10.30 to talk to Lord Leigh about the showing of this house. He is rather annoyed that the Trust is taking so long to consider his offer. Indeed here is a house of first-rate quality, one we simply must save.

Monday, 29th December

I went to Burford Priory. The Southbys were away but I went round the house with the caretaker, and this evening wrote a long report for the Historic Buildings Committee. There are only three rooms of interest, Speaker Lenthall's Chapel of 1660, much restored, the 1583 great chamber with ribbed ceiling, and the Queen Anne staircase. The situation of the house in relation to the town is important, and its general appearance is attractive. It has been very much altered.

Tuesday, 30th December

At Stratford-on-Avon I visited Shakespeare's Birthplace. Last year they had 100,000 visitors at 1s. each. For so small a house I am surprised the trustees do not collect better furniture. The oak pieces I saw all looked fakes without exception. The birth-room, having been a shrine since Isaac Walton's day – his name scratched on a windowpane survives – is affecting. On comparing the building of today with early photographs taken in 1858 and still earlier prints, one sees how much it has been restored and altered.

Lunched at The George Inn, Shipston-on-Stour. The Cotswolds sprinkled gently with snow under a leaden sky, the roads deserted and dead and wild. At Oxford I tried to sell two huge volumes of William Nicholson plates of the colleges to Blackwells but they would make no offer. Strolled to the Divinity Schools. The weird roof is of Henry VI's time, heavy and base I think. The perspective Jacobean panels of the Convocation Room are quite classical. The guide was an awful old man whose ignorance was supreme. Moreover he was proud of it. In the Sheldonian Theatre the guide pointed out, what I should long ago have realised, that Streater's ceiling is meant to imitate the open sky as seen in his day from the Roman Theatre of Marcellus. Wren was responsible for this translation. The awning depicted above the cornice and the gold ribs representing the ropes that would pull it across are in every sense baroque. He said all the carving was Grinling Gibbons's. I seriously question this.

Wednesday, 31st December

Dined at Brooks's with Dick Girouard whom I met there. Walked home to bed at 10.30 and read *Dombey and Son* contentedly. Party-lust seldom irks me nowadays. That is one consolation. Heard the distant cacophony and catcall of sirens, and the cretinous shouting at midnight.

Index

The names and titles of entrants are given as they were in 1946 and 1947. Friends frequently mentioned are cross-referenced under their Christian as well as their surnames.

The names of properties in CAPITALS are those which today belong to the National Trust. Those in *italics* are under a restrictive covenant with the Trust.

Particulars and times of opening (which vary from year to year) may be obtained from the National Trust's "List of Properties" (circulated to members) and the "Historic Houses, Castles and Gardens" guide, which is issued annually.

The county references given are to the old boundaries which existed since Doomsday, and even before, until the hash made by Parliament in adopting the puerile recommendations of the Redcliffe-Maud Royal Commission on Local Government of 1966–9.

264